Third Edition

Archery

STEPS TO SUCCESS

Kathleen M. Haywood, PhD
University of Missouri at St. Louis

Catherine F. Lewis, MEd
Riverview Gardens School District
St. Louis County, Missouri

Human Kinetics

Library of Congress Cataloging-in-Publication Data

Haywood, Kathleen.
  Archery : steps to success / Kathleen M. Haywood, Catherine F. Lewis.-- 3rd ed.
    p. cm.
  ISBN 0-7360-5542-8 (soft cover)
  1. Archery. I. Lewis, Catherine, 1957- II. Title.
  GV1185.H38 2006
  799.32--dc22

                        2005014768

ISBN-10: 0-7360-5542-8
ISBN-13: 978-0-7360-5542-0

The Web addresses cited in this text were current as of November, 2005, unless otherwise noted.

Acquisitions Editor: Jana Hunter; **Developmental Editor:** Cynthia McEntire; **Assistant Editor:** Scott Hawkins; **Copyeditor:** Jan Feeney; **Proofreader:** Ann M. Augspurger; **Graphic Designer:** Nancy Rasmus; **Graphic Artist:** Denise Lowry; **Cover Designer:** Keith Blomberg; **Photographer (cover):** © Getty Images/photo by Robert Laberge; **Art Manager:** Kareema McLendon; **Illustrator:** Roberto Sabas; **Printer:** Sheridan Books

Human Kinetics books are available at special discounts for bulk purchase. Special editions or book excerpts can also be created to specification. For details, contact the Special Sales Manager at Human Kinetics.

Printed in the United States of America   10 9 8 7 6 5 4

Human Kinetics
Web site: www.HumanKinetics.com

United States: Human Kinetics, P.O. Box 5076, Champaign, IL 61825-5076
800-747-4457
e-mail: humank@hkusa.com

Canada: Human Kinetics, 475 Devonshire Road, Unit 100, Windsor, ON N8Y 2L5
800-465-7301 (in Canada only)
e-mail: orders@hkcanada.com

Europe: Human Kinetics, 107 Bradford Road, Stanningley
Leeds LS28 6AT, United Kingdom
+44 (0) 113 255 5665
e-mail: hk@hkeurope.com

Australia: Human Kinetics, 57A Price Avenue, Lower Mitcham, South Australia 5062
08 8372 0999
e-mail: info@hkaustralia.com

New Zealand: Human Kinetics, Division of Sports Distributors NZ Ltd.
P.O. Box 300 226 Albany, North Shore City, Auckland
0064 9 448 1207
e-mail: info@humankinetics.co.nz

Third Edition

Archery

STEPS TO SUCCESS

 Contents

Climbing the Steps to Archery Success

Get ready to climb a staircase, one that will lead you to become an accomplished archer. You cannot leap to the top or skip stairs; you get to the top by climbing one step at a time. The steps to archery success are arranged in order so that you can take each step in an easy transition from the previous one. This new, expanded edition allows you to progress to an intermediate stage and even to specialize in various types of archery, such as competitive target shooting, competitive 3-D shooting, or bowhunting.

Archery is a sport that involves the use of many pieces of equipment. Your first step is to fit the equipment to your unique body structure and strength. Ill-fitting equipment can cause beginners to develop flaws that are difficult to overcome. The next step is to learn how to handle archery equipment safely. Target archers and bowhunters alike must be aware of the harm an arrow can do if they do not exercise care at all times.

The next step is to learn to shoot with good technique, first by mimicking shots and then by shooting arrows. The early emphasis is on building good technique and consistently executing that good technique. Just about any beginner can hit the bull's-eye once if he shoots enough arrows. The goal of the steps to success is to consistently hit the bull's-eye. Subsequent steps allow you to refine your technique and adapt it to both your unique body structure and the type of archery you want to shoot. Accessories are added gradually at just the right time to improve your accuracy. Throughout the steps you can engage in specific learning activities and drills to advance your skill and break the monotony of the typical archery practice session.

Additional steps build your mental skills for shooting and teach you multiple ways to analyze your own performance in order to correct the minor flaws that detract from your accuracy. Upgrades in equipment can help improve your

Meters or Yards?

Shooters who are accustomed to measuring distance in metric may substitute meters for yards for the purpose of learning to shoot. For example, if the text directs you to shoot from 12 yards, you may shoot from 12 meters.

scores, but you need to learn to be a critical consumer. You also will learn to adjust your equipment to achieve smooth arrow flight and to maximize scores. Near the top of the staircase you will learn to prepare and adapt your equipment for specific types of archery, especially competitive target archery, competitive 3-D shooting, and bowhunting.

Whether you want to shoot in a recreational league or in a competitive tournament, to enjoy the bowhunting season or shoot 3-D rounds year-round, you will improve your performance and enjoy shooting more as you develop greater competence and learn more about archery and archery equipment. *Archery: Steps to Success* provides a progressive plan for developing your shooting skills and building confidence in your ability to hit your mark.

Follow the same sequence with each step:

1. Read the explanation of what is covered in the step, why the step is important, and how to execute the focus of the step, which may be a skill, concept, use of equipment, or a combination of the three.

2. Study the illustrations, which show exactly how to execute aspects of the shot.

3. Read the instructions for each drill. Practice the drill and record your score.

4. At the end of the step, review your performance and total up your scores from the drills. Once you've achieved the indicated level of success with the step, move on to the next step.

Make *Archery: Steps to Success* part of your successful climb to the top. Learn the fundamental form that provides a solid foundation on which to build your skill. Use a systematic and gradual approach to advancing your skill and using equipment accessories. You can specialize in a form of archery, but all successful archers and bowhunters use the same basic form. Consistency is the name of the game for archers. Even when you reach the top, the drills and practice activities can keep your shooting sharp. The tools for analyzing your performance can be used no matter what your level, experience, or type of equipment.

The reward for completing the steps to success is a lifetime of opportunity to enjoy the many forms of archery. For some, just the challenge of improving performance is enough. For others, spending hunting season in the woods is their desire. Those who like competition can choose from a variety of archery contests, such as Olympic-style, outdoor shooting at long distances, 3-D animal target shoots, and indoor tournaments with 100 archers on the shooting line. Good luck on this step-by-step journey to developing the physical and mental skills necessary for accurate shooting. Enjoy your climb in *Archery: Steps to Success* to become a successful archer and join legions of men and women throughout history who have learned to hit their marks!

The Sport of Archery

When you pick up a bow to shoot your first arrow, you are partaking in an activity dating back at least 20,000 years. The bow and arrow are pictured in drawings that old on a cave wall in Spain's Valltorta Gorge. Other finds document the long history of archery: flint arrowheads from the period between 25,000 and 18,000 b.c., arrow shafts from approximately 9000 b.c., one-piece yew or elm bows from 8000 to 6000 b.c., and a rock fresco of an Egyptian archer from approximately 7500 b.c. In 1991, the preserved body of a man who lived around 3300 b.c. was found on the Similaun Glacier in the Alps. He carried a quiver of 14 arrows.

The bow and arrow were once critical to humankind's survival. The bow allowed humans to become proficient hunters. Prey provided various raw materials, such as hide, bone, and sinew, for tools, shelter, and clothing and added protein to the diet. Hunting with a bow was safer than using other methods because prey could be shot from a distance. Early bow designs reflected the materials available in the geographic region, the tools available for craftsmen, and the way in which the bow was used. For example, short bows were easier to handle from horseback or a chariot, and long bows were better for shooting distant targets from a fortified encampment.

Early bows also were selfbows made of a single piece of wood rather than the design eventually preferred, gluing together multiple pieces of wood.

Empires rose and fell through the use of the bow and arrow as weapons. The ancient Egyptians established the bow as a primary weapon of war around 3500 b.c. They made bows almost as tall as themselves and arrowheads of flint and bronze. Around 1800 b.c., the Assyrians introduced a new bow design: a short composite bow of leather, horn, and wood with a recurve shape. It was more powerful than the longbow used by the Egyptians and could be handled easily on horseback. This bow gave the Assyrians an edge in battle over their Middle-Eastern rivals. The Hittites also used the short recurve bow in mobile warfare by shooting from the light, fast chariots they developed around 1200 b.c.

Middle-Eastern superiority in archery continued for centuries as the peoples of the area successfully fought Europeans. For example, the Romans, although known as mighty soldiers, used an inefficient draw to the chest when shooting the bow and were outclassed as archers by the third-century Parthians of Asia. The Romans later adopted the draw to the face and improved their archery prowess. The Mongols conquered much of Europe, and the Turks threw back the Crusaders, in part because of their superior recurve bows and better shooting technique.

The samurai warriors of Japan were known for their archery skill. They developed a bow about seven feet long called the *yumi,* made largely of bamboo. A unique feature of the yumi was the placement of the grip about two-thirds the way down the bow. Whether the bow performed better with this placement or whether the shorter, lower limb allowed the bow to be shot more easily from kneeling positions or horseback is unknown.

In the 11th century, the Normans developed a bow that they used to defeat the English (Anglo-Saxons) at the Battle of Hastings in a.d. 1066. In battles of the time, archers avoided carrying large numbers of arrows by reusing their enemies' arrows, but the English had few if any archers and positioned themselves behind a shield wall. The Normans gained an advantage at the end of the day by retrieving many of their arrows lying near enemy lines and shooting them in an arc over the wall.

After the Battle of Hastings, the Norman and Anglo-Saxon cultures were integrated. The English adopted the bow as their major weapon and then improved it. Their famous longbows were about 6 feet long and very powerful. Longbowmen became the core of English armies that would dominate battles for centuries to come. Many ballads of the 13th and 14th centuries, such as the tales of Robin Hood, attest to the archery skill that the English developed with the longbow. English kings would often require Englishmen to practice archery on Sundays and holidays or ban other sports that diverted time from archery.

Although the value of the bow as a war weapon declined swiftly after the invention of firearms in the 16th century, the fun and challenge of archery guaranteed its continued existence as a sport. King Henry VIII promoted archery as a sport in England by directing Sir Christopher Morris to establish an archery society, the Guild of St. George, in 1537. Roger Ascham published the book *Toxophilus* in 1545 to preserve much of the archery knowledge of the time and to maintain interest in archery among the English.

Archery societies were founded throughout the 1600s, and the tournaments they held firmly established archery as a competitive sport. The Ancient Scorton Silver Arrow Contest was first held in 1673 in Yorkshire, England, and continues to be held today. Women joined the men in competition and were first admitted to an archery society in 1787. Contests were held in three major forms of archery: one that resembles today's target shooting to a vertically mounted target; one that was a precursor of clout shooting (long-range shooting to a large target laid out on the ground); and one called *roving* that resembles field shooting today, wherein archers walk along the countryside to shoot at various targets.

On the North American continent, Indians relied on the bow and arrow for hunting. Indian bows, however, were short and weak; the hunter had to get close to game such as bison and elk to be successful. Some Indian tribes hunted from horseback, riding up next to game; others hid in forested areas, waiting for game to come in range. European settlers brought their well-developed knowledge of bowmaking from their native countries and kept alive the interest in target archery in North America. The first archery club on the continent, the United Bowmen of Philadelphia, was established in 1828.

The Civil War spurred greater interest in archery in the United States. When the war ended, the victorious Union prohibited former Confederate soldiers from using firearms. Two veteran brothers, Will and Maurice Thompson, learned archery with the help of Florida Indians. Maurice wrote a book, *The Witchery of Archery,* that helped spread interest in archery across the country. By 1879, the National Archery Association (NAA) was founded and began holding national tournaments. In 1938 Ben Pearson established a company to mass-produce archery equipment. Enthusiasm for field archery (a target archery competition that simulates hunting) and bowhunting itself led to the establishment of the National Field Archery Association in 1939.

Archery first became an official Olympic event at the Paris Olympics in 1900, an appropriate sanctioning because the mythical founder of the ancient Olympic Games was Hercules, an archer. Archery was an event at the 1904 St. Louis Olympics and the 1908 Olympics in England—and female archers were included in both games—but archery did not reappear until

1920 when the Olympics were held in Belgium. Archery failed to appear in any of the Olympic Games held over the next 52 years.

The problem with early archery competition was the lack of a universal set of rules. The host country usually held the archery contest most popular in that country. If archery was not popular in the host country, the event was not even held during athletic meets. To better organize competitive archery, Polish archers worked to establish an international governing body. As a result, the Fédération Internationale de Tir à l'Arc (FITA) was founded in 1931. FITA set up universal rules and designated particular rounds that would be shot in international competitions, including the Olympics. As a result, international competition grew and gained so much momentum in succeeding decades that archery was readopted for the 1972 Olympic Games. It has been a part of the Olympics ever since, and medals are now awarded to men and to women in both individual and team competition.

Technical advances in the design of bows and arrows and the availability of new materials have increased shooting accuracy and, consequently, interest in archery. Two developments have had particular impact. In 1946 Doug Easton developed a process for manufacturing aluminum arrow shafts. The uniformity of aluminum arrows in weight and spine (stiffness) greatly increased the accuracy and enjoyment of shooting for many. Then in the late 1960s, H.W. Allen invented the compound bow in Missouri. The compound bow uses eccentric (off-center axle) pulleys or cams that are mounted in the tips of the bow limbs to reduce the holding weight of the bow for a given draw weight (the number of pounds required to draw any bow a given distance). With the compound bow, archers can hold longer in order to aim, shoot more arrows, and shoot higher poundage, all with less fatigue. These types of bows are popular in North America for target and field archery and especially for bowhunting.

Smaller inventions and improvements also boosted the accuracy and enjoyment of shooting throughout the 1900s. In 1937 bowsights were first used at an NAA tournament. In 1951 plastic vanes were first used to replace the feathers on arrows, and in 1961 the Hoyt Archery Company made bows with attached stabilizers. Release aids came on the scene in national competitions held in 1970.

ARCHERY TODAY

Newer materials such as carbon have led to the design of lighter and therefore faster arrows, more consistent performance of bow limbs, and more flexibility to interchange parts and accessories. Throughout the history of shooting, new innovations in materials and technique boosted interest and participation in archery. New archers today can use modern equipment and accessories to shoot with great accuracy. Even more important, advances in equipment make it possible for more shooters than ever before to be successful in hitting their marks.

Archery is enjoyed today by thousands of people all over the world. Archery appeals to all kinds of people—men and women, children and older adults, and those with and without disabilities (figure 1). Another reason for the popularity of archery is the many ways to enjoy archery, including target shooting and bowhunting.

Target Archery

Target archery has been popular since the days of King Henry VIII of England. The challenge of hitting the mark is timeless. Today, many archers enjoy shooting recurve bows and using their fingers to hold and release the bowstring. Others enjoy shooting compound bows and using mechanical releases (figure 2). Some like to shoot without a bowsight while others enjoy using sights with every possible mechanical innovation.

When compound bows and release aids came onto the archery scene, there was an obvious need to provide separate competition categories for archers, since this equipment provides an advantage in precise shooting. Some archery associations chose to sponsor certain equipment categories and not others and still other associations were founded to provide competitive opportunities for certain new types of equipment. Often, these devices first became popular

Figure 1 Archery is popular with people of all ages and ability levels.

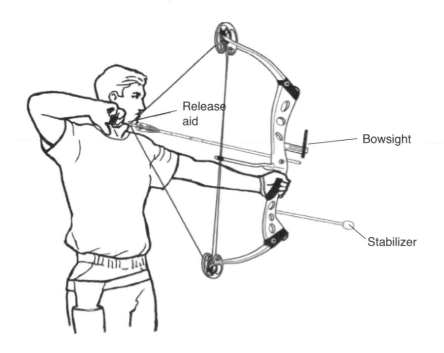

Release aid

Bowsight

Stabilizer

Figure 2 An archer using a compound bow, a bowsight extended from the bow, a release aid, and a stabilizer.

in the United States, and it took time for their use to spread around the world.

Today target archers are lucky to have many choices of equipment styles and competitive formats. Those living in colder climates can often find indoor facilities with shooting distances around 20 yards or meters. Outdoors, target archers can shoot longer distances and classic competitive rounds with all archers shooting from a line to concentric circle targets. Or, target archers can shoot field archery events in which they walk from target to target and shoot from varying distances to ringed targets.

Other Types of Archery

Bowhunting (figure 3) is a very popular activity today. Bowhunters enjoy the challenge of taking game as they help to control the size of game populations whose natural predators have dwindled. The amount of game taken during a season is usually regulated. The majority of bowhunters now use compound bows rather than

recurve bows. Compound bows make bowhunting more humane because a kill is more likely than a wound with the increased arrow speed and the potential for heavier draw weight. The compound bow also allows smaller persons to hunt with the necessary bow draw weight.

Bowhunting has become so popular that bowhunters often hold competitive rounds in the off-season. Field archery simulates hunting in that the shooting distance and terrain vary from target to target. In some field archery rounds, paper animal targets are used instead of concentric ring targets. Silhouette or three-dimensional (3-D) foam targets shaped like animals are popular for hunting rounds. They are placed in wooded or grassy areas at unmarked distances. In hunting rounds, the equipment, especially the bowsight, might be limited to that typical for hunting.

Flight shooting is another type of archery enjoyed in some parts of North America (figure 4). Arrows are shot for distance. Special bows and

Figure 3 Most bowhunters use compound bows. These bows allow a smaller person to hunt with the necessary draw weight. One of the challenges of bowhunting is adapting to the natural terrain.

Figure 4 A flight bow.

arrows are designed for just this purpose. Today's flight bows shoot more than 900 yards.

Bowfishing is yet another way to enjoy archery. From a boat or canoe, fish are shot with an arrow attached to fishing line. A special reel is mounted onto the face of the bow. The breeds of fish taken are often carp, gar, buffalo, sucker, redhorse, stingray, and skate. Most effective shots are taken through a depth of four feet or less because the water quickly slows an arrow.

Novelty shoots are occasionally held for enjoyment and variety. These shoots sometimes take the form of clout shooting in which a 48-foot target is laid on the ground and shot at from 140 to 180 yards. Archery golf, which is similar to regular golf, involves shooting a flight arrow, an approach arrow, and a putting arrow at a four-inch ball. In roving, archers in a small group take turns choosing and then shooting at a target to see who can come the closest.

Some parts of North America also have crossbow competitions. Technical advances in crossbow design and materials have made crossbows very accurate. Today's shooters aim at 60-centimeter target faces from distances as great as 65 meters.

Soon, technological advances will allow archers to shoot at virtual images generated by computer systems. The number and type of games created by such systems could be limitless. No matter which form of archery or what type of equipment you come to enjoy, the same basic form and shot-to-shot consistency lead to shooting accuracy. The equipment and your physical and mental skills must come together to produce the perfect shot.

EQUIPMENT AND ACCESSORIES

Equipment is important to your success in archery. High-quality equipment that's fit to your size, strength, and interest can bring you success for many years. High-quality equipment is also expensive. The more knowledgeable you are about archery tackle, or equipment, the more likely you'll be to choose the type of equipment that matches your size and strength. At the same time, merely spending money on archery equipment is no guarantee of success. You should learn to be a critical consumer since someone will always be anxious to sell you the magic bow or accessory to make you a champion! If you need to improve and refine your technique, no amount of money spent on equipment will make a difference in your scores.

In this section, you will learn about basic archery equipment and accessories, including terms for various pieces of equipment and the advantages and disadvantages of each type of equipment. Information about advanced accessories is also included. You can read about advanced accessories now or come back to this material later.

Choosing a Bow

Two types of bows are commonly used today. One type uses the bow limbs to store the energy to propel the arrow. You will probably encounter two variations of this type in an instructional setting. One variation is a straight-limb bow made of solid fiberglass, and the other is a recurve bow made of laminations of wood and fiberglass. Each variation has its advantages and disadvantages (see table 1). The other type of bow stores energy in an off-center pulley or cam and is known as a compound bow.

The straight-limb fiberglass bow (figure 5) is inexpensive, and both right-handed and left-handed shooters can use the same bow. However, the straight-limb bow design does not provide very much leverage when an archer bends the limbs by pulling back the bowstring. Also, the arrow sits to the right or left of center, and the archer must compensate for this setup when aiming. Straight-limb bows are adequate for beginners because the initial emphasis should be on learning proper shooting form. Serious archers rarely use straight-limb bows, however.

The recurve bow design (figure 6) is more efficient than the straight-limb bow design. A recurve bow in its relaxed position has limb tips that are bent back, away from the archer. The bowstring lies across 2 to 3 inches of the limb. When the bowstring is drawn back, the curves straighten

Table 1   Advantages and Disadvantages of Various Bows

Type of bow	Advantages	Disadvantages
Straight-limb fiberglass	Inexpensive Can be fitted for right-handed or left-handed archers	Little cast Not center-shot
Recurve	Greater cast Greater arrow speed Interchangeable limbs if take-down style	Shooting distance requires high draw weight
Compound	Holding weight is less than draw weight Potentially faster arrow speed	Must be fitted for archer's draw length

to provide leverage. When the string is released, the curves return to their C shape. This series of actions imparts more arrow speed than a straight limb does. The length of the limbs is fitted for an archer's size to maximize the leverage that the limbs provide. This quality is called cast. The terms used to describe the various parts of both straight-limb and recurve bows are given in figures 5 and 6. Note that the back of a bow's limbs is the surface facing away from the archer.

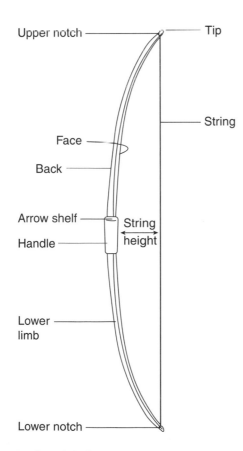

Figure 5   A straight-limb fiberglass bow.

The recurve bows used in competition today consist of a metal handle riser section and removable limbs. Both can vary in size for numerous combinations that fit an archer exactly. The metal handle riser can be made of aluminum or magnesium. Limbs are typically composites of many materials, such as foam cores with carbon overlays, carbon and fiberglass laminations, or wood cores (often hard rock maple) with fiberglass and carbon laminations. Designers of bow limbs strive for an ideal combination of speed, stability, and smoothness in deciding what materials to use and how to combine them.

Compound bows also have a metal handle riser and composite limbs, but they are characterized by an off-center, or eccentric, pulley or cam mounted on each limb tip (figure 7). Some models have a cam on the lower limb and a round wheel on the upper limb. The energy required to rotate the part of the pulley with the long radius is greater than the energy required to rotate the part with the short radius. The pulleys are mounted so that the energy required to pull back the bowstring is the greatest at mid-draw and the smallest at full draw when the archer is holding to aim. When the archer releases the bowstring, this situation is reversed, and the energy applied to the arrow is increased. For example, an archer with a 40-pound (18-kilogram) compound bow of 50 percent let-off, or reduction, holds only 20 pounds (9 kilograms) of resistance at full draw. However, 40 pounds of thrust are imparted to the arrow.

A disadvantage of the compound bow for young people who are growing or for shooters who share a bow (such as families or instructional classes) is the need to fit the bow to the

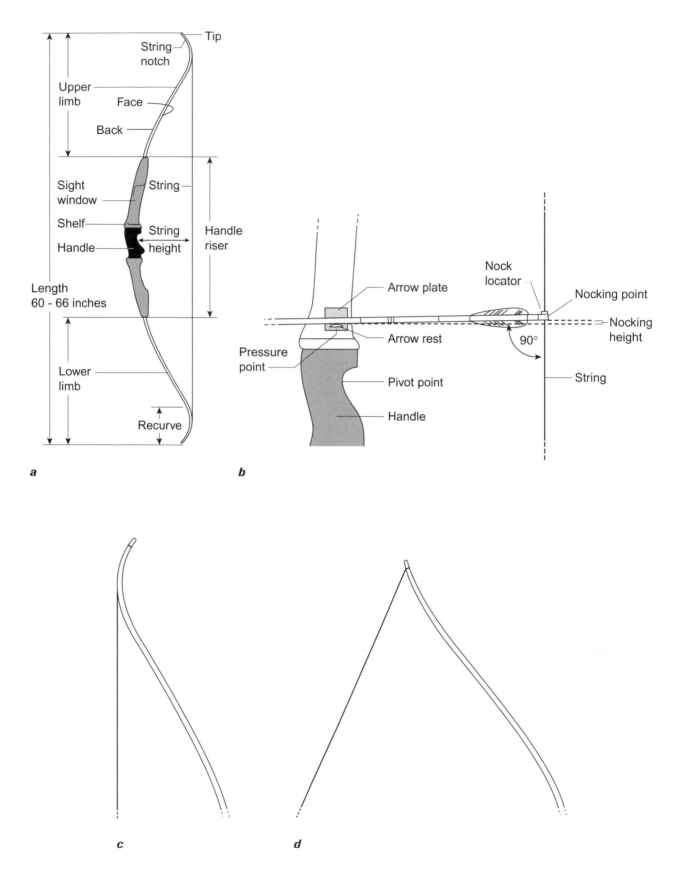

Figure 6 Various views of a recurve bow: *(a)* bow with major parts labeled; *(b)* close-up of arrow rest and nocking point area; *(c)* bow limb in relaxed position; *(d)* bow limb in drawn position.

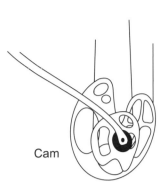

Cam

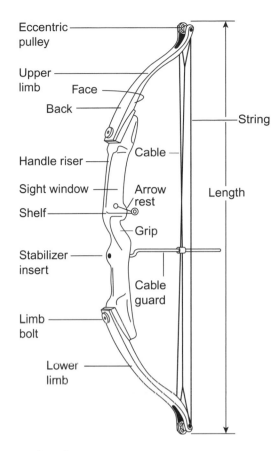

Figure 7 A compound bow. The wheels can be round, eccentric pulleys or cams.

person's draw length. It is necessary to fit the bow to the individual archer's draw length in order for the point of greatest reduction in pounds to correspond to the full draw of the individual archer. A recent innovation in the manufacturing of compound bows addresses this disadvantage for beginners. A light-poundage compound bow with a single cam (there is simply a round wheel mounted on the other limb tip) is now available (figure 8). The bow's poundage is typically 10 to 20 pounds and there is no let-off, or poundage reduction. Shooters with a draw length to about 30 inches can use the bow. This compound bow is ideal for young people (whose draw length will increase with growth) and those in instructional settings. The poundage is adequate for short distance and allows beginners to focus on form.

So which type of bow is right for you? Both modern recurve and compound bows make it possible to shoot with great precision. Your decision about which to use depends in part on whether you would like to enter competitive archery or bowhunting events. Because compound bows allow archers the advantage of shooting arrows with many more pounds of thrust than it takes to hold the bowstring at full draw while aiming, separate competitive divisions are usually held for compound and recurve bow shooters. If your interest is target archery, visit local archery clubs and ranges. Find out if the competitive events in your geographical area include both divisions. This information might influence your decision.

Because most hunters use compound bows, this type of bow typically dominates competitive hunting events. If your goal is primarily hunting, you probably want to choose a compound bow that is camouflaged rather than brightly colored. If you decide you want to use a compound bow, remember that you can still learn to shoot with a recurve bow. You can better attain a precise fit in a compound bow once you have increased your strength and solidified your shooting form. We will discuss fitting a bow to your size and strength in step 1.

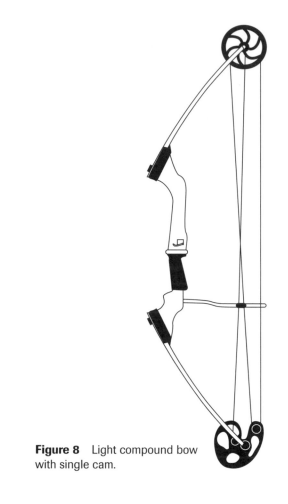

Figure 8 Light compound bow with single cam.

Choosing Arrows

Arrows can be made of five materials: wood, fiberglass, aluminum, carbon, and aluminum-carbon. Just as with bows, the various types of arrows have advantages and disadvantages

(table 2). The basic terminology used to describe the parts of an arrow is the same for each type and is given in figure 9.

Because they are inexpensive, wooden arrows are acceptable for beginning archers, but these arrows are not very durable and they warp easily. Because of differences in the pieces of wood used to make arrows, they cannot be closely matched. As a result, an archer might find variation in flight from arrow to arrow.

Fiberglass arrows are more durable than wooden arrows, and fiberglass arrows can also be sized to fit archers of various arm lengths and strengths. Fiberglass arrows of a given size can be manufactured more consistently than wooden arrows. However, fiberglass arrows break more easily. Now that economical aluminum arrows are available, fiberglass arrows are not very common.

Aluminum arrows can be manufactured so that arrows of a given size meet consistent specifications and consequently are more accurate than wooden or fiberglass arrows. Archers can therefore purchase additional arrows to match their originals at any time. Aluminum arrows are manufactured in a variety of sizes and in different qualities of aluminum alloy. Because you can straighten bent arrows and easily replace damaged arrow points, you can maintain a good set of aluminum arrows for quite some time. Aluminum arrows also can accept various weights and styles of arrow tips and different styles of nocks. Those used for hunting can be fitted with an

Table 2 Advantages and Disadvantages of Various Arrows

Type of arrow	Advantages	Disadvantages
Wooden	Inexpensive	Cannot be matched to each other Not readily matched to archer's draw length and weight
Fiberglass	Can be sized to draw length and weight Can be matched better than wooden arrows	Breaks easily
Aluminum	Can be precisely manufactured Wide range of sizes available Durable Arrow tips can be interchanged	Expensive
Carbon and aluminum-carbon	Fast	Very expensive Carbon layer breaks down if struck

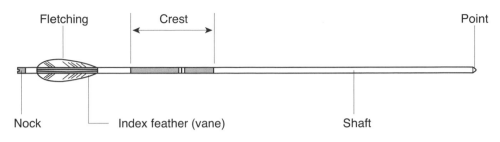

Fletching   Crest   Point

Nock   Index feather (vane)   Shaft

Figure 9 Parts of a target arrow.

insert so that hunters can switch back and forth between target tips and broadheads. Aluminum arrows fletched with feathers can be stripped and plastic vanes applied, or vice versa, so aluminum arrows offer much variety in setup. Their versatility, consistency, and durability make them the arrow of choice even for beginners.

Aluminum-carbon arrows are made of an aluminum core wrapped with carbon. Carbon and aluminum-carbon arrows are smaller and lighter than pure aluminum arrows. However, carbon and aluminum-carbon arrows are more expensive and less durable than aluminum. They are typically used by archers who shoot long distances in outdoor settings. These arrows tend to be impractical for archers who tightly pack their arrows in a target, which is typical when shooting short distances, because the carbon wrapping breaks down when it is struck.

You can begin shooting with economical arrows and later graduate to better arrows as your technique becomes routine. In step 1 you will find out how to select arrows for learning to shoot. In step 8 you will learn how to select arrows that can be "tuned," or finely matched, to your equipment setup.

Choosing Accessories

Several accessories make shooting comfortable and more accurate. One is an arm guard worn on the forearm of the hand holding the bow. This guard provides protection from the bowstring in case the bowstring slaps the forearm on the release of the bowstring. This guard also minimizes the effect on the bowstring and arrow flight should such contact occur.

Another accessory is a finger tab worn over the fingers that hold the bowstring. This tab both protects the fingers and improves the smoothness of the bowstring's release.

A quiver is a handy accessory for holding or carrying arrows. It also minimizes injuries by keeping sharp arrow tips contained. Quivers come in a variety of styles (figure 10). Most archers use a belt quiver. If you're shooting outdoors, a ground quiver that is stuck into or set on the ground might be convenient to use.

An arrow rest (figure 11) is an important accessory. It is mounted on the bow above the bow shelf. You place the arrow on the arrow rest

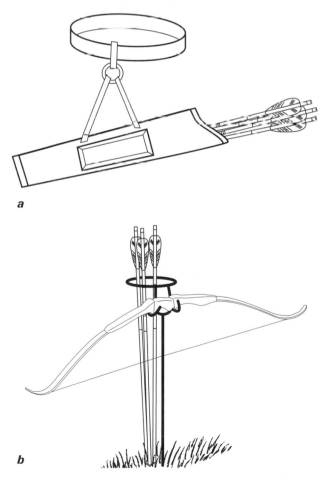

a

b

Figure 10 Two types of quivers: *(a)* belt quiver; *(b)* ground quiver.

and keep the arrow there until you shoot it. The advantage of shooting an arrow off an arrow rest over shooting an arrow off the bow shelf is that the arrow rest allows the fletching on an arrow to clear the bow more smoothly on the arrow's flight toward the target. This advantage results in smoother arrow flight and consequently more accurate shooting. Arrow rests vary in type and cost. The most expensive ones are adjustable so that a bow can be precisely tuned for ideal arrow flight. For your initial experience in archery, a simple arrow rest will suffice. In step 1 you will learn how to install an arrow rest.

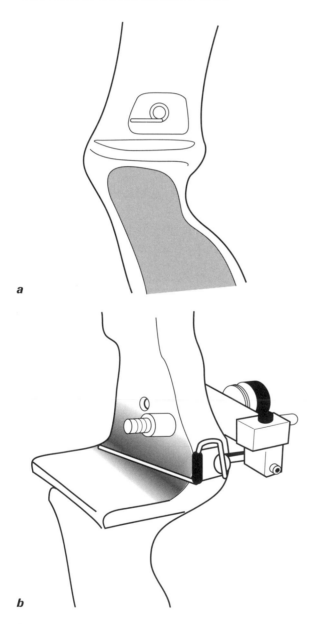

a

b

Figure 11 Arrow rests: *(a)* spring rest; *(b)* rest with collapsible arm.

The bowsight is an attachment to the bow that places a marker, or aiming aperture, in the bow window. To aim, you line up the aperture with the bull's-eye rather than look at the relationship between the arrow and bull's-eye. With a bowsight, you can direct an arrow to the same place, horizontally and vertically, on every shot by controlling the elevation and left–right direction of your bow arm. If the arrow is not directed precisely to the bull's-eye, you can adjust the bowsight by an exact amount for subsequent shots.

A bowsight is attached to the bow so that the aiming aperture is visible to an archer at full draw in the bow window, which is to the left of the upper-handle riser for a right-handed archer. Hunting sights usually have more than one aiming aperture, each of which is set for a different shooting distance. Target sights have one aperture that is repositioned as an archer changes shooting distance.

The aiming aperture should be adjustable, both horizontally and vertically. A vertical scale on the bowsight allows you to record the sight position appropriate for various shooting distances. If the present sight position is directing the arrow slightly high or low for a given shooting distance, a scale also permits you to see exactly how a certain adjustment affects the arrow. Manufactured sights also come with a scale, or you can purchase an adhesive paper scale or even a short metal ruler to mount on the sight.

Target sights can be very simple, inexpensive devices, or they can be elaborate, precisely made tools that extend from the bow (see figure 2, page xii). The difference between sights is typically the ease and accuracy of moving the aperture and durability. The more expensive sights also can accommodate various types of aiming apertures, depending on an archer's preference.

Choosing Optional Accessories

Several additional accessories can improve your scoring accuracy even more. The accessories include a bow sling, stabilizers, a kisser button, a peep sight, a draw check, a release aid, and an overdraw.

The bow sling (figure 12) is a rope or strap that encircles the hand or fingers and the bow so that the bow will not fall to the ground even if the archer releases the grip on the bow handle. A loose grip on the bow handle is an ideal part of sound shooting technique. A bow sling is inexpensive and allows the archer to relax the hand holding the bow without the fear of dropping it.

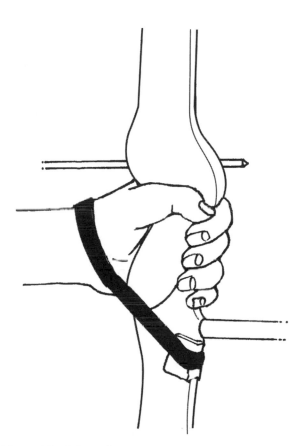

Figure 12   A bow sling.

Various types of bow slings are available. Some attach to the bow, and the hand is slipped through the strap when the archer takes hold of the bow. Others attach to the thumb and forefinger or to the wrist. The type of sling used is a matter of personal preference. All the types work well, and the expense is minimal considering the improvement in shooting accuracy that comes with a relaxed bow hand. You can begin using a bow sling right away or wait until you reach step 4.

A stabilizer (figure 13) is a metal rod with a weight on its end. High-quality bows come with inserts allowing one or more stabilizers to be attached to the face or back of the bow. A stabilizer is beneficial to shooting accuracy because it reduces the tendency of the bow to turn, or torque, in the bow hand. In step 1 you can learn how to select one or more stabilizers for your bow.

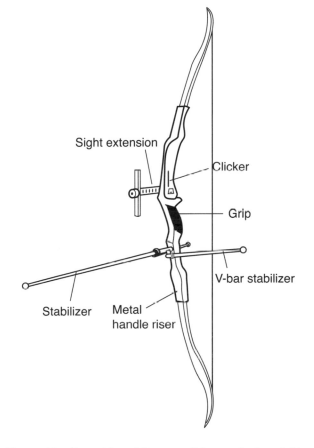

Figure 13   Bow with stabilizers, a clicker, and a bowsight extension attached.

The kisser button is a small, horizontal disc that is attached to the bowstring above the nock locator. The kisser button is set to touch between the lips at full draw. It aids archers in maintaining a consistent anchor. In step 1 you will learn how to position and use a kisser button.

The peep sight is a small plastic or metal disc inserted between the strands of the bowstring. It is always used with a bowsight. The archer looks through the peep sight when aiming. Its function is similar to that of a rear sight on a rifle because the archer lines up the peep sight, the bowsight, and the bull's-eye. If you decide to use a peep sight, step 4 describes how to install one.

A draw check can be helpful to some archers. Even with a solid anchor position, the precise length of the draw may change slightly from shot to shot. A draw check eliminates any variation. There are several types of draw checks; the most common one is a clicker. There is a clicker mounted on the bow pictured in figure 13 (page xxi). We will discuss clickers further in step 10.

Another type of draw check sometimes used by compound bow archers is cable stoppers. Two blocks are clamped onto the bow's cables. As the bow is drawn and the cables move, the two blocks approach each other until they are flush at full draw. The archer cannot move the bowstring farther back, so the draw length is identical from shot to shot. Through trial and error, the blocks are set in position on the cables to meet when the archer is at full draw.

Shooting with a release aid (figure 14) is a popular form of archery for hunters and target archers alike. When used properly, the release aid results in more accurate shooting than is possible with the fingers. A single loop of rope or a small metal rod holds the string just below the arrow nock. When the archer triggers the device, the release is cleaner than three, or even two, fingers coming off the string. The string deflection that occurs with a finger release is minimized, so the arrow takes a straighter path to the target. In competitive events, archers using release aids are almost always placed in different divisions than archers releasing the bowstring with their fingers. Usually archers using release aids shoot compound bows. In step 5 we will go into more detail on shooting with a release.

An overdraw (figure 15) is a device that extends the arrow rest toward the archer to

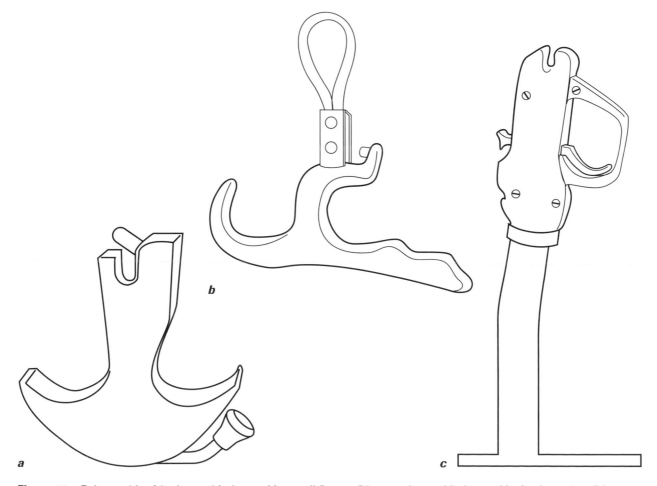

Figure 14 Release aids: *(a)* release aid triggered by small finger; *(b)* rope release aid triggered by back tension; *(c)* release aid triggered by index finger.

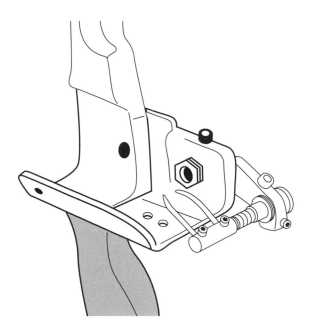

permit use of a shorter, and therefore lighter and faster, arrow. Compound bow shooters who use a release aid are the most likely archers to use an overdraw. Care must be taken with an overdraw because the arrow point is drawn behind the bow hand and could injure the archer if the arrow slipped off the rest at release. If you decide to try an overdraw, be sure it has a tray to catch the arrow should it slip.

Figure 15 An overdraw.

TARGET ARCHERY COMPETITION

Unlike most sports in which a single set of rules governs play, competitive target archery can be shot in many different types of rounds or contests. For example, indoor contests are usually shot at a constant, short distance (20 yards or meters) at a target of a uniform size. Each outdoor contest, though, is usually shot at various distances with targets of variable size, depending on the distance. Some rounds call for just one shooting distance, others call for three or four, and still others require 10 or more. The number of arrows shot in a round also varies. Indoors, 30, 45, or 60 shots is typical, but 56 to 144 shots per round is common outdoors. Tournaments can consist of one or more rounds. Sometimes different types of rounds are shot within the same tournament.

Unless the round simulates hunting, a target of concentric circles is used. The closer an arrow lands to the center of the target, the more points are awarded. One thing is typical of all the various rounds. The score of individual arrows is totaled, and the archer with the highest point total wins the contest. In recent years, some archery tournaments have used head-to-head competition, sometimes after a traditional round to establish seedings, and a winner advances until a single archer is declared champion. These

formats are particularly exciting for spectators. The Olympic Games have adopted this format.

Competitive target archery is also shot with a variety of bows, although archers are often separated into classes within a tournament or into different tournaments based on their equipment. The traditional recurve bow consists of a handle-riser section made of metal, often magnesium. The bow limbs are usually composites of wood and fiberglass, plastic, or carbon. An adjustable sight is mounted on the bow, as are one or more rods called stabilizers, which reduce the tendency of the bow to turn on its long axis upon release of the arrow.

The compound bow also has a metal handle riser, but its limbs might be composite or solid fiberglass. Eccentric pulleys or cams are mounted on the limb tips. Steel cables are attached to the pulleys, and the bowstring, in turn, is attached to the cable. A compound bow can also be equipped with adjustable sights and stabilizers.

The target arrow is usually made of aluminum, carbon, or a combination of the two. It is equipped with a steel tip that is bullet shaped. Real feathers or plastic vanes are attached to the back end of the arrow. In modern target archery, all of an archer's arrows should be identical in size, weight, and length.

Competitive target archery is shot with sophisticated equipment. Yet the variability of a novice's accuracy is often due more to basic form and technique than to equipment. A simple, one-piece, traditional bow and wood or fiberglass arrows are sufficient for learning the basic techniques of archery. Expensive equipment does not guarantee more accurate shooting for a beginner.

SHOOTING RULES

Different archery associations, kinds of equipment, and types of rounds lead to variations in archery rules. You need to be familiar with the specific set of rules that govern any class, range, or contest in which you participate. Many of the rules are similar, however, and the following common archery rules for shooting and scoring will provide a good foundation for your early experiences in archery. Later in this book, you will learn safety rules in more detail.

If you shoot with a class or at an indoor range, the shooting distance will be specified. If there is a shooting line (a straight line marked on the floor or ground), stand with one foot on each side of the line when shooting.

An established number of arrows will be shot in a round. This number is called an *end*. It is both discourteous to shoot more than this number of arrows and a rule violation in competition.

If you are shooting with a group, someone may be assigned to control shooting with a whistle. One blast signals the beginning of shooting. Two blasts indicate archers may go forward to the target to score and collect arrows (figure 16). Four or more blasts indicate that all shooting must immediately cease. If no one is controlling the shooting, be sure to wait until all archers have finished shooting before you go forward to retrieve your arrows.

Archery targets can be of various types, depending on the round shot. Arrows in the official five-colored, 10-scoring-ring target face count as follows from the center out: 10 points, 9 points, 8 points, 7 points, 6 points, 5 points,

Figure 16   Archers advancing to retrieve their arrows after the two-blast signal.

4 points, 3 points, 2 points, and 1 point. If an arrow touches two scoring areas on the target face, the higher score counts. Any arrow missing the target face is scored a zero.

If an arrow drops from the bow as you are nocking, drawing, or letting down, you can reshoot that arrow provided that you can retrieve it without leaving the shooting line. If you cannot reach it, the arrow is considered shot. You can retrieve it when the signal to retrieve arrows is given. It is scored as 0 points.

If you shoot at an outdoor range, shoot from the same distance as any other archers already shooting when you arrive, unless you leave an open target between your target and those of the other archers. In this case you can shoot up to 10 yards closer or farther to the row of targets than the other archers.

ARCHERY RESOURCES

Archery is shot around the world. Many countries have archery associations, and archery periodicals are published worldwide.

International Associations

Fédération Internationale de Tir à l'Arc (FITA)
Avenue de Cour 135
CH-1007 Lausanne
Switzerland
www.archery.org

International Field Archery Association
Hauptstrasse 39
D-57636 Sörth
Germany
www.ifaa-archery.org

International Bowhunting Organization
(fosters the sport of bowhunting and furthers bowhunting education)
3409 Liberty Avenue
Suite 201
P.O. Box 398
Vermilion, OH 44089
www.ibo.net

United States

National Archery Association (USA Archery)
1 Olympic Plaza
Colorado Springs, CO 80909
www.usarchery.org

National Field Archery Association
NFAA Headquarters
31407 Outer I-10
Redlands, CA 92373
www.nfaaarchery.com

Archery Shooters Association (promotes bowhunting and bowhunting education and sponsors competition featuring 3-D animal targets)
P.O. Box 399
Kennesaw, GA 30144
www.asaarchery.com

National Crossbow Hunters Organization (NCHO)
P.O. Box 506
Verona, OH 45378
937-884-5017

Physically Challenged Bowhunters of America, Inc. (PCBA)
RD1, Box 470
New Alexandria, PA 15670
724-668-7439
www.pcba-inc.org

Pro-Am Bowfishing Association, Inc. (PABA)
Route 4, Box 376
New Prague, MN 56071
800-758-5184

United Kingdom

The Grand National Archery Society (governing body for the sport of archery in the UK)
Lilleshall National Sports Centre
Near Newport
Shropshire, TF10 9AT
Great Britain
www.gnas.org

British Long-Bow Society
29 Batley Court
Oldland, Bristol
England BS15 5YZ
www.askarts.co.uk/longbow.html

Canada

Federation of Canadian Archers
200, 2460 Lancaster Road
Ottawa, ON
K1B 4S5
Canada
www.fca.ca

Canadian National Archery Center (NAC)
915 Rue Maisonneuve
Saint-Hubert, PQ
J3Y 7V1
Canada
450-445-2982

Italy

Federazione Italiana di Tiro con l'Arco
Via Vitorchiano 113/115
00189 Roma
Italy
www.fitarco-italia.org

Arcieria Amatoriale (the Italian
Traditional Archery Association)
Associazione per la Tutela dell'Arco
Tradizionale in Italia
00139 ROMA
Via Captrais, 14/q
Italy
06/87188560 0330/918646

Australia

Archery Australia
P.O. Box 54, Panania 2213

Sydney International Archery Park
Bennelong Road, Homebush Bay
Australia
www.archeryaustralia.com

Australian Bowhunters Association
P.O. Box 975
Morayfield QLD 4506
Australia
(07) 5498 3706
www.bowhunters.org.au

Korea

Korea Archery Association
Room 901
Olympic Centre
88, Oryun-dong
Seoul, 138-749
Korea
www.sports.or.kr

Archery Periodicals

The U.S. and International Archer,
www.bowhunting.net/usarcher

Archery Magazine (magazine of the National
Field Archery Association in the United
States), www.nfaaarchery.com

Bow International (quarterly publication for
archers published in Worcestershire, UK),
www.bownet.com

The Field Archer (magazine of the
English Field Archery Association),
www.efaafieldarcher.com

Archery Focus Magazine,
www.archeryfocus.com

The Glade, www.theglade.co.uk

PREPARING YOUR BODY FOR SUCCESS

Archery is not as vigorous as most other sports, but archers must exert force by using the same back and arm muscles on every shot. Strength is an obvious advantage in shooting, as is muscular endurance. Muscular balance and flexibility are advantages as well. Archers should use regular strength and flexibility exercise to offset overuse, imbalances, and injuries from the repetitive motions of shooting.

Try to strengthen your muscles, especially the arm, shoulder, and trunk muscles, through a resistance (weight) training program. It's ideal to perform your routine three times a week. Increased strength allows you to shoot a bow of higher poundage that shoots arrows in a flatter trajectory. Increased muscular endurance allows you to shoot long practice sessions without a breakdown in technique as you tire. Be sure your resistance training routine is a balanced one that covers all of the upper-body muscle groups, both sides of the body, and opposing muscle groups (flexors and extensors) for movement in a given plane. Your emphasis might be on the upper body, but remember that strong legs provide a solid foundation for your shot.

An ideal way to maintain flexibility and muscular balance and to prepare for shooting is to develop a preshooting stretching routine. A few minutes of vigorous activity, such as jogging, rope jumping, walking, or jumping jacks, warms the muscles before you stretch. Try to do a stretch for each direction of movement in the upper-body joints. Stretch slowly into position and hold for 10 seconds. Repeat each stretch three to six times. Avoid bouncing or forceful twisting motions. Breathe normally. After stretching, draw your bow several times without shooting. Ease the string back after drawing; do not release it without an arrow in place.

If time permits, repeat your stretching routine after shooting, too. This is a good time to work on increasing your range of motion because the exercise of shooting promotes increased blood flow to the muscles.

Fitting Equipment

You have probably seen young children trying to hit balls with baseball bats or tennis rackets that are too big for their bodies. That problem is obvious. Poorly fitted archery equipment might not be so obvious to the untrained eye, but such ill-fitted equipment causes frustration all the same. Try as you might, you will not have much success with ill-fitted equipment.

Your first step to success in archery is to get equipment that is matched to your size and strength. The time and effort you put into perfecting your shot technique will yield better scoring results if your equipment is well matched to your body and set up properly. Buy the best equipment you can afford, but keep in mind that the most expensive equipment in the world will not give you better results if it is not matched to your size and strength. In fact, ill-fitted equipment can work against your efforts to learn and refine good shooting form. Be wary of using secondhand equipment unless the drills in this step indicate that the equipment is a match to you! Later in this step, you will learn how to set up your bow to shoot. With properly fitted and prepared equipment, you can concentrate on learning good shooting technique because you know you are getting the most out of your equipment.

In archery, the shooter stores energy in the bow during the drawing of the bowstring.

This energy is transferred to the arrow when the archer releases the bowstring. The more energy you can store in the bow, or the higher the draw weight you can pull, the more energy can be transferred to the arrow and the faster the arrow can fly.

You might think it would be worthwhile to contort your body in all sorts of ways in order to use the highest draw weight possible, if it were not for a rather important thing—accuracy! To shoot accurately, archers must be able to replicate their technique from shot to shot as precisely as possible. To achieve this consistency, you must use a draw weight that is in your comfort range. Draw weight is a function of the physical properties of the bow and the distance of the draw, which is in turn ultimately related to your arm length. For this reason, most bows must be matched to your size and strength.

Later, you will learn more about what happens to an arrow when the bowstring is released. For now, recognize that an arrow can vary in two ways: length and spine (flexibility). For a given bow draw weight and arrow length (both related to your arm length), there is an optimum range of arrow spine. So arrows also must be matched to your size and strength and to your bow.

FITTING YOUR BOW AND ARROWS

Determining the right bow for you involves several steps. First, you should decide whether to shoot right- or left-handed because bows are made either right-handed or left-handed. Then, you should determine your draw length and the best bow size. The drills later in this step will take you through this process.

Choosing Hand Preference

Choosing whether to shoot right- or left-handed might seem obvious to you. Most right-handed archers choose to shoot right-handed, using the left hand to hold the bow and the right hand to pull the bowstring. Certainly right-handed archers with a dominant right eye should shoot right-handed, and left-handed archers with a dominant left eye should shoot left-handed.

If you are cross-dominant, which means you are right-handed but have left-eye dominance or vice versa, you have a choice to make. An archer typically lines up the dominant eye with the target when aiming, so you can shoot on the side of your dominant eye. If you are more comfortable shooting on the side of your dominant hand, you can learn to shoot with your dominant eye closed instead of drawing with your nondominant hand. For example, if you are right-handed and cross-dominant, close your left eye to aim. If you do not, you might line up your left eye with the target and shoot your arrows to the left on some but not all of your shots. Fitting drill 1 (below) will help you determine your dominant eye.

If you are cross-dominant and plan to use a bowsight, closing your dominant eye to aim with the other eye should prove successful. With a bowsight and sight settings for shooting various distances, you do not need the depth perception that binocular vision provides. Many archers use a peep sight, similar to the rear sight of a rifle, placed in the strands of the bowstring with a bowsight. Only your aiming eye can see through the peep sight to line up the bowsight with the target.

Fitting Drill 1. *Determining Eye Dominance*

When determining your hand preference for shooting, you need to know which is your dominant eye. Place one hand over the other so that a small hole is created between your thumbs and fingers. Extend your arms toward a target. With both eyes open, center the bull's-eye in the opening made by your hands (figure 1.1a). Slowly bring your arms toward your face while continuing to look at the bull's-eye with both eyes open. When your hands touch your face, the opening should be in front of the dominant eye (figure 1.1b). If the opening is in front of both eyes, you simply need to repeat with a smaller opening.

An alternative method is to assume the same position, but instead of moving the hands toward the face, keep the arms extended. With both eyes open, center the bull's-eye in the opening, and then close the left eye. If the object remains in view, your right eye is dominant. If not, your left eye is dominant.

Success Check

- Keep the opening in your hands about the size of a nickel.

Score Your Success

Determining your dominant eye = 3 points
Your score_____

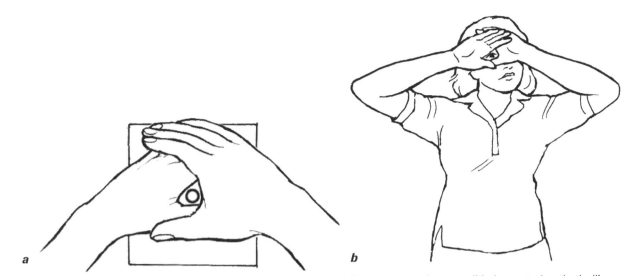

Figure 1.1 Determine eye dominance. *(a)* Put one hand on top of the other to make a small hole, centering the bull's-eye in the hole. *(b)* Bring hands to face, keeping both eyes open.

Determining Draw Length

You need a draw length measurement to fit both the bow and arrows. Draw length is the distance between the nocking point of the bowstring and the grip of the bow handle (the pivot point) at full draw. Your arrows must be longer than your draw length; otherwise, your arrows would fall off the arrow rest as you draw your bow. Your draw length also influences your selection of a properly fitted bow, as you will see later. You need an accurate draw length measure to select both your bow and your arrows.

Fitting drill 2 (below) will help you determine your draw length. It is important to get an accurate measure of your draw length since ill-fitted equipment actually can work against establishing good shooting form. If you decide to purchase your own equipment after your initial archery lessons, remeasure your draw length at that time. If you are purchasing before you begin lessons, be sure to seek expert advice. Fortunately, most bows suitable for competition or for hunting can be adjusted a small amount to precisely match your draw length.

Fitting Drill 2. *Determining Draw Length*

In this drill, you will use two methods to determine your draw length. First, obtain a light-poundage bow and a long arrow. Stand about 8 yards from a target. If you are shooting right-handed, hold the bow in your left hand. Hook onto the middle of the bowstring with the first three fingers of your right hand. Raise the bow and pull the string back (keep your elbow high) until the string above your hand touches your nose. Be sure to stand erect and keep your head erect. Ease the string back. Practice this action several times, making sure your left arm is extended but does not push the bow away.

Now snap the arrow onto the bowstring beneath the nock locator and place the arrow on the arrow rest of the bow. Pointing the bow toward the target, draw the string back with one finger hooked onto the string above the arrow and the other fingers below the arrow. Have someone mark the arrow directly above the arrow rest (figure 1.2). Ease the string back. Measure from the nock slit to the mark. This measurement is your draw length.

Another way to determine your draw length is by using the Pellerite method (Pellerite 2001). Stand with your back to a wall. Extend your arms

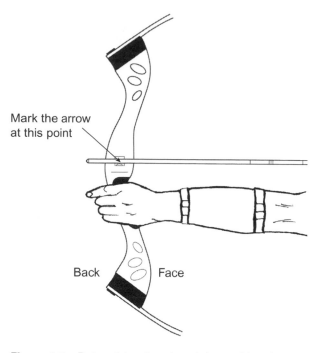

Mark the arrow at this point

Back   Face

Figure 1.2 Determining draw length by marking the arrow.

Pellerite, B. 2001. *Idiot proof archery*. Gahanna, OH: Robinhood Video Productions.

and hands out to your sides at shoulder level. Have someone mark the tip of each middle finger. Measure this distance (that is, your wingspan). If your wingspan is 71 inches, your draw length is 28 inches. For every inch your wingspan is less than 71 inches, subtract 1/2 inch from the 28-inch draw length. For every inch your wingspan is over 71 inches, add 1/2 inch to the 28 inches.

Were the two measurements close to each another? One obvious difficulty with the first method is that the archer needs to have good form to get an accurate measure. This is not always the case with a beginner. For a beginner, the Pellerite method is more accurate.

Success Check

- Stand erect.
- Keep your head erect.

Score Your Success

Determining your draw length = 3 points
Your score_____

Fitting a Recurve Bow

If you will be shooting with a recurve bow, you need to select one that is the proper length and weight. First, determine the ideal bow length for you by using your draw length to find the proper bow length listed in table 1.1. Next, choose a draw weight. Start with a light weight that you can pull and hold easily while developing good form.

If your recurve bow has a handle riser and detachable limbs, keep in mind that bow length

is a function of both riser and limb length. For example, a bow could be 68 inches in length by having a 23-inch riser and long limbs or a 25-inch riser and medium-length limbs. Shorter risers tend to make a bow shoot at a slightly higher draw weight for a given limb length.

Keep in mind that the draw weight printed on the bow or bow limbs is the draw weight at a standard draw length of 28 inches, a draw that is 26 1/4 inches from the throat of the bow grip plus 1 3/4 inches. The bow's draw weight is not as important to you right now as remembering how draw length changes the actual shooting weight of your bow. If your draw length is shorter than the standard, the bow limbs will not deflect as far and you will be shooting fewer pounds than the weight stated on the bow. If your draw length is longer than standard, you will be shooting more pounds than the weight stated. To estimate the actual bow weight you will be shooting, add two pounds for every inch your draw length is above the standard or subtract

Table 1.1 Selection of Bow Length

Draw length	Bow length
24 inches or less	60 to 64 inches
25 to 26 inches	65 to 66 inches
27 to 28 inches	67 to 68 inches
29 inches or more	69 to 70 inches

two pounds for every inch your draw length is below the standard.

Adult archers of average strength typically begin with a bow that weighs 20 to 25 pounds. Stronger archers can begin with 25- to 30-pound bows. Lighter bows of 15 to 20 pounds are appropriate for young archers.

For the early steps to success in archery, you will be shooting short distances to large targets without a bowsight. The goal will be to learn and refine good shooting form. You will not need a heavy bow to get the arrow to the target. Typically it is better to learn good technique with a lighter-poundage bow and then transition to a heavier bow once you have established good form, strengthened the muscles used to draw and hold the bow, and want to shoot from longer distances.

Obtaining the appropriate bow length also is more important when you begin to shoot longer distances. Remember that energy is stored in the bow during the drawing of the bowstring. Recurve bow limbs that are long cannot store very much energy if drawn by someone with a short draw length. The quality of getting the most energy storage in the limbs for bending them a given amount is called *cast*. Archers want the most cast possible for their draw length, and that is why bow length is important in fitting recurve bows.

Most competition-quality recurve bows consist of a handle-riser section and detachable limbs. Limbs of different lengths can be used with the same handle riser so that it is possible to custom-fit the bow length to the archer.

Fitting a Compound Bow

Compound bows for competitive target shooting and for hunting must be fitted first for draw weight and draw length and then for bow length. The holding weight of a compound bow, which is the force that is held at full draw, is a fraction of its peak weight, which is the force that is imparted to the arrow. Obviously, you can select a compound bow of higher draw weight than a recurve bow. You must pull through the peak weight of a compound bow in order to reach the hold weight, so you must have the strength to pull through the peak weight. The archery shop where you purchase your compound bow should have a scale that will measure the bow's peak weight and its holding weight at your draw length.

The size and type of the pulley or cam of a compound bow determines the point in the draw where the holding weight is reached. This point is called the valley because it is the point in the draw of the lowest draw weight. Ideally the valley should correspond to your draw length. Many compound bows today allow an adjustment of approximately 3 inches in draw length with the same-size pulley. This makes it easier to fit a compound bow, but your draw length must fall within the specified range for the bow, and the bow's cables must be placed in the groove of the pulley corresponding to your draw length.

In the past, manufacturers of compound bows adjusted compound bow length to draw length. Draw lengths over 30 inches necessitated a bow at least 40 inches long, axle to axle. Draw lengths of 33 inches or more made the preferable bow length 44 inches or more. Recently, designers have built bows that are very short from axle to axle. These bows shoot arrows at high speeds, but sometimes precision is sacrificed.

Misstep

Based on your draw length measurement, you select a bow that you can't pull all the way back to your face or, with a compound bow, that causes you to lean back to get the bowstring to the valley.

Correction

Your draw length measurement is too short or too long. Try fitting drill 2 (page 3), especially the wingspan measure, to reestablish your draw length and obtain the proper bow for that draw length.

Fitting Drill 3. *Finding Actual Draw Weight*

The poundage given by a recurve bow manufacturer is the poundage at a standard 28-inch draw length. Your draw length is probably different, so your actual draw weight changes by approximately 2 pounds for every inch of difference. Determine the actual or shooting draw weights for each of the combinations shown in table 1.2. (Answers are on page 12.)

Table 1.2 Draw Weight Drill

Case	Draw length (inches)	Draw weight marked on bow (pounds)	Actual draw weight
1	24	25	
2	29 1/2	30	
3	27 1/2	30	
4	30	35	
5	28	40	
Yours			

Success Check

- Add 2 pounds for every inch over the standard 28 inches.
- Subtract 2 pounds for every inch under the standard 28 inches.

Score Your Success

Correctly estimate 4 or 5 draw weights = 3 points

Correctly estimate 2 or 3 draw weights = 2 points

Correctly estimate 1 draw weight = 1 point

Your score_____

Choosing Arrows

Using arrows of proper length is absolutely critical from a safety perspective. Drawing an arrow past the arrow rest can be dangerous, and this situation is likely to happen if the arrow is too short for your draw length. On the other hand, an arrow that is too long does not fly well.

As a beginner, determine your arrow length by adding at least 3 3/4 inches to your draw length, as shown in figure 1.3. When you establish a more consistent form, you can use arrows just 3/4 inch to 1 3/4 inches longer than your draw length.

Figure 1.3   Fitting Arrows

1. Beginning shooters, add 3 3/4 inches to draw length
2. Experienced shooters, add 3/4 to 1 3/4 inches to draw length
3. Determine actual draw weight
4. Choose shaft size

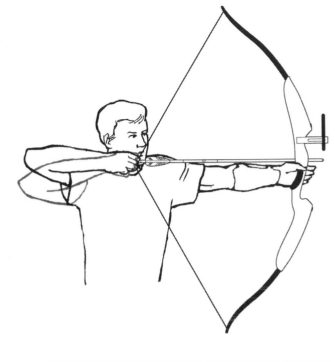

Arrows also vary in shaft size. The rationale for determining the ideal shaft size is presented in step 8, Upgrading, Tuning, and Maintaining Equipment. For now, you can select the size of your arrow shaft from table 1.3 if you are using fiberglass arrows. If you are using aluminum arrows, go to a pro shop or the arrow manufacturer's Web site. Have your bow type, draw length, and draw weight information. A pro shop has a complete arrow selection chart and can assist you in using the chart to find the arrow size you need. If you go to a Web site, you will be able to enter your information and obtain a short list of recommended arrow sizes.

Table 1.3   Shaft Sizes for Fiberglass Arrows

Bow weight at draw length (pounds)	Draw length (inches)								
	23	24	25	26	27	28	29	30	31
20 to 25	0	0	0	1	2	3	4	5	6
26 to 30	0	0	1	2	3	4	5	6	7
31 to 35	0	1	2	3	4	5	6	7	8
36 to 40	1	2	3	4	5	6	7	8	9
41 to 45	1	2	3	4	5	6	7	8	9

Fitting Drill 4. *Arrow Selection*

To select a fiberglass arrow using table 1.3 (page 7), find the weight of your bow, adjusted for your draw length, in the first column. Read across to your draw length to determine your ideal shaft size. Select arrows that have this number printed on the sides of their shafts. To find your ideal aluminum shaft size for this drill, use table 1.4, a simplified aluminum arrow selection chart. Note that this chart requires your arrow length, which is longer than your draw length. For this purpose, you can use the length given as the arrow length. Assume you are fitting arrows for a recurve bow. Move down column 1 to find the bow weight and then across to the designated arrow length to find the four-digit numbers representing the aluminum shaft size. The size of an aluminum shaft is printed on its side. Note that for aluminum arrows, several sizes could be appropriate.

Determine the shaft sizes (for both fiberglass and aluminum) for each of the cases shown in table 1.5. (Answers are on page 12.)

Success Check

- Read across to your draw or arrow length.

Table 1.4 Simplified Aluminum Arrow Selection Chart

Actual recurve bow draw weight	Correct arrow length			
	26 in.	28 in.	30 in.	32 in.
20-25 lbs.	1516 1518	1616 1713 1714	1813 1814 1816	
30-35 lbs.	1616 1618 1713 1714	1716 1813 1814	1818 1914 1916	2016 2114
40-45 lbs.	1716 1813 1814	1818 1914 1916	1918 2016 2114	2018 2115 2213
50-55 lbs.	1818 1914 1916	1918 2016 2114	2018 2115 2213	2216

Score Your Success

Correctly determine 4 or 5 sizes = 3 points
Correctly determine 2 or 3 sizes = 2 points
Correctly determine 1 size = 1 point
Your score_____

Table 1.5 Determining Arrow Shaft Size

Case	Actual draw weight (pounds)	Draw or arrow length (inches)	Shaft size, fiberglass	Shaft size, aluminum
1	25	28		
2	22	26		
3	30	28		
4	40	30		
5	50	32	Not given	
Yours				

Fitting the Arm Guard and Finger Tab

The final step in fitting your equipment is to choose an arm guard and finger tab. An arm guard that covers the forearm of your bow arm (the one that holds the bow) should be sufficient. Some archers find that their particular body structure places the upper arm close to the path of the string upon release. For comfort, they choose a long style of arm guard that covers both the upper arm and the forearm.

The finger tab covers the first three fingers of your draw or string hand (the one that pulls the bowstring). Finger tabs come in several sizes. Choose one that covers the fingers when you form a hook to pull the string but that does not have an excess of leather extending beyond the fingertips. Figure 1.4 shows a properly fitted tab and arm guard.

Figure 1.4 Finger tab and arm guard.

SETTING UP YOUR BOW AND ACCESSORIES

At the very least, you should have a *nock locator* on your bowstring before you begin shooting and an *arrow rest* mounted on your bow. You could also install a *bowsight* now, but since the initial steps emphasize good form and all shots will be at short distances to large targets, a bowsight isn't absolutely necessary. In step 4 you will learn how to install and use a bowsight.

Another helpful accessory is a sling. This is a strap that surrounds the bow and wrist or the bow and the thumb and forefinger. The strap prevents the archer from dropping the bow upon release of the string, given that a relaxed hold of the bow leads to more accurate shots than a tight grip on the bow handle. You will read about the grip in more detail in step 6, but for now it is easy to use a sling. Put it on when you pick up a bow to shoot. It requires no further attention!

A nock locator guides you in placing your arrows on the bowstring. It guarantees that your arrows will be oriented at the same angle on every shot. Even slight variations in the angle can affect accuracy because a small distance at the tail end of the arrow affects the arrow's trajectory to the target. A nock locator often is a small, C-shaped piece of metal lined with rubber or soft plastic to protect the bowstring. A special pair of pliers is used to tighten the locator on the string.

Metal locators are inexpensive and can be repositioned, but some archers simply wrap waxed dental floss around the bowstring to form a nock locator. Most archers place the locator so that the arrow is nocked right below it. The arrow sits at a perfect right angle if they shoot a mechanical release or slightly tail high if they release with the fingers, as shown in figure 1.5a. This preliminary placement should suit you well for your early archery experiences. Installation drill 1 (page 11) shows how to precisely position the nock locator when tuning a bow, something you want to do once your shooting technique is well established.

If you are using a fiberglass, straight-limb bow, the bow handle usually serves as an arrow rest. Some inexpensive recurve bows also are made with a shelf on which the arrow rests. Most other recurve and compound bows, though, are meant to have an arrow rest installed on them. Some of these bows have a cutout section in the handle riser. You must purchase an arrow rest and install it on the handle riser in the proper location, as shown in figure 1.5b. Installation drill 2 will guide you in positioning such a rest. More expensive recurve and compound bows have a hole in the handle riser that allows the rest to be installed at the proper location.

There are many different types of arrow rests. Whether you are using a finger or mechanical release is an important consideration in choosing an arrow rest. Later, as part of the tuning process, you will learn the advantages and disadvantages of some of these arrow rests and how to adjust them precisely.

Figure 1.5 — Setting Up Equipment

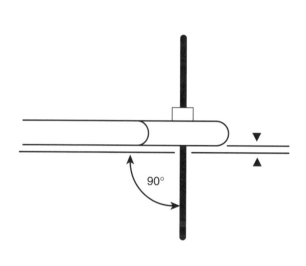

a

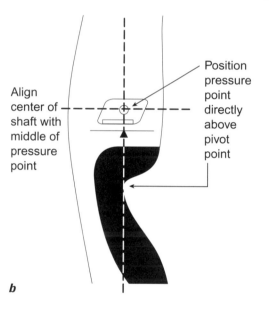

Align center of shaft with middle of pressure point

Position pressure point directly above pivot point

b

NOCK LOCATOR

1. Position bow square on string
2. Mark corner of 90-degree angle on the string
3. Measure a nock width plus 3/8 inch up from the mark
4. Position lower edge of nock locator at the point you have determined
5. Clamp nock locator

ARROW REST

1. Align pressure point over handle pivot point
2. Attach the rest 5/8 inch above arrow shelf

Installation Drill 1. *Nock Locator Setup*

The first step in installing a nock locator is marking the point on the bowstring where the bottom of a nocked arrow forms a perfect 90-degree angle with the string. Bow squares are sold for this purpose, but you can substitute a large mechanical drawing triangle or a carpenter's L.

Position the lower edge of the nock locator 1/2 inch above the square if you are releasing with your fingers. This allows the arrow to clear the bow slightly tail high so that the arrow's fletching does not strike the bow handle. If you are using a mechanical release, position the nock locator so that the arrow is perfectly level or 1/4 inch high. Clamp the nock locator in this position (figure 1.6). Later, when you learn about fine-tuning of a bow, you might adjust this position slightly.

Success Check

- Place bow square so that it gently sits on arrow rest. (See figure 2.2 on page 17)
- Mark string at a perfect right angle.
- Move up 1/2 inch.

Score Your Success

Successfully install nock locator = 3 points

Your score_____

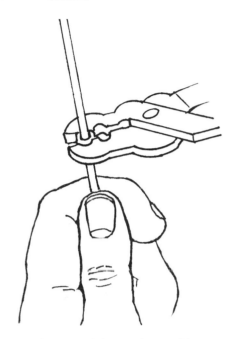

Figure 1.6 Clamp nock locator into position.

Installation Drill 2. *Arrow Rest Installation*

To attach a self-stick arrow rest on a bow not tapped for a removable arrow rest, place the bow on a table. Align the pressure point of the rest over the pivot point (throat) of the bow handle. Position the rest 5/8 inch above the bow shelf to allow room for the arrow's fletching to clear the shelf upon release. Mark this place with several light pencil marks, peel the paper from the back of the rest, and press it into place.

If you are installing an arrow rest on a handle riser that is tapped for a removable arrow rest device, you likely will decide on the type of arrow rest based on whether you release with your fingers or with a mechanical release. If you release the bowstring with your fingers, you will probably use what is called a *shoot-around* rest. If you use a mechanical release, you will probably use a *shoot-through* rest.

With a shoot-around rest, you will insert a cushion plunger into the hole tapped for that purpose.

Place an arrow on the bowstring with your bow on its side on a table and align the center of the arrow with the center of the plunger. Attach your arrow rest to the bow so that the arrow sits in this position when the bow is held upright.

With a shoot-through rest, attach the rest so that the launcher arms support a nocked arrow in a position so that it would not strike the handle riser upon release. Later, in considering fine-tuning, you will adjust the cushion plunger or launcher.

Success Check

- Align pressure point over pivot point.
- Place rest 5/8 inch above shelf.

Score Your Success

Install an arrow rest = 3 points

Your score_____

STABILIZERS

A stabilizer is a rod, often with a weight at the end, mounted on the bow at approximately a right angle to the long axis of the bow. The stabilizer can be long or short. Archers can choose how many stabilizers they prefer to use and how to configure them.

Stabilizers minimize the torque, or turning, of the bow around its long axis as you release the bowstring and send the arrow on its way. The arrow can push slightly against the bow especially when you hold and release the bowstring with the fingers. The arrow pushing against the bow can cause the bow handle to turn, affecting the flight of the arrow. Attaching a weight a distance from the axis of rotation resists the turning. The resistance is a product of the amount of weight and its distance from the axis of rotation. Archers can get the same dampening effect from lighter weights farther from the axis and heavier weights closer to the axis.

Additionally, archers tend to grab the bow handle or push or pull it at release if they think their aim is slightly misdirected. These actions detract from accuracy, but stabilizers tend to dampen these movements such that the effect of the movement is diminished. The weight of stabilizers simply adds to the inertia of the bow to movement. The weight also dampens small movements during aiming, allowing archers to settle on the bull's-eye.

As a novice archer choosing stabilizers, you should first consider the amount of weight added to the bow itself. While the weight of stabilizers can dampen movements during aiming and release, too much weight can fatigue the shoulder muscles over a shooting session and have the reverse effect. Add a stabilizer to your bow only when you feel you have the strength to hold your bow long enough to settle and aim every shot over your entire practice session.

It is best to begin with a single stabilizer with a light weight on the end. As your muscular strength and endurance build with practice, you can add weight easily since the weights on the end of the stabilizer rods are usually interchangeable. Later, you can experiment with V stabilizers that angle back and out from the main stabilizer or with additional stabilizers. Bowhunters usually prefer short stabilizer rods since they carry their bows through brush and wooded areas.

To use a stabilizer, you must have an insert on your bow so that the threads on the end of the stabilizer rod can be screwed into the insert. On bows that have a metal handle riser and wood, fiberglass, or composite limbs, these inserts are in the metal handle riser section. The most common configuration is a stabilizer that extends toward the target from the bow handle just below the grip. Usually, the V configurations are mounted onto this main stabilizer.

Answer Key

Fitting Drill 3. *Finding Actual Draw Weight*

Case 1: 17 pounds

Case 2: 33 pounds

Case 3: 29 pounds

Case 4: 39 pounds

Case 5: 40 pounds

Fitting Drill 4. *Arrow Selection*

Case 1: fiberglass #3; aluminum 1616, 1713, 1714

Case 2: fiberglass #1; aluminum 1516, 1518

Case 3: fiberglass #4; aluminum 1716, 1813, 1814

Case 4: fiberglass #8; aluminum 1918, 2016, 2114

Case 5: fiberglass not given; aluminum 2216

SUCCESS SUMMARY OF FITTING EQUIPMENT

You now know how to select a bow that fits you, to select arrows that fit you and are matched to your bow, and to select accessories that fit. You also know how to prepare your bow for shooting. The time spent in selecting appropriate equipment and setting it up for shooting is a good investment in your future success and enjoyment.

A properly fitted bow that matches your hand preference, draw length, and strength is more comfortable to shoot than a poorly fitted one. Properly fitted arrows minimize your errors and enable you to have the most scoring success.

For each of the drills presented in this step, you can earn points to chart your progress. Enter your score for each drill and add them up to rate your total success. If you scored at least 16 points, you are ready to move to the next step on safety. If you scored fewer than 16 points, be sure to complete the drills on determining your eye dominance and draw length and to install a nock locator and arrow rest to earn the needed points.

Fitting and setting up equipment properly also contribute to safe shooting. Selecting arrows of proper length makes shooting safe for you, and installing a nock locator makes shooting safer for those around you. Because safety is a great concern in archery, you must now turn your attention to safety, even before you shoot.

Fitting Drills

1. Determining Eye Dominance ___ out of 3
2. Determining Draw Length ___ out of 3
3. Finding Actual Draw Weight ___ out of 3
4. Arrow Selection ___ out of 3

Installation Drills

1. Nock Locator Setup ___ out of 3
2. Arrow Rest Installation ___ out of 3

Total ___ *out of 18*

Shooting Safely

When we were kids, the local police department gave a demonstration on the park archery range. A policeman filled a gallon jug with sand and placed a balloon behind it. He fired a handgun into the jug. The sand stopped the bullet. An archer then shot an arrow into the jug. It passed through the sand and popped the balloon. The policeman made his point to would-be archers: An arrow can be lethal when shot from a bow.

In archery, safety should always come before shooting. In this step, you will learn how to shoot safely to protect both yourself and others. Safety rules apply before you shoot, while you shoot, and as you retrieve your arrows.

SAFE EQUIPMENT

The first step in safe shooting is choosing equipment that fits properly, as emphasized in step 1. Ill-fitted equipment can be a hazard to you and to others around you because it can cause you to shoot unsafely. Once you have the proper equipment, you must routinely inspect it to assure yourself that it has not been damaged or become so worn that it is unsafe. Equipment failure during a shot can put you and others at risk of injury.

The first step in making your shooting safe is to be fitted for equipment that is matched to your size and strength. This allows you to be in control of every shot. Next, you must inspect your equipment to make sure it is in good working order before every shooting session. This step is particularly important with older equipment,

but it should be a regular part of your shooting preparation in any case. Finally, check what you are wearing. Although archery does not require a certain type of clothing, some clothing and accessories can be problematic.

Keep the following points in mind when selecting your equipment. Have an instructor or pro shop employee verify that your arrows are long enough for you. Overdrawing a short arrow is dangerous because the arrow can shatter if it lodges behind the bow; the arrow can even embed itself in your arm (figure 2.1). If you lend your arrows to other archers, make sure the arrows are long enough for the other archers. Choose a bow draw weight that you can draw easily and hold at least several seconds without tiring.

Figure 2.1	Dangerous Practice: Overdrawing a Short Arrow

1. Arrows should be of the proper length
2. Bow weight should be comfortable
3. Bow limbs and arrows should be free of cracks
4. Make sure bowstring is intact
5. Do not overdraw arrow

Misstep

Your bow dry-fires (arrow falls to your feet on release).

Correction

Inspect the arrow nock for cracks. Replace cracked nocks.

Before shooting, inspect your equipment carefully. First inspect your bowstring. If it is frayed or if any strand of the string is broken, replace the bowstring. Check the serving on your bowstring. If it is unraveling, tie it off, have it re-served, or replace the string.

Next, inspect your bow. If there is a crack in the limbs, do not shoot your bow. Have an instructor or employee at a pro shop inspect it. A cracked bow could break at full draw and cause an injury.

If you are shooting with a recurve bow, check the string or brace height to make sure that it is at least 6 inches (figure 2.2). Attach a bow square to the bowstring and set the arm of the bow square on the arrow rest. Read the number of inches marked on the arm of the bow square at a point exactly above the deepest part of bow handle or grip (pivot point). If the brace height is shorter than 6 inches, the bowstring might slap your wrist. Step 8, Upgrading, Tuning, and Maintaining Equipment, explains how to adjust brace height.

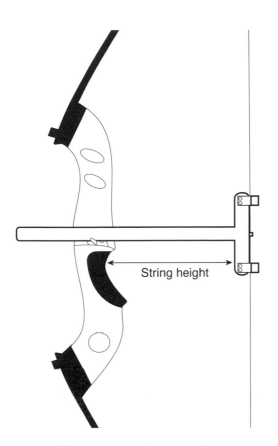

String height

Figure 2.2 A bow square positioned to allow you to check the string or brace height.

If you are shooting with a compound bow, make sure that the steel cables are routed properly on the pulleys and that the bowstring is securely attached to the cables.

Inspect your arrows. Wood arrows with cracks should be broken into two pieces and discarded. Extremely bent aluminum arrows should be straightened before shooting. Each arrow should have a properly installed tip.

Inspect your arrows' nocks. Remove and replace cracked nocks immediately because a damaged nock can slip off the string before release.

ATTIRE

Archery requires no particular uniform, but archers avoid clothing that could catch the bowstring. Shoes, arm guards, and finger tabs help prevent injuries.

When dressing to shoot, avoid baggy shirts, baggy sleeves, and chest pockets with buttons for trim. Remove pens and pencils from shirt pockets (figure 2.3). Also avoid necklaces, dangling earrings, and pins. A bowstring could catch on any of these. If you have long hair, you may want to tie it back so that it does not become caught in the bowstring.

Wear shoes when shooting. If you drop an arrow on your bare foot or step on it in the grass, it could cause an injury. Wear an arm guard and use a finger tab. They protect you from abrasions and blisters.

Figure 2.3   Dangerous Practice: Attire

1. Wear shoes and close-fitting clothing
2. Wear an arm guard and finger tab
3. Remove jewelry and objects, such as pens, from pockets

Safe Equipment Drill. *Equipment Inspection*

Develop an inspection routine that you conduct before every shooting session. Follow these steps:

1. Inspect bow limbs for cracks.

2. Inspect arrow rest for breakage or slippage.

3. Make sure bowstrings and compound bow cables are seated properly.

4. Inspect bowstring and its serving for fraying or breakage.

5. Check arrows for cracks in shafts or nocks, and make sure the arrows' points are in place.

Success Check

- Cracked equipment is set aside.
- Bowstring and cable are properly seated.
- Bowstring and its serving are without frays.

Score Your Success

Demonstration of your inspection routine = 3 points

Your score_____

SHOOTING SAFELY

As you learn about the sport of archery, you must always be aware that you hold a lethal weapon in your hand when you shoot. Before shooting your first arrow, learn safety rules and follow them rigidly. Keep safety in mind when shooting. Safety should be a matter for conscious attention at all times; never relegate it to the subconscious. Accidents often happen because people do not give their full attention to the task at hand. You must shoot with safety in mind.

Most of the following safety rules point out in specific ways that a bow is a lethal weapon and that you must be very careful in its use. Anticipate dangerous situations.

Take your position on the shooting line when instructed to do so, making sure you straddle the line so that you and all shooters are standing in one straight line (figure 2.4). Nock your first arrow only after the signal to shoot is given (usually one whistle blast).

| **Figure 2.4** | **Shooting Safety** |

1. Straddle shooting line
2. Point arrow at ground or target
3. Make sure area around and behind target is clear
4. Shoot only at target
5. Restart shot if arrow falls off rest
6. Stop on emergency signal

 Misstep

You nock your arrow and then turn to talk to another shooter or a spectator.

Correction

Be sure to keep your bow with a nocked arrow pointed at the ground or at the target. If you turn away from the target, remove your arrow from the bowstring.

Point a nocked arrow at the ground until the target area is declared clear and you are ready to draw the bowstring. Even an arrow released from a partially drawn bow can cause serious injury. Nock your arrow only at the nock locator.

If shooting on your own, check the target area to make sure that it is clear at least 40 yards behind and 20 yards to each side of the target before each shot.

If an arrow falls off the arrow rest, restart the shot rather than attempting to replace the arrow at full draw. Otherwise, you may release the bowstring because of fatigue before getting the arrow into proper position.

Learn to shoot without holding the arrow on the bow with your index finger. You could puncture or scratch your finger if you hold the arrow on the bow with your index finger.

If any of your equipment falls forward of the shooting line when you are shooting in a group, rake it toward you with your bow or an arrow (figure 2.5) rather than crossing the shooting line to retrieve it.

Always shoot arrows toward the target; never shoot arrows straight up into the air. Stop

Figure 2.5 Use a bow to rake fallen arrows toward you. Do not cross the shooting line to retrieve any equipment that falls.

shooting immediately if you hear an emergency signal. Three or more whistle blasts are often used as the emergency signal.

Misstep

You are ready to release when someone walks into the target area from the side or from the shooting line.

Correction

You must let down (ease the string forward) immediately if someone walks into the target area or in front of the shooting line. Remind other archers to wait for the signal or all other archers to finish.

RETRIEVING ARROWS SAFELY

It is tempting to think that the risk associated with archery is over once the arrows are shot. Yet, more archers are injured when retrieving and carrying an arrow than when shooting. Not only do arrows have sharp points, but they also could cause injury by poking. The broadheads used for hunting deserve the utmost caution. They are razor sharp and can cause severe, life-threatening injury. Adherence to the following rules should help prevent such injuries.

Step back from the shooting line when you finish shooting your arrows. However, if an archer next to you is at full draw, it is courteous to remain in place so that you do not distract the other archer.

Place your bow on a bow rack or in a designated area while you retrieve your arrows. Someone could trip over a bow left on the ground or floor.

Cross the shooting line to retrieve your arrows only when given the signal to do so (usually two whistle blasts). If no one is providing signals, move forward only after all other archers have stepped back from the shooting line to indicate that they have finished shooting.

Walk, don't run, to the target and approach it with caution (figure 2.6a). Tripping into the nock end of an arrow can cause a serious injury, especially to your eyes.

Retrieve low arrows that landed in the grass short of the target as soon as possible on the walk to the target. If the fletching is embedded in the grass, pull the arrow forward and out of the grass to keeping from damaging the fletching (figure 2.6b).

Be sure there is no one behind you as you pull your arrows from the target. Place one hand flat against the target face to prevent it from ripping, and then grasp the arrow shaft close to the target with the other hand (figure 2.6c). Twist the arrow back and forth to remove it. This twisting keeps the arrow from bending and prevents you from creating a large, forceful backward thrust that could strike someone nearby with the nock end of the arrow. To help prevent eye and head injuries, use caution when retrieving notepads, pens, or other objects below the target.

Figure 2.6   Retrieving Arrows Safely

APPROACHING THE TARGET

1. Wait for the signal before crossing the shooting line
2. Walk to the target
3. Watch for arrows in the grass

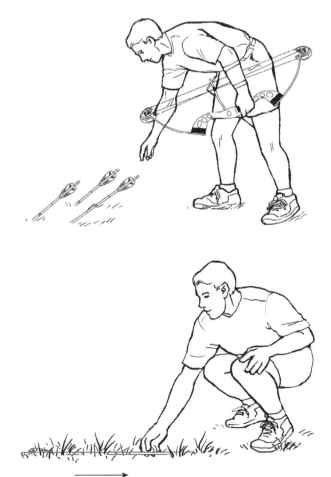

RETRIEVING ARROWS

1. Pull forward any arrows embedded in the grass
2. Leave equipment in front of the target if you walk behind the target

(continued)

Figure 2.6 *(continued)*

REMOVING ARROWS FROM THE TARGET

1. Make sure no one is behind you when removing arrows from the target
2. Twist arrows to remove them from the target
3. Carry arrows in a quiver

Misstep

You are shooting alone and you carry your equipment with you as you search behind the target for a lost arrow.

Correction

Leave your bow in front of the target as a signal to other archers.

Be careful with arrows because the points are sharp. Carry them in a quiver or with the points in your palm (target points only).

When you have to retrieve arrows behind the target, you must be sure no one else will shoot at it. One archer should remain in front of the target while the others look for the lost arrows. If you are shooting alone, leave your bow or quiver in front of the target. This action is especially important on a field course or bowhunting practice range where brush might hide you from the view of archers arriving to shoot the target.

Safe Shooting Drill. *Safety Test*

You should demonstrate your knowledge of the safety rules of archery before shooting your first arrows. For your sake and the sake of others learning archery with you, you must know and obey the safety rules. Use the following questions to check your safety knowledge. Answers are on page 23.

1. What should you do if you find a crack in your bow limb?

2. What should you do if you find a crack in a wooden arrow?

3. What should you do if you find a crack in the plastic nock on your arrow?

4. How should you dress for shooting?

5. What should you check for on your bowstring?

6. When is it safe to nock an arrow when shooting with a group?

7. When is it safe to nock an arrow when shooting on your own?

8. What does one whistle blast mean?

9. What do two whistle blasts mean?

10. What do three whistle blasts mean?

11. When is it permissible to step across the shooting line?

12. What should you do if your arrow falls off the arrow rest as you are drawing (pulling the bowstring back) or aiming?

13. When is it permissible to hold an arrow on the bow with your index finger?

14. What should you do when you finish shooting your arrows?

15. How should you approach the target?

16. When should you retrieve arrows that fall short of the target?

17. When should you retrieve arrows that land behind the target?

18. What should you check for before pulling your arrows from the target?

Success Check

- Review the rules of safety if you missed any of the questions.

Score Your Success

18 correct = 10 points

17 correct = 7 points

16 correct = 4 points

15 correct = 1 point

Fewer than 15 correct = 0 points

Your score_____

Answer Key

Safe Shooting Drill. *Safety Test*

1. Do not shoot. Seek advice at a pro shop.

2. Break it into two pieces and discard.

3. Remove cracked nock and replace it.

4. Wear close-fitting clothing and remove jewelry and pocket items. Tie long hair back.

5. Check for fraying or a broken strand and a frayed serving.

6. After the signal (one whistle blast) it is safe to nock an arrow when shooting with a group.

7. After you check for a clear target area it is safe to nock an arrow when shooting on your own.

8. It is permissible to nock an arrow and begin shooting.

9. It is permissible to cross the shooting line to retrieve arrows.

10. Stop shooting immediately. This is an emergency situation.

11. After two whistle blasts, or when all archers have stepped back from the line, it is permissible to step across the shooting line.

12. Ease the string forward and start the shot over.

13. It is never permissible to hold an arrow on the bow with your index finger!

14. Step back from the line and place your bow in the designated area.

15. Approach the target at walking speed, watching for arrows that landed in the grass.

16. On the way to the target, retrieve arrows that fall short of the target.

17. After positioning a fellow archer or your bow or quiver in front of the target, retrieve arrows that land behind the target.

18. Check for archers or spectators standing in the way before you pull your arrows from the target.

SUCCESS SUMMARY OF SAFETY

Every archer wants shooting to be an enjoyable experience. You should never place another archer in harm's way. Despite the inherent danger of the bow and arrow, shooting can be safe when you do two basic things: methodically and regularly inspect equipment and anticipate unsafe shooting conditions in order to correct them before shooting.

For both of the drills presented in this step, you can earn points to chart your progress. Enter your score for each drill and add them up to rate your total success. If you scored at least 12 points, you can move to the next step.

Safe Equipment Drill	
1. Equipment Inspection	___ out of 3
Safe Shooting Drill	
1. Safety Test	___ out of 10
Total	___ **out of 13**

Preparation is often a key to doing something well. You have prepared to shoot by obtaining equipment fit to your body size and strength and by learning how to participate safely. Now you are ready to learn how to shoot. In the next step you will begin by learning to draw and anchor your bow without an arrow. Once comfortable with the draw and anchor, you can safely learn to shoot your first arrows.

Shooting With Good Form

Some sports and sport skills are fun to play and watch because you never know what's going to happen next. Wrestlers have an ongoing interchange of attack and counterattack; soccer players switch from offense to defense and back to offense within seconds; volleyball players dig the ball one minute and spike it the next.

Other sports and sport skills are performed well only if they are executed the same way, correctly, every time. Like a great free-throw shooter whose every attempt looks like a replay of the one preceding it, a successful archer is a consistent archer. An archer's goal is to establish perfect form, called T-form, and then reproduce it on every subsequent shot.

Note that we're referring to consistency in technique, not outcome, at least at first. So don't be distracted by the flight of the arrow or scoring your shot. Instead, learn the T-form shooting technique taught in this step, and practice the drills to develop a shot pattern you will use every time you take aim. If you think that sounds boring, just think how bored you'll be with bull's-eye after bull's-eye!

UNDERSTANDING T-FORM

The body's muscular structure can maintain good T-form alignment of the arms and trunk with less effort than with other positions. Muscle groups on opposite sides of the limbs and trunk pull evenly in T-form. Archers who assume bent positions at full draw are pulling more with one muscle than another. They may find it difficult to assume that exact position on subsequent shots, especially when they are fatigued or nervous.

Remember that in shooting archery, you maintain your position for several seconds to aim while holding the bow up and the bowstring back against many pounds of resistance. The nervousness you may feel from wanting to shoot well in a contest, or the excitement you may feel as a deer is approaching, also could cause a breakdown in your form. You need a shooting style that is easy to reproduce, even under pressure.

It is also easier for you to visualize placing your body into the T-shape than a bent shape (figure 3.1). You have an exact visual image of the straight lines and right angles of the T. If your body or limbs are in a bent position, you can more easily adjust to a straight position than to a degree of bend. So you can monitor your own form more easily when your goal is T-form.

You may see other archers experiencing some degree of success in shooting without T-form. This success might be short-lived. In the long run, archers with T-form are more comfortable and relaxed and shoot more accurately than archers without this alignment. Practicing T-form and making it a habit are well worth the effort in your early experience with archery.

Figure 3.1 Visualizing T-form.

MIMICKING A T-FORM SHOT

The best way to learn the basic T-form shot is to first mimic it without actually shooting an arrow. Mimicking gives you the chance to make the motions of shooting habitual and to get used to the equipment gradually. Mimicking contributes to safe shooting, too. You can make sure you are handling the bow and arrow safely and not overdrawing the arrow.

First mimic T-form without an arrow. Take a stance with your bow arm side toward the target, feet shoulder-width apart, and weight even. Check your stance by imagining a straight line going through the toes of each foot. If this line would continue toward your target, you are in good position (figure 3.2a). If it would not, adjust your position. Stand straight and keep your shoulders square over your feet. Avoid twisting your trunk.

Hold the bow at the handle straight up and down in front of you. Form a hook with the middle three fingers of your string hand. Hook the bowstring in the end joint of the fingers with one finger above the nocking point and two below it (figure 3.2b).

Raise and extend your bow arm at shoulder level toward the target. Look over your front shoulder. Draw the string by pulling your elbow back in one fluid motion. The shoulder blade of the drawing arm should move toward your spine. Remember, you will need to exert enough muscular force to overcome the draw weight of the bow. Bring the string hand back to your anchor position and rotate your bow elbow down and out. The anchor position is under your chin, with the top finger and chin touching and the string touching the tip of your nose and your chin.

Hold this position for a few seconds, noticing how it feels, and then ease the string forward to the bow's relaxed position (figure 3.2c). Never release a bowstring unless there is an arrow in the bow because dry-firing might damage the bow. Relax before repeating the process.

Figure 3.2   Mimicking T–Form

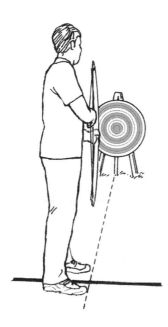

a

b

c

STANCE

1. Position your side toward target
2. Align feet and keep weight even
3. Stand straight
4. Keep bow in front
5. Shoulders are square
6. Mouth is closed and teeth are together

DRAW AND ANCHOR

1. Set bow in V of thumb and index finger
2. Set string hand hook
3. Look over front shoulder
4. Raise bow toward target
5. Rotate bow elbow down
6. Relax string hand and wrist
7. Draw string elbow back at shoulder level
8. Position chin on hand and string on chin and nose

EASE DOWN

1. Concentrate on target
2. Ease string forward

Misstep

The bow arm elbow turns in to the anticipated path of the bowstring.

Correction

Make sure your bow hand is directly behind the bow handle and then rotate your elbow down and out.

You might be tempted to skip mimicking, but remember that learning T-form before you start worrying about where the arrow will go will reap benefits later. When an archer shoots with a draw position based on straight lines and right angles, accuracy is sure to follow. Some world-class archers mimic their shots as a warm-up before their shooting sessions, so don't be afraid to make mimicking a regular part of your archery practice.

Mimicking Drill 1. *Bow Arm Practice*

It is helpful to practice rotating your elbow down and out while there is pressure against your hand. Approach a doorjamb and extend your bow arm. (If you are outdoors with nothing to lean against, you can have a partner provide resistance.) Place the heel of your hand against the doorjamb (thumb toward ceiling) and lean against the doorjamb slightly (figure 3.3a). Rotate your elbow down and around without moving your hand so that the wider part of your arm is vertical (figure 3.3b). Be sure to keep your bow shoulder down, not hunched. You can check your position by now bending your arm at the elbow. If your hand is at chest level, your elbow position has been correct. If your hand is at face level, your elbow position has been incorrect. Repeat nine more times.

To Increase Difficulty

- Hold your bow and extend it toward a target.
- Hook the bowstring with your string hand and rotate the elbow down.

To Decrease Difficulty

- Hold your bow arm out to the side at shoulder level, palm down. Keeping your arm in place, rotate your hand to a vertical position. Your bow arm should be in proper position. Relax, and then try to achieve this position while performing this drill.

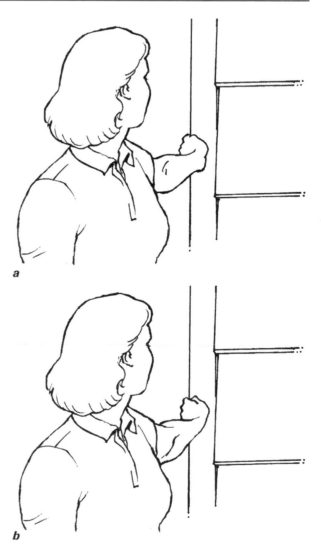

Figure 3.3 Bow arm practice: *(a)* Press heel of hand against doorjamb; *(b)* rotate elbow down without moving hand.

Success Check

- Level the shoulders.
- Keep hand vertical.
- Rotate elbow down and out.

Mimicking Drill 2. *Looking in a Mirror*

Standing diagonally in front of a mirror with a bow, practice setting your bow hand and a relaxed hook with your draw hand fingers (figure 3.4). Raise the bow and draw by moving your elbow straight back at shoulder level. Keep your draw wrist straight and relaxed. Be sure to anchor with the bowstring touching the middle of your nose and chin. Check your position for T-form by looking in the mirror; move just your eyes, not your head. Slowly ease the string back. Repeat nine more times.

To Increase Difficulty

- Repeat this drill, drawing with your eyes closed so you can focus on the feel of T-form before you check the mirror.

To Decrease Difficulty

- Perform this drill without a bow or with a bow much lighter in poundage than your shooting bow.

Success Check

- Keep shoulders level and head erect.
- Move draw elbow back at shoulder level.
- Touch chin with string hand.
- Touch nose and chin with string.

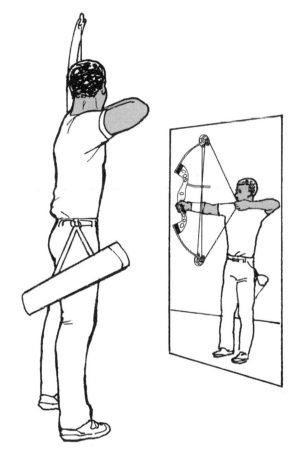

Figure 3.4 Check your form in a mirror.

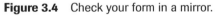

MIMICKING WITH AN ARROW

The next step is to mimic T-form with an arrow (figure 3.5). Take your stance as before. Nock an arrow just below the nock indicator on the string. The index (odd-colored) feather or vane should be toward you. Place the shaft on the arrow rest. Form your string hand hook and place one finger above the arrow and two below it. Draw to your anchor position as before. Remember not to go past your anchor position because you might pull the arrow off the arrow rest. Hold this position for a few seconds, and then ease the bowstring forward. Rest, and then repeat this mimic until you are comfortable handling the bow and arrow. Although the intention here is to mimic and not actually shoot an arrow, you should always practice in front of a target butt just in case you accidentally release the string.

Figure 3.5 Mimicked T-Form Shot With Arrow

 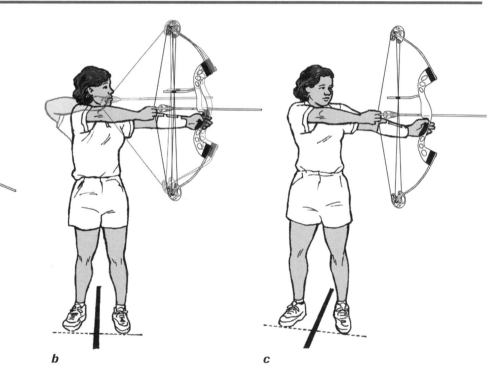

a *b* *c*

STANCE

1. Position your side toward target
2. Align feet and keep weight even
3. Stand straight and square to target
4. Nock arrow against nock locator
5. Position index feather toward you

DRAW AND ANCHOR

1. Set bow hand, and then draw hand
2. Put one finger above and two fingers below arrow
3. Raise bow toward target
4. Rotate bow elbow down
5. Relax hands and draw hand flat
6. Move draw elbow back
7. Place chin on hand, with string touching chin and nose

EASE DOWN

1. Align string and arrow shaft
2. Keep the bow level
3. Ease string forward

Misstep

Arrow falls off rest during draw.

Correction

Keep the wrist and first knuckles of the draw hand straight throughout the draw without cupping your hand. Use the hand only as a hook, moving the arm with the back muscles. Keep the bow vertical.

Mimicking With Arrow Drill 1. *Partner Check*

For this drill you will need a partner who is somewhat familiar with T-form. Mimic six shots with an arrow. Your partner should watch you from the side and back and try to catch you varying your form. You will probably find it more difficult to maintain form on your later arrows as you tire.

To Increase Difficulty

- Mimic 10 shots in a row.

To Decrease Difficulty

- Mimic three shots in a row.

Success Check

- Keep the bow arm and draw arm at shoulder level.
- Anchor. String touches nose and chin.

Score Your Success

5 or 6 repetitions with consistent form = 3 points

3 or 4 repetitions with consistent form = 2 points

2 repetitions with consistent form = 1 point

Your score_____

Mimicking With Arrow Drill 2. *Mirror Drill*

Standing diagonally in front of a mirror with a bow, practice nocking your arrow and setting your bow hand with a relaxed hook with your draw hand fingers. Raise the bow and draw by moving your elbow straight back at shoulder level. Keep your draw wrist straight and relaxed. Be sure to anchor with the bowstring touching the middle of your nose and chin. Check your position for T-form by looking in the mirror; move just your eyes, not your head. Slowly ease the string back. Complete a total of six repetitions.

To Increase Difficulty

- Mimic the shot with your eyes closed after you set your draw hand hook, and then open them to check the mirror.

To Decrease Difficulty

- Mimic the shot with a bow much lighter in poundage.

Success Check

- Keep shoulders level and head erect.
- Move draw elbow back at shoulder level.
- Touch chin with string hand.
- Touch nose and chin with string.

Score Your Success

5 or 6 repetitions with consistent form = 3 points

3 or 4 repetitions with consistent form = 2 points

2 repetitions with consistent form = 1 point

Your score_____

Mimicking With Arrow Drill 3. *Bow Hand Check*

Obtain two small dot stickers or pieces of colored tape. Place one on the middle of the bow handle just above where you place your hand. Take your bow hand position and place the second sticker on your hand right below the other dot on the bow. Shoot two ends of six arrows each (a total of 12 repetitions). Before drawing for each shot, take your bow hand position and check to see whether the stickers or pieces of tape are aligned (figure 3.6).

Success Check

• Centerline of arm intersects center of bow.

Score Your Success

10 to 12 repetitions with the stickers aligned = 4 points

8 or 9 repetitions with the stickers aligned = 3 points

6 or 7 repetitions with the stickers aligned = 2 points

4 or 5 repetitions with the stickers aligned = 1 point

Your score_____

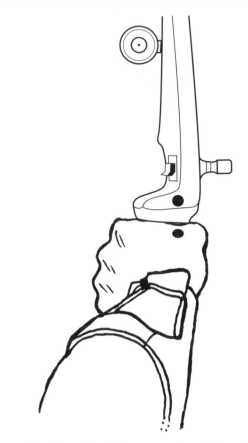

Figure 3.6 Does the sticker on your hand align with the sticker on the bow?

EXECUTING THE T-FORM SHOT

Once you are comfortable mimicking T-form with an arrow, you need only add the release to shoot an arrow. Stand close (10 to 15 yards) to a target butt. You can place a large target face or just a paper plate on the target butt for a focus point. At first, don't worry about where your arrows land.

Remember your safety rules. When you are sure the area behind and to the side of the target butt is clear, take your stance as in mimicking (figure 3.7a). Set your bow and string hands just as before. Draw and anchor (figure 3.7b). Now tighten your back muscles and simply relax your fingers to release the string (figure 3.7c). Keep your bow arm up and head still. The bow will do the rest!

Figure 3.7   T-Form Shot

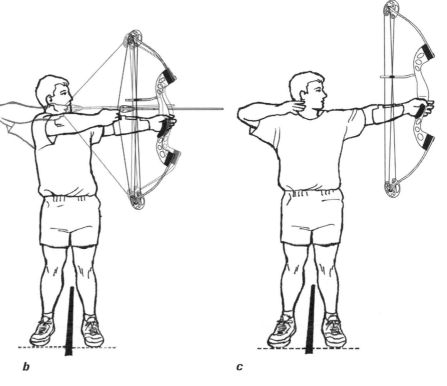

a

b

c

STANCE

1. Position your side toward target
2. Align feet and keep weight even
3. Stand straight and square to target
4. Nock arrow against nock locator
5. Keep index feather toward you

DRAW, ANCHOR, AND AIM

1. Set bow hand, then draw hand
2. Place one finger above and two fingers below arrow
3. Raise bow toward target
4. Rotate bow elbow down
5. Relax hands and draw hand flat
6. Move draw elbow back
7. Position chin on hand; string touches chin and nose
8. Align string and arrow shaft and level bow
9. Tighten back muscles
10. Maintain relaxed bow and draw hands
11. Count to three

RELEASE AND FOLLOW-THROUGH

1. Relax the draw hand to release string
2. Draw elbow pulls back on release
3. Keep bow arm up, toward target
4. Maintain head position
5. Draw hand finishes over rear shoulder

Misstep

The hips slide forward or the front shoulder scrunches up during the draw or while aiming.

Correction

Stand straight and use the back muscles to draw by moving the draw elbow back. If you cannot make this correction, switch to a bow that is lighter in draw weight.

After you have practiced the basic shot enough that you are comfortable drawing and releasing, add a predraw aim to your routine. A predraw aim places the bow arm at a height where the arrow tip is aligned with a spot about 18 inches below your focus point. After anchoring, align the bowstring (which appears fuzzy when your aiming eye is focusing on the target butt) and the arrow shaft. Check the bow limbs through your peripheral vision to ensure that the bow is vertical. These two additions give you consistency in aiming your arrows vertically and horizontally.

T-Form Drill 1. *Release Mimic*

Without equipment, form your string hand hook. Hook it into the forefinger of your bow hand and anchor under your chin (figure 3.8). Tighten your back muscles, leaving your draw hand relaxed. Now relax your fingers to "release." Your draw hand should be carried back toward your rear shoulder by your back tension. Practice six consecutive releases. You can do this drill anywhere, anytime.

Success Check

• Keep string hand wrist and first knuckles straight.
• Tighten back muscles.
• Relax string fingers.

Score Your Success

Complete 5 or 6 repetitions, developing muscular tension only in the back = 3 points

Complete 3 or 4 repetitions, developing muscular tension only in the back = 2 points

Complete 1 or 2 repetitions, developing muscular tension only in the back = 1 point

Your score_____

Figure 3.8 Mimicking the release.

T-Form Drill 2. *Grouping*

Experienced archers know that grouping arrows is more important than shooting occasional bull's-eyes. One can always aim at a different place to "move" the group into the bull's-eye. The score used in this drill emphasizes shooting a group of arrows. Using T-form consistently should lead to grouping. Shoot an end of six arrows from 10 yards at an empty target butt. You don't need a target face. Take a tape measure to the target. Wrap the tape around all your arrows to obtain the smallest measurement possible. Record the distance needed to surround your arrows.

To Increase Difficulty

- Shoot with your eyes closed. For safety, have a friend watch for safety hazards and make sure your bow is pointed toward the target butt.
- Move back to 15 yards.

To Decrease Difficulty

- Shoot only four arrows per turn.

Success Check

- Relax bow hand and arm.
- Maintain follow-through position until arrow hits the target.

Score Your Success

Distance needed to surround arrows is 35 inches or less = 4 points

Distance needed to surround arrows is 36 to 48 inches = 3 points

Distance needed to surround arrows is 48 to 60 inches = 2 points

Distance needed to surround arrows is 60 to 72 inches = 1 point

Your score_____

T-Form Drill 3. *Hit or Miss*

Our emphasis has been on establishing good form rather than "scoring" shots. If you are anxious to see how accurately you can shoot now, even without using an aiming sight, place a piece of paper 2 feet by 2 feet on the target butt. To establish a standard, shoot an end of five arrows from a distance of 10 yards and note how many land on the paper. Now shoot four more ends.

To Increase Difficulty

- Draw a tic-tac-toe pattern on the paper with a broad-marking pen. Write point values in the squares. Record the number of points earned by arrows landing in the squares. Arrows touching a line can take the higher point value.
- Use a smaller piece of paper.

To Decrease Difficulty

- Use a larger piece of paper.

Success Check

- Relax the draw hand to release.
- Maintain T-form.

Score Your Success

Four ends with an equal number or more hits than your standard (first) end = 4 points

Three ends with an equal number or more hits than your standard end = 3 points

Two ends with an equal number or more hits than your standard end = 2 points

One end with an equal number or more hits than your standard end = 1 point

Your score_____

T-Form Drill 4. *Balloon Pop*

Blow up six balloons and mount them on a target butt. Shooting five arrows per end from a distance of 10 yards, try to pop as many balloons as possible. Repeat the drill four times, replacing balloons as needed on each end.

To Increase Difficulty

- Use fewer balloons.

To Decrease Difficulty

- Use more balloons.
- Place balloons closer together on the target butt.

Success Check

- Use proper T-form.
- Relax bow and string hands.

Score Your Success

Pop five balloons or more = 4 points

Pop four balloons = 3 points

Pop three balloons = 2 points

Pop two balloons = 1 point

Your score_____

DEVELOPING A MENTAL CHECKLIST

A mental checklist is a helpful way to proceed through shot setup. It reminds you to attend to the necessary aspects of shot preparation and leaves you little time to think about other things or be nervous. If you tend to repeat the same form error, a checklist can include a specific reminder to avoid the error.

A mental checklist helps you methodically and precisely prepare every shot in the same way. Your checklist points can vary on a daily basis with shooting conditions. For example, an archer shooting at a target on a sloping hillside often unwittingly cants the bow. The addition of a mental checklist reminder to level the bow helps the archer check for a level bow on every shot.

Begin the development of your personal checklist by identifying the keys to success pertinent to your shooting style. Figure 3.9 gives a skeleton list of the keys to success. It assumes that some of the simplest aspects of shooting have already become routine for you. Remember, a mental checklist is highly personalized. It can reflect your unique shooting style and address the bad habits into which you tend to fall. Adapt this checklist for yourself. Feel free to add anything you tend to overlook or do incorrectly.

Figure 3.9 Mental Checklist

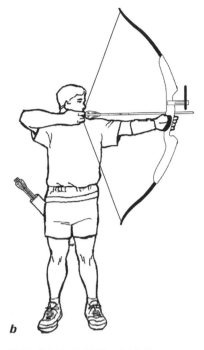

a

b

c

STANCE

1. Assume stance
2. Nock arrow

DRAW AND AIM

1. Set bow hand
2. Set draw hand hook
3. Raise bow and then draw
4. Anchor
5. Level the bow
6. Steady the bow

RELEASE AND FOLLOW-THROUGH

1. Tighten back muscles
2. Relax draw hand to release
3. Keep bow arm up and steady

Misstep

You overlook important steps in your shot preparation. You make the same mistake on a majority of your shots.

Correction

Practice your mental checklist without shooting. Next, practice it while mimicking shots. Then, shoot several ends with a written checklist, as in mental checklist drill 1 (see page 38).

Mental Checklist Drill 1. *Learning Your Checklist*

Copy the keys to success that you have chosen for your personal checklist onto a long, narrow sheet of paper that you can attach to the face of your upper or lower bow limb. As an alternative, copy the list with large lettering onto a large index card and lay the card on the ground in front of you (figure 3.10). (Anchor it on a windy day when shooting outdoors.) Use your written checklist for your next two practice sessions, then see whether you can recite your checklist to a friend without reading it. When you can do so, shoot without the written list, but remember to mentally go through your checklist on every shot.

Success Check

• Say every point on your checklist.

Score Your Success

Recite all points = 3 points

Recite all points but one = 2 points

Recite all points but two = 1 point

Your score_____

Figure 3.10 Write down your checklist and anchor it to the ground in front of you.

Mental Checklist Drill 2. *Rehearsing Aloud*

Shoot four ends of five arrows each at 20 yards. On each arrow, recall the items in your checklist aloud as you perform them up until you anchor. Saying the checklist aloud reminds you to attend to each item. Go through the items during the anchor and aim silently. After you release the bowstring, recall aloud your cues for maintaining follow-through.

Success Check

• Include every point from your checklist.
• Push other thoughts out of your mind.

Score Your Success

Complete 18 to 20 shots, remembering every step = 3 points

Complete 15 to 17 shots, remembering every step = 2 points

Complete 12 to 14 shots, remembering every step = 1 point

Your score_____

SUCCESS SUMMARY OF SHOOTING FORM

You have been practicing the archery shot with T-form, which stresses straight lines and right angles. The sooner you make T-form a habit, the sooner you will achieve success in hitting your target!

The practice drills in this step provide a variety of ways to make T-form a habit, so by now you should be comfortable getting a shot off. Your mental checklist also should be helping you execute each shot consistently. Following the mental checklist you designed should improve your consistency from shot to shot. This checklist also keeps your mind focused on the task at hand and gives negative thoughts little opportunity to invade your thinking.

You probably noticed that the more consistent your T-form became, the more your arrows grouped rather than scattered on the target. An experienced archer can group arrows even if blindfolded, just by relying on the feel of habitually practiced T-form. See how close you are getting toward this goal.

For each of the drills presented in this step, you can earn points to chart your progress. Enter your scores and add them up to rate your total success. If you have 24 or more points, you can advance to the next step. If you have fewer than 24 points, repeat some of the drills to increase the number of repetitions you have practiced and the number of points earned before moving on.

Mimicking Drills

　1. Bow Arm Practice ___ out of 3

　2. Looking in a Mirror ___ out of 3

Mimicking With Arrow Drills

　1. Partner Check ___ out of 3

　2. Mirror Drill With Arrow ___ out of 3

　3. Bow Hand Check ___ out of 4

T-Form Drills

　1. Release Mimic ___ out of 3

　2. Grouping ___ out of 4

　3. Hit or Miss ___ out of 4

　4. Balloon Pop ___ out of 4

Mental Checklist Drills

　1. Learning Your Checklist ___ out of 3

　2. Rehearsing Aloud ___ out of 3

Total ___ **out of 37**

In this step, we stressed that accurate shooting begins with learning good form—T-form—and then using it repeatedly to execute the archery shot. In many sports, though, individual athletes often adopt movements and positions that work better for them than the basics they might have learned first. This occurs in archery, too. It is possible that variations of the square stance and bow hand position you learned in this step are better for your body structure. In step 4 you will have an opportunity to try some variations in order to decide which one works best for you.

Refining Technique

Few sports can take as many forms as archery takes—target shooting, field shooting, distance shooting, bowhunting, and bowfishing. You are probably anxious to try one or more of these forms. As you choose a specific type of archery, you will need to individualize your T-form to be the most compatible with the goal of that style of archery. For example, getting a shot off quickly is more important in bowhunting than in target archery. Establishing an anchor position quickly becomes crucial to success in bowhunting.

Individualizing your shooting form to a personal style also accommodates your body shape and structure. For example, you might choose a certain bow hand position because it is the most comfortable and consistent for your arm and wrist or a certain stance because you have a larger chest than the average shooter. Refining the more detailed aspects of your shooting style will take your performance to a higher level. Practice drills must emphasize exact positions and replication of each aspect of your refined form. In this step, you will refine two other parts of your shooting style: stance and bow hand position.

STANCE

As part of basic T-form, you take a stance with feet about shoulder-width apart and toes along an imaginary line that goes straight to the target. This stance is known as the *square stance*. The square stance is a good stance for beginners because it is natural, easy to establish, and easy to duplicate. However, every archer also has a unique natural stance, a stance that feels the most comfortable. Your body build often dictates that one stance is better than another for you. You must experiment to find the stance that enables you to naturally direct

the bow straight to the target without drifting right or left.

The three basic archery stances are square, open, and closed. Each stance has advantages and disadvantages (table 4.1).

If you are planning to shoot target archery, you should strive to use an identical stance from shot to shot and from session to session. Three or four archers often shoot at the same target butt, so you might not always be able to stand directly in front of your target. You must learn to adapt so that an imaginary line through your

Table 4.1   Advantages and Disadvantages of Various Stances

Type of stance	Advantages	Disadvantages
Square	Natural position Easy to duplicate	Small base of support in front-to-back plane Body can sway, especially in windy conditions Minimizes string clearance, especially for large-chested shooters
Open	Provides stable base of support Minimizes tendency to lean away from target Provides more string clearance than other stances	Promotes tendency to twist upper body to face target Promotes tendency to use arm more than back muscles to draw
Closed	Provides stable base of support Promotes good alignment of arm and shoulder in direct line to target	Minimizes string clearance; string may strike body or clothing Promotes tendency to lean away from target or overdraw

stance points to the target even if you are standing slightly to the right or left. If you are planning to shoot field archery or to hunt, you likely will find times that your footing is uneven. You will have to adapt to the lay of the land.

In this step, you might first want to determine your preferred stance so that you can assume that stance whenever possible. Then, practice shooting with various stances while striving to maintain the alignment of your shoulders and the target. A drill for this has been included.

The square stance (figure 4.1a) places the toes on a straight line to the target. The open stance (figure 4.1b) moves the rear foot up across this imaginary line, a position that opens the body to the target. The closed stance (figure 4.1c) moves the front foot up across this line. You should determine whether to open or close your stance and by how much.

Figure 4.1   Stances

SQUARE

1. Feet are shoulder-width apart
2. Toes are aligned
3. Body is erect
4. Weight is even

Target

a

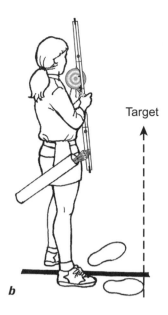

Target

b

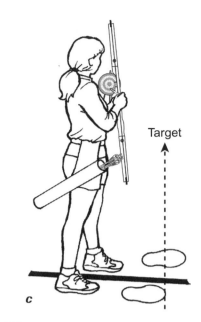

Target

c

OPEN

1. Front foot is turned outward 45 degrees
2. Rear foot is forward 6 inches
3. Body is erect
4. Shoulders are square
5. Weight is evenly distributed
6. Line to target intersects middle of rear foot and toes of front foot

CLOSED

1. Front foot is turned outward 45 degrees
2. Front foot is forward 6 inches
3. Body is erect
4. Weight is even
5. Line to target intersects toes of rear foot and middle of front foot

Misstep

You feel tension in your draw arm when using the open stance.

Correction

You might be opening your shoulders too much and need to square your shoulders to the target enough to use your back muscles to draw.

To determine your natural stance you should attach a bowsight to your bow. Or, you can tape a toothpick onto the back of the bow so that one end extends into your line of sight. Stand 20 yards from a target with a square stance. Without actually shooting an arrow, draw and anchor, aim, and then close your eyes and count to three. Open your eyes and note whether the sight has drifted to the left or right. If it drifted to the right (and you are shooting right-handed), open your stance a little; if it drifted to the left, close your stance a little. Repeat this process, correcting your foot position a little each time, until your bow remains steady. Once you find this natural stance, you may want to use foot markers to promote consistency until the stance becomes second nature. If you are outdoors, take your stance and then insert two golf tees into the ground in front of the toes of each shoe. You can accomplish the same thing indoors with two pieces of tape or a light chalk mark.

Misstep

Your foot position varies from shot to shot or from end to end.

Correction

Use foot markers. Golf tees work outdoors; use chalk or tape indoors.

Stance Drill 1. *Impact-Variation Drill*

This drill demonstrates how stance influences the accuracy of shooting. With a square stance, shoot an end from 12 yards. Note and place a small mark at the center of your arrow grouping on the target face. Now, shoot an end with a closed stance. Again mark the center of your arrow group. Shoot a final end with an open stance and mark the center of your arrow group.

Success Check

* Body is erect
* Weight is evenly distributed

Score Your Success

Six repetitions with the square stance = 1 point

Six repetitions with the closed stance = 1 point

Six repetitions with the open stance = 1 point

Your score_____

Stance Drill 2. *Alignment Check*

This drill gives you an opportunity to determine which stance provides the best alignment to the target for you. Stand approximately 15 yards from the target. Without actually shooting an arrow, come to full draw and aim at the bull's-eye. Close your eyes and count to three. Open your eyes and note whether your bow has drifted to the left or right. If it drifted to the right, open your stance a little; if it drifted to the left, close it a little (if you are left-handed, transpose). Change your foot position approximately an inch at a time until you find a stance that does not result in drifting. When you have found the position that results in no drift, add a cue to your mental checklist to remind yourself to use this stance on every shot.

Success Check

* Weight is evenly distributed.

Score Your Success

Three successive draws without drifting = 3 points

Two successive draws without drifting = 2 points

One draw without drifting = 1 point

Your score_____

Stance Drill 3. *Golf Tee Drill*

With two golf tees in hand, take a stance on the shooting line. Push the golf tees into the ground at your toes. Now move behind the shooting line. Sight down the golf tees to see whether an imaginary line through your stance goes straight to the target. Repeat this exercise by moving several steps up the shooting line and then several steps down the line from your first position. Often three or four archers shoot at a target at one time. You must learn to take a correct stance even if you cannot stand squarely in front of the target.

Success Check

* Stand with feet shoulder-width apart.
* Stand with shoulders square to target.

Three repetitions with perfect alignment = 3 points

Two repetitions with perfect alignment = 2 points

One repetition with perfect alignment = 1 point

Your score_____

Stance Drill 4. *Partner Stance Check*

Choose a partner. Take your natural stance in front of the target from about 12 yards away. Shoot an arrow. Have your partner stand behind you, looking down the range, and sight down the imaginary line that would intersect your front and back shoulder to see whether it points to the bull's-eye as you come to full draw. Shoot arrows from different positions along the shooting line. Have your partner check you each time.

To Increase Difficulty

- Find a hilly area to walk on with your partner. Bring your bow but no arrows. Along your walk, stop and pick out various objects for targets. Draw as if you were shooting at that object, adapting your stance to the lay of the land. Have your partner check to see that your shoulders are aligned to the target, even if your stance is uneven.

Success Check

- Stand with shoulders square to target.

Score Your Success

Three repetitions with perfect alignment = 3 points

Two repetitions with perfect alignment = 2 points

One repetition with perfect alignment = 1 point

Your score_____

BOW HAND POSITION

You can use one of several bow hand positions: the low wrist, the high wrist, or the straight wrist. Each wrist position has advantages and disadvantages (table 4.2). With each bow hand position, archers strive to maintain a relaxed bow hand so that they resist the push of the bow on the bow arm as the bowstring is drawn rather than grip the bow. Archers choose the hand position that best allows them to maintain a relaxed hold, given their strength and bone and muscular structure. If you have not yet used a finger or bow sling, do so now (see Sport of Archery, page xxi). With a sling, you are not as tempted to grip the bow out of fear of dropping it as you would be without a sling.

Any movement of the bow as the arrow is clearing the arrow rest can cause a deviation in where the arrow lands. Consider that pushing the tail end of an arrow just 1 degree off center can make it land far from the bull's-eye. You want to avoid any movement of the bow at the time of release. If your bow hand is tense or grips the bow in a tight hold, you are more likely to move upon release than if your bow hand is relaxed. Archers who take a grip in which the hand is not directly behind the bow handle also have a tendency to bend the wrist during the draw. Usually these archers can't maintain the exact wrist position until the arrow clears the bow. The wrist moves, and the arrow's flight is affected.

Table 4.2 Advantages and Disadvantages of Wrist Positions

Wrist position	Advantages	Disadvantages
Low	Allows wrist to relax backward completely Does not require great wrist strength	Promotes tendency to grab bow if wrist and fingers are not relaxed
High	Minimizes area of hand contacting bow handle Minimizes bow torque Minimizes tendency to grab bow on release	Difficult to maintain over long shooting session without great strength Promotes tendency to move wrist at release with fatigue
Straight	Consistent from shot to shot Makes deviations in position easy to feel	Difficult to maintain over long shooting session without great strength Pressure against skin web between thumb and forefinger promotes tendency to wrap fingers around bow

Many archers also have a tendency to grab the bow as they release the string, even if the bow hand is relaxed during draw and aiming. This turning of the bow, or torque, can still affect the tail end of the arrow as it clears the arrow rest. Also, beginning archers sometimes anticipate the release so that the bow is moving throughout the release of the bowstring. Only dedicated practice in relaxing the bow hand throughout the shot and follow-through can help you overcome these errors.

Another reason for maintaining a relaxed bow hand is that your two hands tend to mirror one another in tension level. If your bow hand is tight, your string hand tends to be tight as well. If your bow hand is relaxed, your string hand tends to be relaxed, too, resulting in a cleaner release of the string or trigger of a mechanical release.

The three bow hand positions put the wrist at a different height in relation to the bow hand. The low position (figure 4.2a) places your arm below your bow hand. The high position (figure 4.2b) places your arm above your hand. The arm and hand form a line in the straight wrist position (figure 4.2c). In the low and straight positions, the hand is placed so that the pressure is along the inner side of the thumb muscle.

Figure 4.2   Wrist Positions

LOW WRIST

1. Hand is on bow, pressure is along inner side of thumb, knuckles are at 45-degree angle
2. Bow rests on base of thumb
3. Centerline of arm intersects center of bow
4. Wrist is relaxed backward as bow is drawn
5. Hand and fingers are relaxed

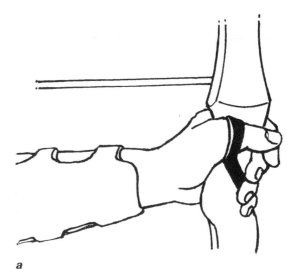

a

HIGH WRIST

1. Centerline of arm intersects center of bow
2. Wrist is higher than hand
3. Pressure of bow is on small area of hand
4. Hand and fingers are relaxed

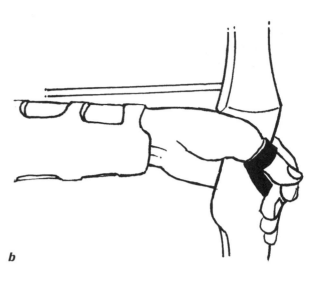

b

STRAIGHT WRIST

1. Centerline of arm intersects center of bow
2. Wrist is level with hand
3. Pressure of bow is on web of hand
4. Hand and fingers are relaxed

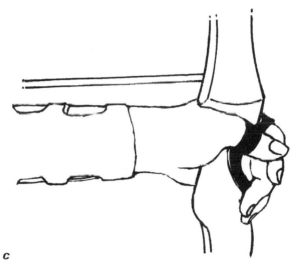

c

Misstep

Your bow hand is so tense that you either grip the handle tightly and your knuckles turn white or you extend your fingers and lock them into position.

Correction

Relax the fingers of your bow hand. If you are afraid of dropping the bow, use a bow sling.

Misstep

You hold the bow handle to the side.

Correction

Be sure to center your hand behind the bow and relax your fingers; the imaginary line down the center of your arm should intersect the center of the bow.

Regardless of which wrist position best minimizes torque and bow movement for you, the three positions have common features. First, an imaginary line running down the center of the bow arm should intersect the center of the bow. This alignment brings the line of pressure closest to the line of pressure exerted by the bowstring, making torque easier to control. Second, your hand and fingers must be completely relaxed so that the bow jumps forward upon release (and is caught by the bow sling) rather than turning to the right or left. As a result, the bowstring should travel a straighter line as it accelerates the arrow, and the arrow should clear the bow without interference.

Which position you use is largely a matter of preference, but you may find that your physical strength and structure lend themselves to a particular bow hand position. Also, the shape of the bow's handle or grip can determine a particular bow hand position. Some bows are made with removable hand grips so that you can install the hand grip shape that allows you to use your preferred bow hand position. Experiment with the various bow hand positions to determine the best one for you. Once you find your preferred position, if your bow has interchangeable hand grips, install the one for your preferred bow hand position.

Hand Position Drill 1. *Choosing a Bow Hand Position*

This drill provides an opportunity to try the various bow hand positions. Shoot six arrows from approximately 15 yards with a high wrist. Then do the same with a straight wrist and then with a low wrist. Make sure the centerline of your arm intersects the center of the bow (figure 4.3). Changing your bow hand position might change where your arrows land on the target, but you need not be concerned about that now. Merely note how comfortable the bow hand position feels and where the arrows land (in a smaller or bigger group) on the target. The bow hand position that produces the tightest group and feels the most comfortable is probably the one you should use. Add a cue to your mental list to remind you to use this bow hand position on every shot.

Success Check

- Centerline of arm intersects center of bow.
- Hand and fingers are relaxed.

Figure 4.3 Arm line intersects the center of the bow.

Score Your Success

Six repetitions with a high wrist = 1 point

Six repetitions with a straight wrist = 1 point

Six repetitions with a low wrist = 1 point

Your score_____

Hand Position Drill 2. *Tension Demonstration*

In this drill you can purposely contrast a tense bow hand with a relaxed one to see how tension influences your performance. Shoot three arrows from approximately 15 yards with your bow hand fingers rigidly extended and tense. Note where your arrows land. Now shoot three arrows by purposely gripping the bow handle tightly throughout the shot. Again, note where your arrows land. Finally, shoot three arrows with a relaxed hold. Which condition produced the best shots?

Success Check

* Relax hand and fingers.

Score Your Success

Three repetitions with rigid fingers = 1 point

Three repetitions while gripping the bow = 1 point

Three repetitions with a relaxed hand = 1 point

Your score_____

Hand Position Drill 3. *Consistency Check*

Obtain two small pieces of tape or two dot stickers. Place one on the middle of the bow handle just above where you place your hand. Take your bow hand position and place the second sticker on your hand right below the other dot on the bow. Shoot two ends from approximately 15 yards. Before drawing for each shot, take your bow hand position and check to see whether the stickers or pieces of tape are aligned.

Success Check

* Centerline of arm intersects center of bow.

Score Your Success

9 to 12 repetitions with good alignment = 3 points

5 to 8 repetitions with good alignment = 2 points

1 to 4 repetitions with good alignment = 1 point

Your score_____

Hand Position Drill 4. *Torque Check*

Without an arrow, take your stance and grip your bow as usual while an observer watches from a few feet down the range (figure 4.4). As you draw the string back, the observer should note whether the back of the bow always faces the target or turns to the right or left. The observer can also watch a stabilizer attached to the bow to see whether it points right or left during the draw. If the bow turns right or left, change your hand position on the handle until you can draw without torquing the bow.

Figure 4.4 A partner checks your alignment from in front.

Success Check

• Draw straight back.
• Draw close to bow arm.

Score Your Success

Five draws without torquing the bow = 3 points

Four draws without torquing the bow = 2 points

Three draws without torquing the bow = 1 point

Your score_____

SUCCESS SUMMARY OF INDIVIDUALIZING FORM

You have been refining and individualizing your archery shot yet maintaining T-form. The drills in this step provided you with opportunities to find the stance and bow hand position most comfortable for you. Chart your progress in individualizing and "grooving" your form by noting your drill scores.

Recall that you developed a mental checklist in a previous step. Add steps to your checklist to remind yourself to use the stance and bow hand position you determined to be the best for you.

For each of the drills presented in this step, you can earn points to chart your progress. Enter your score for each drill and add them up to rate your total success. If your total is at least 16 points, move on to the next step. If it is less than 16, repeat some of the drills with the goal of scoring higher.

Stance Drills

   1. Impact-Variation Drill   ___ out of 3

   2. Alignment Check   ___ out of 3

   3. Golf Tee Drill   ___ out of 3

   4. Partner Stance Check   ___ out of 3

Hand Position Drills

   1. Choosing a Bow Hand Position   ___ out of 3

   2. Tension Demonstration   ___ out of 3

   3. Consistency Check   ___ out of 3

   4. Torque Check   ___ out of 3

Total   *___ out of 24*

In the two previous steps, we stressed accurate shooting through good form, T-form, adapted for your body structure. Once you can consistently repeat the archery shot with good form, you can achieve even more accuracy by using a bowsight. A bowsight allows you to direct the arrow at the same place from shot to shot. In step 5, you will learn how to install a bowsight, how to adjust a bowsight, and how to use it to aim your shot. Combining consistent form with the use of a bowsight will improve the accuracy of your shooting.

Sighting and Aiming

At the 1993 World Target Championships, archer Park Kyung-Mo found himself shooting against a former world champion in the semifinal match. From 70 meters, he shot his first two arrows into the 10 ring, which is the inner part of the gold bull's-eye. The next arrow was a 9, landing in the outer part of the bull's-eye, but the remaining nine arrows all landed in the 10 ring. Park Kyung-Mo's score of 119 out of 120 possible points took first place, establishing a new world record that stands today.

Many years of practice helped Park Kyung-Mo establish a world record, but undoubtedly such accurate shooting at a long distance would be very difficult without a bowsight. A bowsight helps you direct your bow in a consistent direction from shot to shot. Once archers establish sight settings for various distances, a bowsight allows them to step up to a new distance and hit the bull's-eye with the very first arrow! Although some archers enjoy the challenge of shooting without a bowsight, most target archers and

bowhunters use one. In this step, you will learn how to aim with a bowsight.

With a bowsight, you can direct your arrows to the same spot on the target from shot to shot. You can reproduce the alignment used on any one shot because you align an aiming aperture on the bowsight with the bull's-eye. If your arrows hit outside the bull's-eye, you can use the bowsight as a calibrated means of adjustment for subsequent shots. You can adjust the bowsight both horizontally and vertically; you must establish through trial and error just how great an adjustment is needed. When you change shooting distance, move the bowsight vertically—down for a greater distance, up for a shorter distance. This adjustment changes the height of your bow arm and consequently the trajectory of the arrow. The horizontal adjustment allows you to accommodate slight changes in shooting form that direct the arrow to the right or left and to adjust for shooting conditions, including wind.

INSTALLING A BOWSIGHT

The bowsight is an attachment to the bow that places a marker or aiming aperture in the bow window. You line up the aperture with the bull's-eye to aim rather than looking at the relationship between the arrow and the bull's-eye.

The bowsight helps you direct an arrow to the same place horizontally and vertically on every shot by dictating the elevation and left-to-right direction of your bow arm. If your arrows are not landing around the bull's-eye, the sight gives you a systematic way to adjust until you zero in on the bull's-eye. Unless you enjoy the challenge of shooting barebow (without a bowsight), you will find the bowsight an indispensable accessory to your shooting.

Target sights can be very simple, inexpensive devices or they can be elaborate, precision-made tools extending from the bow (figure 5.1). Simple sights do a good job of directing the arrow as you desire. The difference between expensive and inexpensive sights is typically the ease and accuracy of moving the aiming aperture. Your choice of bowsight should be dictated in part by the style of archery you want to shoot.

Target archers typically choose a sight that accommodates one aiming aperture. This aperture can be adjusted up or down, directing the bow lower or higher, and left or right. Since target archers have time to change a sight setting between shots, one aiming aperture is sufficient. Bowhunters, on the other hand, not only don't have the time to adjust a sight, but they also don't know ahead of time how far their game will be from their location. Sights for bowhunting typically accommodate three to five aiming apertures, each one set for a different distance.

Extending the sight out in front of the bow makes aiming more precise. If the distance from the eye to the aiming aperture is short, a small error in aiming at the moment of release causes a larger error in where the arrow lands than if the distance from the eye to the aiming aperture is longer. Target archers undoubtedly like to extend the bowsight away from the bow. Bowhunters must take into account the ease of transporting their equipment through wooded areas, up to tree stands, and so on, so bowhunters typically

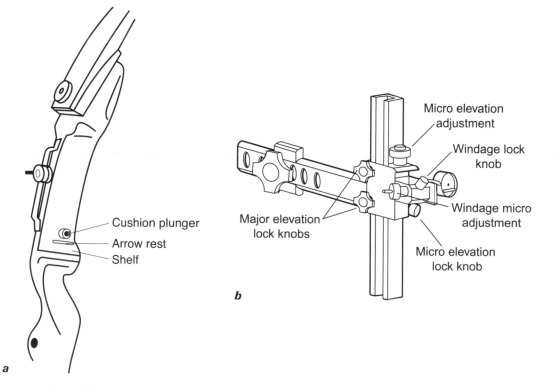

Figure 5.1   Bowsights: *(a)* inexpensive target sight; *(b)* tournament-quality bowsight.

extend the sight just a short distance from the bow handle.

You also must choose an aiming aperture (figure 5.2). Examples of apertures that are aligned with the middle of the bull's-eye include a simple post with a small round ball on the end, a ring with crosshairs, a ring with a post, or a magnifying lens with a dot or circle in the center.

Many archers prefer an open ring. They find

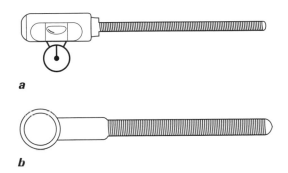

a

b

Figure 5.2 Two aiming apertures: *(a)* drop-pin aperture with a level; *(b)* open-ring aperture.

it is natural to line up the round bull's-eye center inside the ring. Some magnifying lenses have a circle at the center instead of a dot; like the open ring, the circle allows archers to line up the bull's-eye.

Aiming apertures can incorporate a level so that you know you are holding your bow level, but some competition categories restrict the use of levels as well as magnifying lenses. On most

bowsights, the various types of aiming apertures can be interchanged. Start with one that is simple, such as a post or an open ring. You can try other types later. It is probably best to delay using a magnifying or scope sight. While these make the bull's-eye appear larger, they also accentuate your movements during aiming. Some archers react to this by trying to force the bow still, and that typically has the opposite effect on steadying aim!

A bowsight is attached to the bow so that the aiming aperture is visible in the bow window when the archer is at full draw, to the left of the upper bow limb for a right-handed archer. Bowsights can be simple, handmade devices or they can be purchased from a commercial supplier. Purchased sights come in two types. One is permanently affixed directly to the handle riser on the back side of the bow (away from the archer) and along the bow window. The other type attaches to the side of the handle riser. It is either attached to a mounting bracket or screwed into an insert placed there for that purpose. This is typical of bows with metal handle risers. This arrangement makes it easy to change from one sight to another or to vary the distance the sight extends from the bow. The farther the sight extends, the more precise the aiming can be but the more accentuated any bow arm movement appears to the archer during aiming. New archers probably should use a short distance. With increased strength and endurance and consequently steadier aim, the sight can be extended farther from the bow.

Installing Drill 1. *Making a Simple Bowsight*

It is interesting to make your own sight to demonstrate how this simple accessory can improve your accuracy. Obtain a piece of felt or foam about 5 inches long, plastic tape, and a long straight pin with a ball head. If you find self-adhesive 1/2- or 3/4-inch insulating foam, you won't need to tape it on. Position the felt or foam on the back of your bow (the side away from you) along the sight window above the arrow rest. Place a piece of plastic tape along

the felt or foam so that you can mark every half centimeter on the tape with a permanent marker (figure 5.3). Stick the straight pin into the foam or felt so that it is visible in the sight window. The pin serves as your aiming aperture. You can stick the pin in higher or lower and move it in or out to adjust your sight setting. The marks help you note how far you have moved the pin and what locations on your sight correspond to various shooting distances.

Figure 5.3 A handmade target sight with a pinhead as an aiming aperture.

Now shoot two ends of five arrows each. Stand approximately 12 yards from a backstop without a target face. Place a small circle about 4 inches in diameter on the backstop as a target. On the first end, remove the pin on your handmade sight and aim at the circle as you have been. On the second end, replace the pin about two-thirds of the distance up the bow window. On every shot, align the pinhead with the circle. Don't worry about hitting the circle; just focus on aiming there. On each end, note how tight a group your shot arrows are on the target backstop.

Success Check

- Align the pinhead with the aiming spot.

Score Your Success

Tighter group with the bowsight than without = 2 points

Groups that are equally tight = 1 point

Your score_____

PEEP SIGHTS

A peep sight (figure 5.4) is a small round or oval disc with a hole in the middle. It is placed between the strands of the bowstring at eye level.

Figure 5.4 The peep sight.

A peep sight acts as a rear sight, precisely aligning the bowstring and the tail of the arrow with the bowsight and target. Sighting is more precise when two locations between the archer's eye and the bull's-eye are aligned than when just one is aligned.

Obviously a peep sight will improve aiming accuracy. However, not all archers use peep sights. If you will compete in archery tournaments, check to see that peep sights are allowed in your anticipated classification. Also, peep sights can be bothersome. They must be positioned so that you can look through the small opening. Archers who tend to twist the bowstring when positioning their fingers or even those who use mechanical releases sometimes find that the peep sight rotates. Devices that hold the peep sight in the desired orientation are available. Yet, it is time consuming to set up these devices and it is an additional step to anchor in such a way that you can see through the peep sight. It is more difficult to get a shot off quickly when using a peep sight. Beginning archers might want to wait to use a peep sight until shooting form and shot setup are established and routine. Then you can add a peep sight without letting it be a distraction from the other aspects of good shooting.

To install a peep sight, first place it between the strands of the bowstring above the nock locator at about the height of your aiming eye. Draw to your anchor and note whether you can look through the peep sight to see your bowsight. Ease the bowstring back and slide the peep sight up or down as needed. You may have to turn either the peep sight or the bowstring so that the peephole is fully open to your eye. This is a process of trial and error.

Once you have the peep sight at the correct height, mark the bowstring at this location. You might also want to measure and record the distance between the peep sight and your nock locator. Tie the peep sight into the string so that it will not move. There are several methods for doing this, but they require practice to complete well, so you may want to take your bow to a pro shop and have an expert tie in your peep sight.

Installing Drill 2. *Installing a Peep Sight*

You might not want to use a peep sight for shooting at this time. Yet it is good to see what is involved in using one should you decide to add it at a later time. Obtain a peep sight and install it as directed. You might have to draw several times and adjust the height of the peep sight after each draw. When you have the correct height, stand 12 yards in front of a target. Without an arrow, draw and look through the peep sight to align the sight aperture with an aiming spot on the bull's-eye on the target. After a count of two, ease the string back. If the peep sight was turned and you could not look through it, try twisting the bowstring or taking the peep sight out and reinserting it at another angle. Be sure to merely hook onto the bowstring with the fingers of your draw hand rather than twisting the string with your fingers as you draw and hold. Twisting the string can turn the peep sight such that you cannot see through it. Perform five successive draws, align-ing the sight aperture through the peep sight and letting down to rest after each draw. If you would like to continue using the peep sight, clamp or tie it in. If not, you can remove it after the drill.

Success Check

- Keep the back of the draw hand flat.
- Looking through the peep sight, align the sight aperture with the bull's-eye.
- Allow the sight to settle on the bull's-eye.

Score Your Success

Successfully aim through the peep sight for five draws = 2 points

Successfully aim through the peep sight for three or four draws = 1 point

Your score_____

USING A BOWSIGHT

The principles of using a bowsight are the same whether you have a simple, handmade sight, a hunting sight, or a sophisticated tournament sight. You aim the sight aperture at the bull's-eye on every shot. Your shooting form is basically the same as what you have been practicing, but you need to add several steps to your shot sequence that are related to aligning the bowsight.

After taking your stance (figure 5.5a), drawing, and anchoring, align the sight aperture and bull's-eye using the eye on the draw hand side of your body. Remember that if your other eye is dominant, you may need to close it so that you use only the string side eye for aiming. Level the bow by using the level mounted on your sight or by checking that the bow limbs are vertical in your peripheral vision. Your eye should bring the bull's-eye into focus, permitting the aperture and bowstring to blur slightly.

Aligning your eye, the sight aperture, and the target is necessary, but recall that the tail end of the arrow is attached to the bowstring. Ideally, you want to align the string, too! One way to do this is to use a peep sight. You can look through the peep sight to align the sight aperture with the target. The arrow is aligned with this line of aim because you are looking through the center of the bowstring.

If you decide not to use a peep sight or to wait until later to use one, you must adjust your head position so that you see the string running down the middle of the bow limbs and handle. For a right-handed archer, the string should be just to the right of the aperture (figure 5.5b).

Wait to release until the sight aperture is steady in the middle of the bull's-eye. This usually takes several seconds. When the aperture is steady and aligned, tighten your back muscles and relax your string hand to release the string (figure 5.5c). You will be able to hold the sight more steadily as you practice and develop greater muscular strength. However, archers can rarely stop the aperture "dead" in the bull's-eye; attempting to do so usually results in too much tension in the bow and string hands. You can shoot very accurately if the aperture is steady and oscillating around the bull's-eye. It does not need to be perfectly still.

Figure 5.5   Shooting With a Bowsight

STANCE

1. Assume stance
2. Nock arrow
3. Set bow and string hands

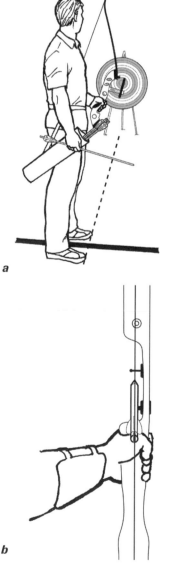

a

DRAW AND AIM

1. Draw and anchor
2. Close eye opposite string side, if necessary
3. Level bow
4. If using a peep sight, look through opening
5. If not using peep sight, adjust head to see string bisecting bow and aligning just to right of aperture
6. Align string side eye with sight aperture and bull's-eye
7. Focus on bull's-eye
8. Steady sight aperture in center of bull's-eye

b

RELEASE AND FOLLOW-THROUGH

1. Tighten back muscles
2. Relax string hand to release
3. Keep bow arm up
4. Keep head steady and focus on bull's-eye

c

Misstep

Some of your arrows land to the right or left of the bull's-eye and you are not using a peep sight.

Correction

Align the bowstring with the middle of the bow limbs and just to the right of the sight aperture on every shot.

Misstep

Your arrows horizontally spread across the target.

Correction

If you shoot with both eyes open, recheck for your dominant eye to ensure it is on the same side as your string hand. If it is not, try closing your bow side eye.

Sighting Drill 1. *Aligning and Aiming Mimic*

Some archers tend to release the bowstring as soon as the sight is on the bull's-eye instead of steadying the aperture and aiming. Without using an arrow, practice drawing, aligning your string and sight, steadying your aperture, and aiming from a distance of 20 yards. Aim for a count of at least three, and then ease the string back. Remember that steadying means settling the aperture so that it oscillates in small movements around the bull's-eye; it does not necessarily mean stopping the aperture in the bull's-eye. Complete 10 repetitions.

Success Check

- Level your bow.
- Align your bowstring on every shot.
- Let the sight aperture settle in the bull's-eye.
- Focus on the middle of the bull's-eye.

Score Your Success

9 or 10 repetitions with sight settling on bull's-eye = 3 points

7 or 8 repetitions with sight settling on bull's-eye = 2 points

5 or 6 repetitions with sight settling on bull's-eye = 1 point

Your score_____

Sighting Drill 2.   *Aiming Mimic on a Three-Spot*

Here is another way to practice aligning your string and sight aperture and aiming. Obtain a three- or four-spot target face (figure 5.6). This is a target face that has the inner rings from a larger target printed three or four times on one face. Very accurate archers who rarely have a shot land in the outer rings use this type of target face.

For this drill, use the target face for aiming. Draw and align your string and sight aperture on the upper or upper-left bull's-eye. Aim and allow the sight aperture to settle on the bull's-eye. Count to two and then move to another bull's-eye. Check your string alignment, then again aim at this bull's-eye, settle, and count to two. If you tire, let down, rest, and repeat this exercise. Otherwise, continue to move to another bull's-eye. Do six sets of aiming.

Success Check

- Align eye, sight aperture, and bull's-eye.
- Focus on bull's-eye.
- Let sight aperture settle.

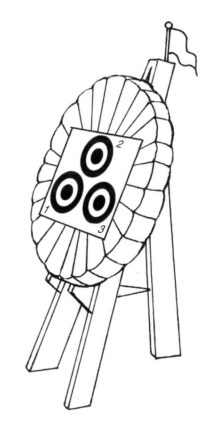

Figure 5.6   Three-spot target face.

Score Your Success

5 or 6 sets, settling on at least two bull's-eyes = 3 points

3 or 4 sets, settling on at least two bull's-eyes = 2 points

1 or 2 sets, settling on at least two bull's-eyes = 1 point

Your score_____

ADJUSTING THE AIMING APERTURE

You establish the proper horizontal and vertical position of the aiming aperture for a given shooting distance by trial and error. If you have aimed the sight at the bull's-eye but the arrows land elsewhere, you must adjust the aiming aperture.

After you shoot several arrows, observe their location on the target face. Move the aperture in the direction of error (figure 5.7). For example, if the arrows group low, move the sight aperture down. Sighting through a lower aperture results in your holding your bow arm and, consequently, your bow higher. If the arrows group high, move the sight aperture up. If the arrows group left, move the aperture left. Be sure to make adjustments to the left or right with the bowsight oriented to the target. It is easy to be confused if you turn the bow around!

Figure 5.7 | **Aiming Aperture Adjustment**

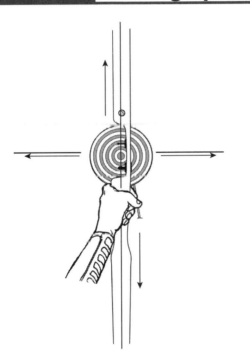

1. Move bowsight up if arrows group above bull's-eye
2. Move bowsight down if arrows group below bull's-eye
3. Move bowsight left if arrows group left of bull's eye
4. Move bowsight right if arrows group right of bull's-eye

 Misstep

Your arrows group farther away from the bull's-eye after a sight adjustment.

Correction

Move your sight in the direction of the group of arrows with your bowsight oriented toward the target.

 Misstep

You aim the sight aperture off center to compensate for your sight setting.

Correction

Aim at the center of the bull's-eye on every shot and patiently move your sight until you have a good sight setting.

When a sight setting is off, some archers are tempted to aim outside the bull's-eye to compensate rather than adjusting the position of the sight. Aiming off center is less desirable than moving the sight, unless sight movements are restricted by the rules for a particular class or style of competitive shooting. Consistently finding any position on a target other than the center of the bull's-eye is almost impossible. Don't hesitate to move your sight. That is why it is adjustable! However, if you feel that you varied from T-form on a particular shot, don't make a sight adjustment based on where that arrow landed. Wait to analyze the position of an arrow shot with good T-form.

If you move to a longer distance, you need to move your bowsight down so that your bow arm is directed to give your shot a higher trajectory. Naturally, if you move closer, you need to raise your sight. How far you move your sight for a given change in distance is established first by trial and error. Thereafter, you can keep a written record of the setting for a particular distance. Target archers often carry a written table of their sight settings for given shooting distances.

Changing distances does not necessitate a horizontal adjustment of your sight. Small errors in the position of your sight, though, have a more apparent effect at longer distances. For example, if your arrows fall on the right side of, but still in, the bull's-eye when you shoot from 20 yards, they likely would fall to the right of, but outside, the bull's-eye at 50 yards. Therefore, some horizontal adjustment of your bowsight might be necessary as you change distances.

Target archers typically use a bowsight with a single aperture that slides up and down the sight. A scale on the sight enables archers to establish a chart of sight positions corresponding to various distances. Bowhunters do not have the time to reposition their sights for a given distance, even if the game is nice enough to stand still! A hunting sight usually has four- or five-pin apertures that can be positioned for those distances the archer is likely to need. The hunter estimates the distance to game and selects the appropriate pin to use in aiming.

Adjusting Drill 1. *Sight Adjustment Practice*

In this drill, you practice designating the direction of sight adjustment. The location of a group of arrows is stated in terms of a clock face. Fill in the directions of sight adjustment that you need in order to bring subsequent shots to the center of the target. For example, for a group at 4 o'clock, move the sight aperture right and down. Answers are on page 65.

1. For a group at 6 o'clock, how would you move the aperture?

2. For a group at 8 o'clock, how would you move the aperture?

3. For a group at 1 o'clock, how would you move the aperture?

4. For a group at 3 o'clock, how would you move the aperture?

5. For a group at 11 o'clock, how would you move the aperture?

Success Check

- Orient bowsight toward target, as when shooting.
- Adjust in the direction of the arrow group.

Score Your Success

Five adjustments correct = 5 points

Four adjustments correct = 4 points

Three adjustments correct = 3 points

Two adjustments correct = 2 points

One adjustment correct = 1 point

Your score_____

Adjusting Drill 2. *Sighting In*

Shoot from a short distance of 15 yards, using an 80-centimeter target face. Shoot three arrows using an initial sight setting with the aperture high on the sight bar. Note where the three arrows land and adjust your sight. Continue shooting and adjusting until your arrows group around the bull's-eye. Record the location of this sight setting by the rule or scale on the bowsight in table 5.1. Now move to 20 yards and repeat this process. When you have established a sight setting, record it. Continue this process, moving back in 5-yard increments to a distance of 35 yards. You can anticipate the needed sight adjustment by moving your sight down a small amount each time you increase your distance from the target.

To Increase Difficulty

- Move to 40 yards and record your adjustment of sight setting.

Success Check

- Move your sight down as you move back.
- Move your sight left or right as needed.
- Make sight corrections after shots with good form, not bad.

Table 5.1 Sight Adjustments

Yards	Sight setting
15 yards	
20 yards	
25 yards	
30 yards	
35 yards	

Score Your Success

Establish all five sight settings = 5 points
Establish four sight settings = 4 points
Establish three sight settings = 3 points
Establish two sight settings = 2 points
Establish one sight setting = 1 point
Your score_____

Adjusting Drill 3. *Quick Sight Move*

For this drill, place an 80-centimeter target on the target butt and shoot six-arrow ends. Start at 30 yards and shoot an end using your sight setting from the previous drill. Record your score in table 5.2, then follow suit for ends at 25 yards, 20 yards, and 15 yards. Now shoot another end at 15 yards, recording your score, then 20, 25, and 30 yards likewise. Your two scores for the same distance should be similar, provided your form has been consistent.

To Increase Difficulty

- Add 35 and 40 yards.

To Decrease Difficulty

- Use a larger target face.

Success Check

- Move your sight up as you move closer to the target.
- Focus on the bull's-eye and let the sight settle.

Table 5.2 Scores for Quick Sight Move

Yards to target	First end	Second end
30 yards		
25 yards		
20 yards		
15 yards		

Score Your Success

First and second end totals are within 5 points for all four distances = 4 points

First and second end totals are within 5 points for three distances = 3 points

First and second end totals are within 5 points for two distances = 2 points

First and second end totals are within 5 points for one distance = 1 point

Your score_____

Adjusting Drill 4. *Subtraction*

This drill is done with a partner. Place an 80-centimeter target on the target butt. Each of you should place a piece of tape around one of your arrows. Shoot six arrows from 30 yards, using your 30-yard sight setting. On each of four ends, total your five unmarked arrows. Then, subtract the value of your marked arrow from your opponent's score. (A sample is shown in figure 5.8.) Record your scores in table 5.3.

To Increase Difficulty

- Shoot from 35 yards.

To Decrease Difficulty

- Shoot from 25 yards.
- Use a larger target.

Table 5.3 Scores for Subtraction Drill

End	Total of 5 arrows	Minus points for marked arrow	Your points	Partner's points
1		–		
2		–		
3		–		
4		–		
Total				

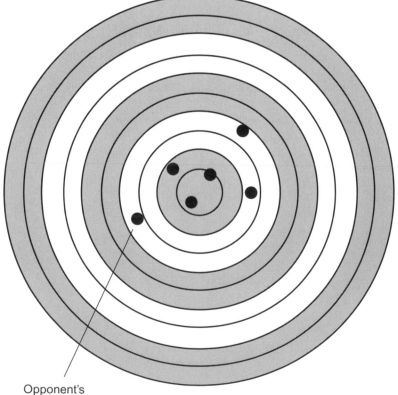

Figure 5.8 Sample result of subtraction drill.

Opponent's marked arrow

Success Check

- Align your bowstring on every shot.
- Let the sight aperture settle in the bull's-eye.
- Focus on the middle of the bull's-eye.

Score Your Success

Outscore your opponent on four ends = 4 points

Outscore your opponent on three ends = 3 points

Outscore your opponent on two ends = 2 points

Outscore your opponent on one end = 1 point

Your score_____

Answer Key

Adjusting Drill 1. *Sight Adjustment Practice*

1. Down.
2. Left and down.
3. Up and right.
4. Right.
5. Up and left.

SUCCESS SUMMARY OF SIGHTING AND AIMING

After you learn to use a bowsight in this step, your shooting should be more accurate than before, especially at longer distances. Don't forget to update your mental checklist for sighting and aiming with a bowsight. Consider the points for aiming listed in figure 5.5 (page 58). Select cues from that list to add to your checklist. As you practice and some of these steps become habit, you can continue to refine your mental checklist.

Of course, simply having a bowsight does not mean you will always hit the bull's-eye. Continue to refine your basic T-form. Make sight adjustments only after well-executed shots.

For each of the drills in this step, enter the points you earned. Total your points to rate your success in learning to use a bowsight. If you have earned at least 19 points, you can move to the next step. Otherwise, repeat the adjusting drills and earn additional points.

Installing Drills

1. Making a Simple Bowsight   ___ out of 2
2. Installing a Peep Sight   ___ out of 2

Sighting Drills

1. Aligning and Aiming Mimic   ___ out of 3
2. Aiming Mimic on a Three-Spot   ___ out of 3

Adjusting Drills

1. Sight Adjustment Practice   ___ out of 5
2. Sighting In   ___ out of 5
3. Quick Sight Move   ___ out of 4
4. Subtraction   ___ out of 4

Total   **___ out of 28**

While watching experienced archers, you might have noticed that they anchor in a different position than you have been using. The anchor position you learned in step 3 is a basic one, and many archers continue to use it. Other archers deviate from that position, sometimes because they find another position more comfortable and sometimes because of the type of archery they wish to perfect. In the next step to success, you will make one final adjustment in your shooting in order to put all of the basics in place to score well. You will decide on a preferred anchor position and whether you want to shoot with a mechanical release instead of using your fingers to release the bowstring.

Anchoring

To this point you have been using an under-chin anchor point. You have been anchoring your string hand under your jaw bone. This is an excellent anchor position for beginning archers. It minimizes the possibility of overdrawing and lodging an arrow in the face of the bow or in the bow hand. It also provides several contact points between the string or hand and the face, maximizing consistency from shot to shot.

Now that you have practiced enough to make your form more consistent, you might consider another anchor position or even whether you want to use a mechanical release. Whether you change or not can be related to your body shape, the accessories you want to use, and the type of archery you wish to shoot—bowhunting, Olympic-style target archery, or professional target archery, for example. Keep this in mind as we review your choices, beginning with various anchor positions for finger shooters and ending with the various types of mechanical release aids.

The purpose of all anchor positions is consistency of both the draw length (which ultimately influences the amount of thrust imparted to the arrow and thus vertical accuracy) and left-to-right alignment in aiming (which ultimately influences horizontal accuracy). The more precise the anchor position, the better. An archer who draws but does not anchor on any part of his body cannot be sure he is aligned, either vertically or horizontally, the same way on every shot. Likewise, even if an archer anchors on his face or chin but lets the anchor vary from shot to shot, he cannot be assured of accurate alignment.

In general, the more points on the face or neck the draw (string) hand and bowstring touch, the more precise the anchor position can be. There is a trade-off between establishing a very precise anchor and shooting quickly, as in hunting, or in difficult climates, such as extreme cold. Additionally, the numbers and types of accessories archers wish to use can influence the anchor positions they use. Peep sights and kisser buttons are good examples. As a first step, we will learn how to install and adjust a kisser button.

KISSER BUTTONS

A kisser button (figure 6.1), a small plastic disc attached to the bowstring, is an inexpensive accessory. A kisser button helps you position your anchor consistently from shot to shot. The kisser button is positioned on the bowstring so that it's between the lips when you anchor—hence its name.

Figure 6.1 The kisser button.

If an archer tends to let the string hand float at full draw (that is, not come to an identical anchor position from shot to shot), the kisser button will not be aligned between the lips on each shot. The archer can adjust to align the kisser button and ensure a consistent anchor position from shot to shot.

Some archers have a tendency to let their jaws drop on some of their shots rather than keeping their jaws closed. If the string hand is anchored on or under the jaw, this results in the tail end of the arrow being higher or lower from shot to shot. A kisser button helps archers to realize they have dropped their jaws on a shot because the button would not touch both lips.

To position the kisser button properly, slide it onto the bowstring approximately 2 inches above the nock locator. Draw the string back until the string touches your nose. Feel for the kisser button. Ease the string back. If the kisser button was above or below your lips, adjust it and draw again. Repeat these adjustments until the kisser button touches between your lips. You may then want to repeat coming to full draw several times, making sure that you are using the anchor position you want. Once you are satisfied with the location of the kisser button, mark its place on your bowstring and record its distance from your nock locator. In this step you will experiment with different anchor positions, so you will want to move your kisser button. Variations in anchor position or the use of a mechanical release can affect the position of the kisser button. Once you have decided on the anchor position you will use from now on, you can clamp down the kisser button so that it will not move. For a nominal cost, you can buy a small clamp that you can squeeze down over the end of the kisser button with a pair of nocking pliers.

Kisser Button Drill. *Installing a Kisser Button*

Have your bow ready and obtain a kisser button. Adjust the position of the kisser button as explained previously. Now shoot three ends of five arrows each and note how many times the kisser button is in the correct position when you first anchor.

Success Check

- Bowstring touches nose.
- Kisser button touches both lips.

Score Your Success

14 or 15 shots anchored correctly = 3 points

12 or 13 shots anchored correctly = 2 points

10 or 11 shots anchored correctly = 1 point

Your score_____

VARIATIONS ON ANCHOR POSITION

Now we will review three general types of anchor positions (table 6.1). The first is the under-chin, low anchor position you have been using thus far. We will discuss this anchor position in more detail, along with a slight variation of it. The second is the side-of-face, high anchor position. Finally, we'll consider the anchors used by archers who use mechanical releases.

Using the Under-Chin Anchor

The under-chin, low anchor position is common and it is probably the anchor used by most target archers, but it may not be the one best suited for your body structure or the type of archery you prefer.

In the under-chin anchor, the string always touches the tip of the nose and the chin. The bowstring therefore crosses the mouth, offering archers the opportunity to use a kisser button and gain an additional touch point for this anchor. The kisser button is positioned so that it is between the lips where the bowstring crosses the mouth. The use of the kisser button is a good check against opening the jaw, something that causes a vertical variation in the anchor position and the orientation of the arrow. Remember that the knuckles of the index finger on the draw hand are tight under the jaw.

There are two variations of the under-chin anchor. In one, the bowstring touches the tip of the nose, the center of the lips, and the center of the chin. Placing the string in the center of the chin necessitates tipping the head, which is an uncomfortable position for some archers. Archers with large hands or short necks sometimes find it difficult to use this version of the under-chin anchor. Archers also need time to position this anchor, which is a disadvantage in bowhunting. It might be difficult to use a peep sight with this anchor, yet this can be a very precise anchor, with three touch points centered on the face.

In the more popular variation of the under-chin anchor, archers bring the bowstring to the tip of the nose or sometimes slightly to the side of the nose, the corner of the mouth, and the side of the chin. Hence, the head can be more upright and the draw hand can be tucked under the jaw more to the side of the neck (figure 6.2). If a kisser button is used, it is placed between the lips in the corner of the mouth. The precision of the touch points might not be as fine as with the centered version, but it is easy to use a peep sight with this anchor, and most archers shooting in classifications that allow peep sights use them with this anchor position. This anchor position also results in a slightly longer draw length than the centered version. Remember that a longer draw with a given bow, especially a recurve bow, provides a little more thrust.

Table 6.1   Advantages and Disadvantages of Various Anchors

Type of anchor	Advantages	Disadvantages
Under chin	Multiple "touch points" Prevents overdrawing	Takes time to position Less comfortable for some archers
Side of face	Can be established quickly Allows barebow archers to sight down arrow shaft	Not as precise Sometimes leads to plucking of bowstring
With mechanical release	Very accurate Allows elbow to be aligned with arrow at release	Takes time to set and position Scoring standards in competition are very high Release aid must be adjusted and set for each person

Figure 6.2　　Under-Chin Anchor

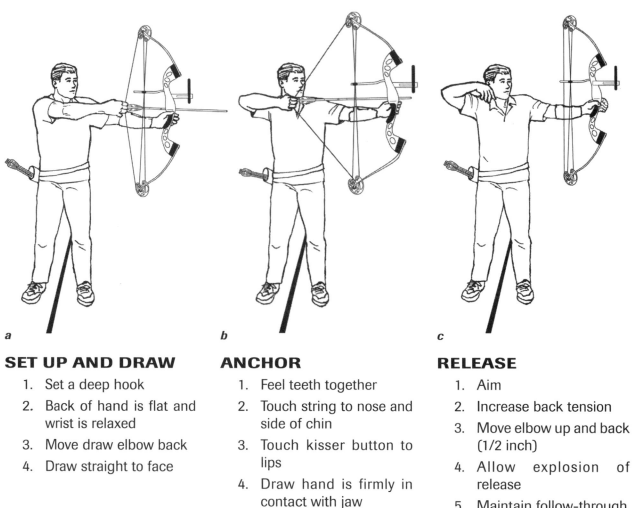

a　　　　　　　　　　　*b*　　　　　　　　　　　*c*

SET UP AND DRAW

1. Set a deep hook
2. Back of hand is flat and wrist is relaxed
3. Move draw elbow back
4. Draw straight to face

ANCHOR

1. Feel teeth together
2. Touch string to nose and side of chin
3. Touch kisser button to lips
4. Draw hand is firmly in contact with jaw
5. Center target in peep sight, if used

RELEASE

1. Aim
2. Increase back tension
3. Move elbow up and back (1/2 inch)
4. Allow explosion of release
5. Maintain follow-through

Misstep

You move your head forward to meet the bowstring.

Correction

Keep your head erect, imagining T-form alignment, and bring the bowstring to the face for consistent shooting.

Misstep

You draw with your fingertips and have a cupped string hand.

Correction

Set your string hand hook deep, at least in the first joint, and relax your hand to keep the hand and wrist flat.

With any anchor, your draw should be straight back in the plane intersecting the target, not out and then in. The anchor position should be firmly in contact with the face or jaw and identically positioned on every shot. Make the draw come to your face rather than tipping the head to meet the draw hand. When you use proper back tension, the follow-through of the release will always be back over the rear shoulder, no matter what type of anchor you use. Keep in mind that the rear position of the arrow influences the trajectory of the shot. Varying the trajectory by varying the anchor from shot to shot sends each arrow to a different place on the target. Once you select your anchor position, keep and perfect it.

This is a good time to check your string hand hook. Set your hook so that the string is in the first joint of the fingers or even deeper. This helps you keep your hand and wrist flat (extended) and relaxed throughout the shot. Holding the string with your fingertips tends to cup the hand and put more tension in it. This typically causes more oscillation of the bowstring as it travels forward after release. Go deeper to keep the back of the hand flat and relaxed. If you held the handle of a heavy briefcase in the first or second joints of your fingers, the weight would straighten your hand and wrist. This stretched, straightened position is what archers desire for their string hands. The more relaxed the hand, the better the bowstring clears the hand at release and the less the bowstring oscillates. Research has shown that some champion archers relax the fingers to release and some champion archers extend their fingers to release (Ertan, Kentel, Tumer, and Korkusuz 2003). One is not known to be better than the other, as long as the string hand is relaxed.

Most archers do not hold equally with all three fingers. They tend to hold more with either the top two fingers and lightly with the bottom or more with the bottom two fingers and lightly with the top. You can do whatever is most comfortable. Do not try to hold equally with all three fingers. As with all things in archery, it is important to do the same thing on every shot. The string hand hook should be set the same way on each shot and the draw to anchor should be executed the same way on each shot.

Ertan, H., Kentel, B., Tumer, S.T., and Korkusuz, F. 2003. Activation patterns in forearm muscles during archery shooting. *Human Movement Science* 22: 37-45.

Under-Chin Anchor Drill 1. *Mimicking With Eyes Closed*

Work with a friend or partner. Take only your bow and assume your stance, bow hand hold, and hook. Raise the bow and draw to an under-chin anchor with your eyes closed. Feel for the proper position, hold for a count of three while maintaining relaxed hands, and then ease the string back. This drill establishes your feel for proper anchor position. Repeat the draw and anchor for a total of 10 repetitions, having your partner look for consistency on every shot. (Your partner can use the success checks as guidelines.)

Success Check

- Hook is deep.
- Head is erect.
- String touches nose.
- String touches chin.
- Kisser button, if used, is between lips.
- Draw hand is flat and relaxed.
- Index finger of draw hand is under jaw.

Score Your Success

10 repetitions with correct form = 5 points

8 or 9 repetitions with correct form = 3 points

6 or 7 repetitions with correct form = 1 point

Your score_____

Under-Chin Anchor Drill 2.

If you have made a slight change in your under-chin anchor, you need to check your sight settings. Start at 15 yards. Shoot until you attain an accurate sight setting. Move back to 20 yards, and then move back to 25, 30, 35, and 40 yards, shooting until you have an accurate sight setting. There is likely to be more difference in your setting at a longer distance than at a shorter distance.

To Increase Difficulty

- Add 45- and 50-yard settings.

To Decrease Difficulty

- Start at 10 yards and stop at 30 yards.

Sight-Setting Check

Success Check

- Touch string to nose.
- Touch string to chin.
- Touch kisser button to lips.

Score Your Success

Attain new sight settings for 6 to 8 yardages = 3 points

Attain new sight settings for 5 yardages = 2 points

Your score_____

Using the Side-of-Face Anchor

While the under-chin anchors are very precise, they do take time to position properly. Some archers prefer to anchor on the sides of their faces (figure 6.3). The common way to anchor on the side of the face is to draw back to the side of the face and position the tip of the index finger in the corner of the mouth. The draw hand is thus tight against the face, providing the consistent "touch" on the face. Sometimes the thumb is tucked under the jaw. This anchor position can be set very quickly, making this anchor popular with some bowhunters. A kisser button is not used, but a peep sight can be used.

Figure 6.3   Side-of-Face Anchor

SET UP AND DRAW

1. Set deep hook
2. Back of hand is flat and wrist is relaxed
3. Move draw elbow back
4. Draw straight to face

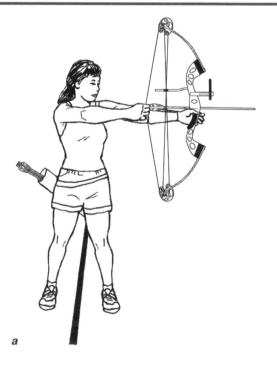

a

ANCHOR

1. Feel teeth together
2. Touch string to nose
3. Touch tip of index finger to corner of mouth
4. Draw hand is firmly in contact with face

b

Misstep

You "pluck" the bowstring, flinging the fingers open and moving the string hand out from the face. Or you use a "dead" release, opening the fingers without increasing back tension, and allow the bowstring to move forward before it comes off the fingers.

Correction

Concentrate on aiming and increase back tension so that the release is a surprise rather than anticipated. Keep the string hand relaxed so that the follow-through is a natural continuation of the string arm up and back.

Another group of archers who prefer this anchor position is those shooting barebow (without a sight). Since the nocked arrow is positioned right under the draw-side eye with this anchor position, barebow archers feel they can shoot more instinctively by sighting right down the arrow shaft. Recall that barebow archers cannot use kisser buttons or peep sights. Many learn how to raise or lower the anchor position to actually vary the distance of the shot. This is called *facewalking*.

The reminders about the draw and string hand hook discussed for the under-chin anchor apply to the side anchor as well. The draw should be straight back to the erect head with a deep string hand hook and relaxed hand. Set the draw hand and draw to anchor the same way on every shot.

To release, aim and increase back tension. Move the elbow up and back about 1/2 inch. Allow the explosion of the release, and maintain the follow-through.

Side-of-Face Anchor Drill 1. *Mimicking With Eyes Closed*

Work with a friend or partner. Take only your bow and assume your stance, bow hand hold, and hook. Raise the bow and draw to a side-of-face anchor with your eyes closed. Feel for the proper position, hold for a count of three while maintaining relaxed hands, and then ease the string back. This drill establishes your feel for proper anchor position. Repeat the draw and anchor for a total of 10 repetitions; your partner looks for consistency on each shot. (Your partner can use the success checks as guidelines.)

Success Check

- Hook is deep.
- Head is erect.
- String touches nose.
- Tip of index finger is between lips at corner of mouth.
- Draw hand is flat and relaxed.

Score Your Success

10 repetitions with correct form = 5 points

8 or 9 repetitions with correct form = 4 points

6 or 7 repetitions with correct form = 3 points

Your score_____

Side-of-Face Anchor Drill 2. *Attaining New Sight Settings*

If you are interested in switching to a side-of-face anchor position, you need to reestablish your sight settings. Start at 15 yards. Shoot until you attain an accurate sight setting. Move back to 20 yards, and then move back to 25, 30, 35, and 40 yards, shooting until you have an accurate sight setting. If you are using a new anchor, there is likely to be more difference in your setting at a longer distance than at a shorter distance.

To Increase Difficulty

- Add 45- and 50-yard settings.

To Decrease Difficulty

- Start at 10 yards and stop at 30 yards.

Success Check

- Touch bowstring to nose.
- Place tip of index finger between lips at corner of mouth.

Score Your Success

Attain new sight settings for 6 to 8 yardages = 3 points

Attain new sight settings for 5 yardages = 2 points

Your score_____

Side-of-Face Anchor Drill 3. *Shooting Barebow*

Although your initial archery experiences in steps 3 and 4 were without a sight, you were using an under-chin anchor. Even if you anticipate shooting with a sight, a good way to appreciate the accuracy of archers who shoot barebow is to try this type of shooting. If you have a bowsight on your bow, remove it, or move the aiming aperture up to the top of the sight so that you don't use it. From a distance of 12 to 15 yards, shoot three ends of six arrows barebow and with a side-of-face anchor at a standard target face.

To Increase Difficulty

- Shoot from 20 yards.

Anchoring With a Mechanical Release

The obvious advantage of using a mechanical release is a cleaner release than can be achieved using the fingers. Rather than three fingers holding the string, a loop of rope, a metal pin, or a set of metal jaws (caliper) holds the string. The bowstring is less deformed than when held with three fingers and is released with much less interference. It travels forward from a mechanical release with less oscillation and therefore the arrow itself travels forward more directly (see step 8 for a discussion of the archer's paradox). In archery events, separate classifications are formed for archers using finger releases and archers using mechanical releases.

As with many things in archery, there are several types of mechanical releases, each with advantages and disadvantages. Each archer must find the release that works best for him or her. Some mechanical releases actually have a trigger (or two!), while others release the bowstring when an archer continues to use back tension to move the draw arm slightly. Some releases are triggered with the index finger; some are triggered with the thumb or with the little finger. With some releases the string hand is horizontal, palm down, while with others the hand is almost vertical, palm out. Archers pull some releases with two fingers and others with all five. Some releases have a wrist strap and others do not.

When selecting a mechanical release, remember that back tension is as important in shooting a mechanical release as it is with a finger release. Release shooters without good back tension tend to anticipate the release and begin to "punch" the release, resulting in a jerky release and less-than-accurate results. They often are focused on making the release happen by triggering their releases rather than focusing on aiming. For this reason, champion target archers often prefer mechanical releases triggered by back tension over trigger releases. Some archers can shoot a trigger release well, but certainly any archer who falls into the habit of punching a trigger release should consider changing to a back-tension release.

Back-tension releases typically consist of a half-moon cam that triggers the bowstring release when it is rotated under tension. A loop of rope is placed around the bowstring just under the nocked arrow and hooked around a pin on the release. Some archers tie a string loop onto the bowstring, one end above the nocking point and the other below it, and actually hook the release onto this string loop rather than directly around the bowstring (figure 6.4).

To shoot with a back-tension release, grasp the release with a deep hook rather than with the ends of the fingers. Just as with a finger

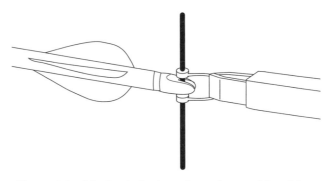

Figure 6.4 Mechanical release looped around the string loop rather than around the bowstring.

release, you want the string hand to be relaxed; grasping the release deep in the hand helps you stay relaxed. With the palm out at about a 45-degree angle to vertical, draw the string straight back to your nose, the back of the string hand firmly in contact with the side of the face (figure 6.5a). Most release shooters use a peep sight, and in addition to having the string touch the nose and corner of the mouth, archers center the target in the peep sight to achieve a precise anchor position.

The release occurs by increasing back tension, moving the string hand elbow up and back about 1/2 to 3/4 of an inch. This rotates the cam and releases the bowstring. Archers often tend to rotate the handle of the release with their hands, but it is preferable to only squeeze the back muscles to rotate the cam.

Some back-tension releases are made with a pin or other means that allow you to draw without fear of accidentally triggering the release prematurely. You set up with the elbow slightly forward of perfect alignment with the target. You then rotate the handle of the release to "activate" it, increase back tension to move the elbow up and back, and consequently trigger the release with the elbow in perfect alignment (figure 6.5b). Obviously, you can adjust the "travel," or extent of cam movement before release, to achieve the proper positions.

Figure 6.5 | Anchor With a Mechanical Release

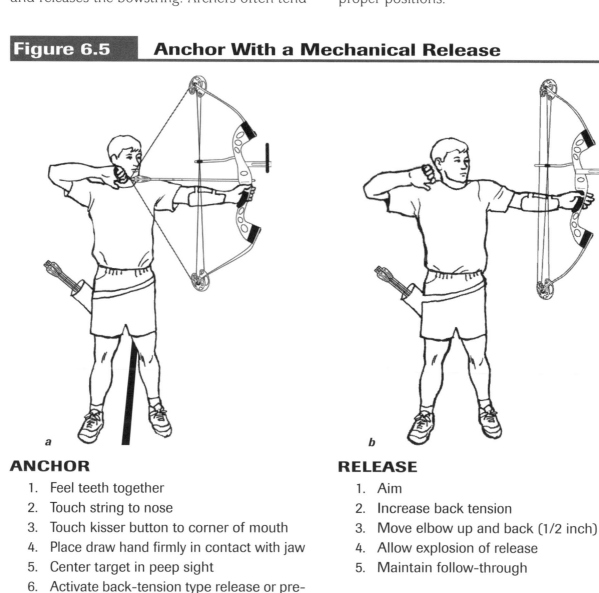

a
b

ANCHOR

1. Feel teeth together
2. Touch string to nose
3. Touch kisser button to corner of mouth
4. Place draw hand firmly in contact with jaw
5. Center target in peep sight
6. Activate back-tension type release or pre-load trigger release

RELEASE

1. Aim
2. Increase back tension
3. Move elbow up and back (1/2 inch)
4. Allow explosion of release
5. Maintain follow-through

Misstep

You punch (jerk) the release.

Correction

Punching comes from anticipating the release rather than maintaining total focus on aiming. Be sure that the release is set with minimal travel (movement to get the release to happen), since a long travel encourages you to anticipate release.

Misstep

You pull the bowstring tightly into your face at anchor.

Correction

This causes left-to-right oscillation of the bowstring as it moves forward and therefore causes left-to-right errors. You might have to adjust the rope on the mechanical release, the string loop, or your anchor so that the bowstring lightly touches the nose and the draw hand contacts the side of the face or jaw.

Target archers achieve great consistency with a back-tension release because it prevents the archer from anticipating the release. A back-tension release, though, can be too slow and complicated for a bowhunter. Bowhunters often choose a caliper-type release (one of these is pictured in figure 6.4) that clamps directly onto the bowstring and has a trigger. Wrist straps prevent the release from being misplaced or dropped from a tree stand.

If you decide to use a trigger release, you can choose a model that is triggered with the thumb, index finger, or little finger. In all cases, set the release so that the trigger pressure required in order to release is firm, 3 to 7 pounds, but the travel, or movement of the trigger to release, is very small. Triggers that are very light or have a long travel eventually tend to cause archers to punch the release or anticipate when the release will occur. The result is arm, hand, or head movements on the release that influence the flight of the arrow and therefore the accuracy. With firm pressure, you can place your finger on the trigger and actually "preload," or partially deflect, the trigger. Once you aim and are committed to the shot, increasing back tension hinges the hand and moves the finger to bring about the release without anticipation.

Index-finger releases are often grasped with the palm down (figure 6.6). You should select a release that allows the wrist and hand to be straight and relaxed rather than bent. Ideally,

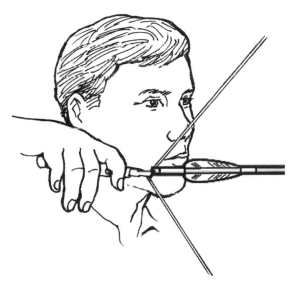

Figure 6.6 An index-finger release.

the first crease of the index finger should be on the trigger, so you must adjust the length of the release according to the size of your hand.

If you decide to change your anchor or use a mechanical release, you will need to determine new sight settings. Anything that changes the position of the rear end of the arrow changes its orientation and trajectory in flight. As with finger shooting, consistency is important in shooting with a release. The mechanical release allows for very accurate shooting, so the scoring in the competitive classifications that allow a release is quite high. Shot-to-shot variations of any type or extent are costly to success!

Anchoring With a Mechanical Release Drill 1. *Mimicking With Eyes Closed*

Work with a partner. Take only your bow and assume your stance and bow hand hold, and hook your release aid onto the bowstring. Raise the bow and draw to anchor with your eyes closed (figure 6.7). Feel for the proper position, hold for a count of three while maintaining relaxed hands, and then ease the string back. This drill establishes your feel for proper anchor position. Repeat the draw and anchor for a total of 10 repetitions, having your partner look for consistency on every shot. (Your partner can use the success checks as guidelines.)

Figure 6.7 Mimicking an anchor position for a mechanical release with eyes closed.

Success Check

- Deep hook is used on release aid.
- Head is erect.
- String touches nose.
- Draw hand is flat and relaxed.

Score Your Success

10 repetitions with correct form = 5 points

8 or 9 repetitions with correct form = 3 points

6 or 7 repetitions with correct form = 1 point

Your score_____

Anchoring With a Mechanical Release Drill 2. *Adjusting Your Peep Sight*

Most archers who shoot with a mechanical release also use a peep sight. Perhaps you have been shooting with a peep sight, but its position was set for an under-chin anchor with a finger release. It is likely that you will have to adjust the position of your peep sight for your anchor position with a mechanical release. Draw to anchor with your mechanical release and see if you can center the target in your peep sight. If not, untie the peep sight and install the peep sight again (see step 5).

Success Check

- Set anchor position.
- Center target and sight aperture in peep sight.

Score Your Success

Five draws while successfully aiming through the peep sight = 2 points

Three or four draws while successfully aiming through the peep sight = 1 point

Your score_____

Anchoring With a Mechanical Release Drill 3. *Attaining New Sight Settings*

If you have decided to shoot with a mechanical release, you need to reestablish your sight settings. Start at 15 yards. Shoot until you attain an accurate sight setting. Move back to 20 yards, and then move back to 25, 30, 35, and 40 yards, shooting until you have an accurate sight setting. If you are using a new anchor, there is likely to be more difference in your setting at a longer distance than at a shorter distance.

To Increase Difficulty

- Add 45- and 50-yard settings.

To Decrease Difficulty

- Start at 10 yards and stop at 30 yards.

Success Check

- Hook release onto bowstring or string loop.
- Grasp release with deep hook.
- Keep hand and wrist relaxed.
- Touch string to nose.
- Touch back of draw hand to face.
- Center target in peep sight.

Score Your Success

Attain new sight settings for 6 to 8 yardages = 3 points

Attain new sight settings for 5 yardages = 2 points

Your score_____

SUCCESS SUMMARY OF ANCHORING

Anchoring is an important aspect of archery technique. A precise anchor helps you establish both horizontal and vertical consistency from shot to shot, while a variable anchor position leads to variable success! In anchoring, you'll want to establish as many touch points as practical for your body shape and size and the type of archery you are shooting.

No matter what anchor position you use and no matter whether you release with the fingers or with a mechanical release aid, certain features of the shot are the same. You will want to draw with the back muscles and maintain good back tension throughout the shot. Your attention should be on aiming, and you'll need to trust that the release will come at the proper time. Anticipating the release typically gets you into trouble, because you'll gradually and often subtly start moving during or even before the release.

For each of the drills presented in this step, you can earn points to chart your progress. Enter your score for each drill and add them up to rate your total success. If you earned 17 points or more, move to the next step. If you did not, repeat the drills for the anchor position you anticipate using from now on.

Kisser Button Drill

1. Installing a Kisser Button   ____ out of 3

Under-Chin Anchor Drills

1. Mimicking With Eyes Closed   ____ out of 5

2. Sight-Setting Check   ____ out of 3

Side-of-Face Anchor Drills

1. Mimicking With Eyes Closed   ____ out of 5

2. Attaining New Sight Settings   ____ out of 3

3. Shooting Barebow   ____ out of 5

Anchoring With a Mechanical Release Drills

1. Mimicking With Eyes Closed   ____ out of 5

2. Adjusting Your Peep Sight   ____ out of 2

3. Attaining New Sight Settings   ____ out of 3

Total   ____ *out of 34*

You now have all the pieces of the shooting puzzle. You can continue to practice and to improve your scoring. Like all athletes, though, you need a way to monitor your performance and to identify the errors that gradually come into every athlete's performance. Moreover, you need a guide for correcting errors, to once again achieve good form and get back on the road to successful scoring. In step 7, you'll see how you can learn to detect and then correct errors.

Analyzing Performance

Some of the most famous people in sports are coaches: Joe Gibbs in football, Joe Torre in baseball, Pat Summitt in basketball. Such coaches are known for their success in helping their athletes reach their full potential. Like any other athletes, archers also benefit from coaching. An archery coach can note flaws in shooting technique and suggest corrections. Unfortunately, archery coaches are not as plentiful as baseball and basketball coaches. Perhaps more than other athletes, archers must learn to detect and correct their own errors.

Archers rely on two sources of information for correcting performance mistakes. They analyze where their arrows land in relation to the bull's-eye where their shots are aimed. That is, they analyze the outcome of their performance. They also check their technique, their actual positions and movements, by evaluating the feel of their shots or watching videos of their techniques. Successful archers, no matter what type of archery they shoot, learn how to check their own shooting and make adjustments in their techniques. The technology available today even makes this evaluation fun!

Any archer would probably seize the opportunity to work with a good coach. Even archers lucky enough to have a coach, though, spend many hours shooting without coaches when practicing, competing, or hunting. The sooner an error can be corrected, the better. Remember that most types of archery involve repetitive shooting. Archers who can quickly adjust their techniques to overcome mistakes will score more consistently than those who cannot.

ANALYZING ARROW PATTERNS

You can use two basic methods to monitor errors that may develop in your shooting. The first method is to observe the result of your performance. In archery, this method involves an analysis of the pattern your arrows form on the target face. Form errors can cause consistent directional errors. For example, if several arrows in each of your ends land to the right of your other arrows, that pattern may indicate one of several shooting flaws. If all your arrows land to the right of the bull's-eye despite repeated corrections of your sight setting, you can pinpoint one of these shooting flaws as the cause.

The second method for checking performance is to observe your own technique. Check your stance, draw, anchor, hold, release, and follow-through for alignment, consistency, and proper execution.

Arrows land in the bull's-eye if they are both vertically and horizontally accurate. Repeated errors in technique result in a consistent directional error. You can identify the error by checking the pattern of the arrows on the target face. If you frequently make the same error, perhaps once in each end with one arrow landing away from the rest, you will be reminded of the error and will need to continue monitoring for that aspect of your shot execution. Consistent directional errors also can be related to equipment. In step 8 you will learn how to adjust your equipment in order to eliminate directional errors caused by equipment setup.

To help describe shot locations, the target face is often compared to a clock face as you view it from the shooting line. Arrows landing to the right of the bull's-eye, for example, are described as 3 o'clock errors. Arrows landing right and slightly high are called 2 o'clock errors, and so on. Obviously you should analyze only well-aimed shots. If you aim a shot at 6 o'clock and it lands at 6 o'clock, there is no need to look for errors in technique!

Horizontal Patterns

The performance errors that affect horizontal accuracy generally include horizontal movements of the bow or bow arm, misalignment of the bowstring and bowsight, misalignment in addressing the target, and releases that give the bowstring too much horizontal movement or oscillation (figure 7.1). Horizontal bow movements can occur if you do the following:

- Cant (tilt) your bow
- Move the bow to the right or left when you release the bowstring

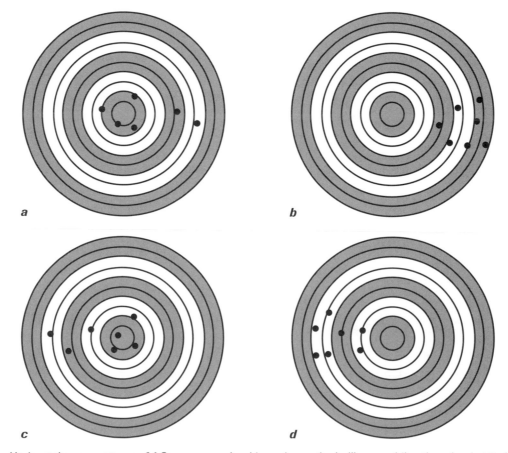

Figure 7.1 Horizontal arrow patterns: *(a)* Some arrows land in and near the bull's-eye while others land at 3 o'clock; *(b)* arrows group at 3 o'clock; *(c)* some arrows land in and near the bull's-eye while others land at 9 o'clock; *(d)* arrows group at 9 o'clock.

- Allow your bow arm wrist to break upon release
- Hold the bow handle to the side

Many archers are so anxious to see their arrows hit the target that they move the bow sideways upon release. To prevent yourself from making this mistake, make sure you use your back muscles to draw, keep your arms in alignment with the target, center your bow arm behind the center of the bow handle, and follow through in T-form.

Misalignments of the bowstring and bowsight often occur when the archer varies the anchor position, changes the eye that aligns the bowstring and bowsight from shot to shot, or varies the pattern of alignment between the bowstring and the bowsight from shot to shot.

Because the arrow is snapped onto the bowstring, changing the position of the bowstring in relation to the aiming aperture changes the orientation of the arrow to the bull's-eye from shot to shot. To avoid these misalignments, use a consistent anchor, use at least the tip of the nose as a touch point for the bowstring, and establish a consistent bowstring and bowsight vissual pattern from shot to shot. The preferred bowstring and bowsight pattern is to see the string just to the right of the aiming aperture. A peep sight automatically gives you a consistent pattern, but it is prohibited in some competition classifications.

Misalignments in addressing the target usually affect the accuracy of the shot because muscles on one side of the body are working harder than those on the other side. The tensed muscles tend to cause horizontal movements upon release, especially as you tire. When addressing the target, establish a solid base of support with your stance without using a very open or closed position, and keep your body aligned to the target by drawing close to the bow arm with the back muscles. Also avoid bows with a draw weight so heavy that you need additional movements to get to full draw.

Releases that give the bowstring unnecessary horizontal movement affect accuracy because they send the tail of the arrow farther to the side than necessary. Remember that the arrow remains in contact with the bowstring for most

of its path forward. The release most likely to cause horizontal errors is plucking the string, which means the hand flies away from the face rather than recoiling over the rear shoulder. Arrow flight also is affected if you nock the arrow backward so that the index feather strikes the arrow rest or bow window or if the bowstring catches on clothing or jewelry as it moves forward.

Vertical Patterns

Performance errors that affect vertical accuracy include the following:

- Moving your bow arm up or down upon release
- Varying your anchor position vertically
- Varying the pressure of the fingers on the bowstring
- Holding the bow too high or too low on the handle
- Deviating from T-form
- Varying your effective draw length (figure 7.2)

Dropping or raising the bow arm on release can affect the tail end of the arrow as it clears the bow. Always follow through by slightly pushing the bow arm to the bull's-eye until the arrow hits the target.

Varying the anchor position vertically orients the arrow differently from shot to shot. Beginning archers often anchor with the mouth open and vary how wide the mouth is open with each shot. Avoid this error by keeping your teeth together on every shot. Varying the pressure of the three fingers on the bowstring also changes the orientation of the arrow. Releases that cause vertical errors are those in which the wrist rotates up or down so that the pressure of the upper or lower finger lessens just before release.

Holding the bow at the same location on the handle on every shot minimizes vertical errors. Holding the handle too high or too low is likely to cause you to move the bow when you release the bowstring. For example, you could heel the bow with the base of the palm and tilt the bow backward as a result.

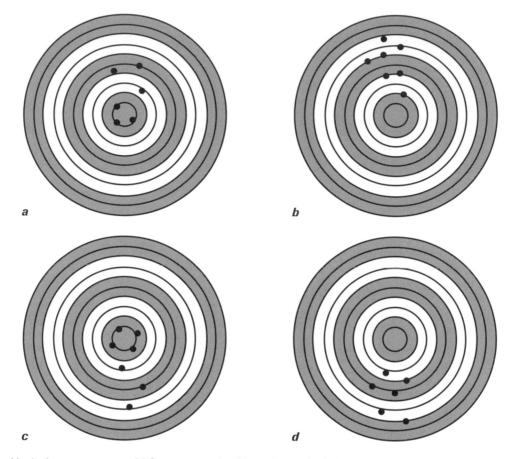

Figure 7.2 Vertical arrow patterns: *(a)* Some arrows land in and near the bull's-eye while others land at 12 o'clock; *(b)* arrows group at 12 o'clock; *(c)* some arrows land in and near the bull's-eye while others land at 6 o'clock; *(d)* arrows group at 6 o'clock.

Deviating from T-form can also contribute to vertical errors, especially if you hunch the front shoulder, slide the hips forward, tilt the head forward or backward, or lean forward or backward. These form errors contribute to vertical bow arm movement and variation in the effective draw length. Even small variations in draw length can affect vertical accuracy by changing the pounds of thrust imparted to the arrow. For example, if your arrows land at 6 o'clock, you may be moving your draw hand slightly forward at release (creeping), bending the bow arm, tilting the head forward, or punching (moving forward) when triggering a mechanical release.

Maintaining T-form and using the back muscles to draw prevent these deviations. Increasing the back tension during the aim and then releasing the bowstring by relaxing the fingers produce the most consistent draw and release.

Mixed Patterns

Several situations could result in arrow patterns of mixed vertical and horizontal errors, such as 10 o'clock or 4 o'clock errors. An archer may make multiple errors, some causing vertical errors and some causing horizontal errors. Such a pattern also results from moving the bow arm diagonally rather than just vertically or horizontally.

If your arrows form a mixed pattern, make sure you maintain a loose grip on the bow and push the bow arm straight to the bull's-eye throughout the aim, release, and follow-through. If your arrows still form a mixed pattern, look for errors that affect both horizontal and vertical accuracy. For example, if your arrows land at 4 or 5 o'clock, look for errors that cause a right, horizontal error and a low, vertical error.

Misstep

Some of your arrows group around the bull's-eye and some land at 9 o'clock.

Correction

Develop a relaxed bow hand (see the drills in step 4). When the bow hand grip is tight, archers tend to flex the finger upon release, an action that turns the bow handle. With a relaxed bow hand grip, the bow is free to jump slightly forward upon release and not affect the arrow either horizontally or vertically. Using a bow sling helps to prevent archers from feeling that they have to hold the bow so that it will not fall.

Misstep

Your arrows spread from 12 o'clock to 6 o'clock.

Correction

Check your anchor position to be sure it is consistent. Check your head position to be sure you draw to your face rather than push your head forward to meet the string. Changes in your anchor can change your draw length and impart varying thrust to the arrow from shot to shot.

Arrow Pattern Drill 1. *Analysis of Arrow Pattern*

Shoot several ends from 20 yards. Before pulling your arrows, plot each arrow's location with an X on the targets provided in figure 7.3. When you finish, look for your most common directional errors. Using the clock face terminology, record where your errant arrows land. Then identify several potential causes of your errors. Shoot several more ends, and try to avoid the errors you identified. Plot these ends on additional targets to see whether you have eliminated or reduced directional error.

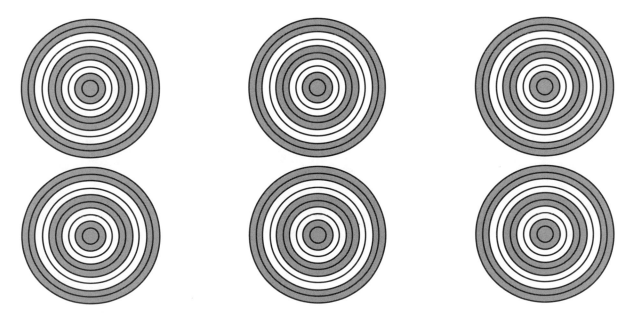

Figure 7.3 Plot arrow locations on these targets.

Success Check

- Maintain T-form.
- Establish consistent bow hand and anchor positions.
- Follow through to target.

Arrow Pattern Drill 2. Analysis of Arrow Pattern From a Distance

Directional errors often become more noticeable as you shoot from longer distances. Once directed off center, the arrow continues over a longer distance on a line that results in its landing farther from the bull's-eye.

Shoot several ends from 30 yards. Before pulling your arrows, plot each arrow's location with an X on the targets provided in figure 7.4. When you finish shooting and plotting, look for your most common directional errors. Using the clock face terminology, record where your errant arrows land. Then identify several poten-

tial causes of your errors. Shoot several more ends, and try to avoid the errors you identified. Plot these ends on additional targets to see whether you have eliminated or reduced directional error.

Success Check

- Align stance and shoulders toward target.
- Maintain T-form by drawing with back muscles.
- Stand erect.

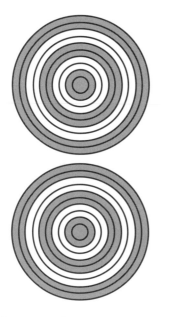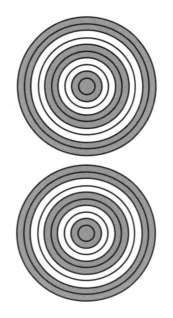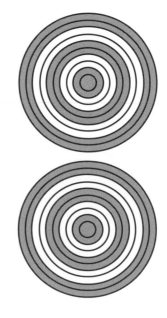

Figure 7.4 Plot arrow locations on these targets.

Score Your Success

Identify at least two causes for each of two directional errors = 4 points

Identify one cause for each of two directional errors = 3 points

Identify at least two causes for one directional error = 2 points

Identify one cause for one directional error = 1 point

Your score_____

Arrow Pattern Drill 3. *Checking Aiming Errors*

Aiming errors are difficult to detect by observation. Another method of detecting errors is required. The following list of items could make up your mental checklist for aiming. Shoot an arrow, and then look down the list. Did you forget any items? Continue shooting until you can execute an entire end without forgetting a step.

1. Close your dominant eye if it's not on the same side as your string hand.

2. Line up the bowstring just to the right of the aiming aperture (figure 7.5) or center the aiming aperture in the peep sight.

3. See the bowstring bisect the bow limbs in your peripheral vision (or check the bubble in the level).

4. Exhale before aiming and releasing.

5. Let the bowsight settle in the bull's-eye before you release the bowstring. Note that the sight doesn't have to stop dead in the bull's-eye.

Success Check

• Establish consistent string and sight pattern.

• Allow sight to settle in bull's-eye before release.

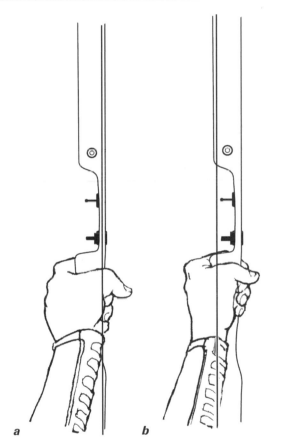

Figure 7.5   Aiming errors: *(a)* bowstring too far to the right of the aiming aperture; *(b)* bowstring too far to the left of the aiming aperture.

Score Your Success

Execute second end without forgetting a step = 3 points

Execute third end without forgetting a step = 2 points

Execute fourth end without forgetting a step = 1 point

Your score_____

ANALYZING TECHNIQUE

The second method for checking performance is to observe your technique. Observe your stance, draw, anchor, hold, release, and follow-through for alignment, consistency, and proper execution. You can identify technique errors in your shooting by examining videotapes or pictures of yourself or asking a knowledgeable friend to observe. Watch carefully for T-form in back and front views. Watch for alignment along a line straight to the target in views from behind, looking down range. You also may be able to feel yourself making a technique error, although archers often do not realize how they are positioning their bodies and limbs.

Errors That Affect Horizontal Accuracy

Many technique errors that cause horizontal errors are detected from a camera or observer behind the archer, viewing down range (figure 7.6a). From this angle, check for positions or movements that cause horizontal variations in arrow flight:

- The body leans right or left, perhaps falling off that direction upon release.

- The shoulders are angled down range.

- The bow arm appears to the right or left from behind the trunk upon release.

- The bow tilts right or left.

- The bow turns right or left upon release.

- The string hand or arm flies away from the face upon release.

Sometimes a rear view from a location above the archer is helpful in detecting these flaws in technique (figures 7.6b and 7.6c). Extend your tripod or have your observer stand carefully on a ladder.

A few aspects of form that affect horizontal accuracy can be observed by a close-up of the face and draw hand. Watch for slight variations in establishing the anchor position, such as touching the bowstring to the tip of the nose on one shot but the side of the nose on another.

Figure 7.6	Horizontal Accuracy

DOWN-RANGE VIEW

1. Stand erect
2. Keep bow vertical
3. Keep string hand and wrist relaxed
4. Use back muscles

a

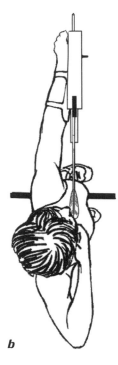

b

c

OVERHEAD VIEW

1. Align the shoulders toward target
2. Increase back tension

CLOSE-UP ON BOW HAND

1. Align bow hand behind bow handle
2. Relax bow hand

Errors That Affect Vertical Accuracy

Technique errors that cause vertical errors are most often detected from an observer or camera position down the shooting line, directed toward the front of the body (figure 7.7a). An ideal setting would have vertical and horizontal references in the background so that deviations from T-form could be easily identified. From this perspective, check for these positions or movements that cause vertical variations in arrow flight:

- The shoulder line is uneven.
- The body leans toward or away from the target.

- The hips slide forward and the upper body tilts back.
- The bow arm moves up or down upon release.
- The anchor position varies from shot to shot.
- The bow hand grip varies from shot to shot.
- Finger pressure varies from shot to shot.

Zoom in on the string or bow hand to see whether its position varies from shot to shot (figure 7.7b). A person also can stand behind you as you're shooting to observe your form by looking at your back (figure 7.7c).

 **Figure 7.7**   **Vertical Accuracy**

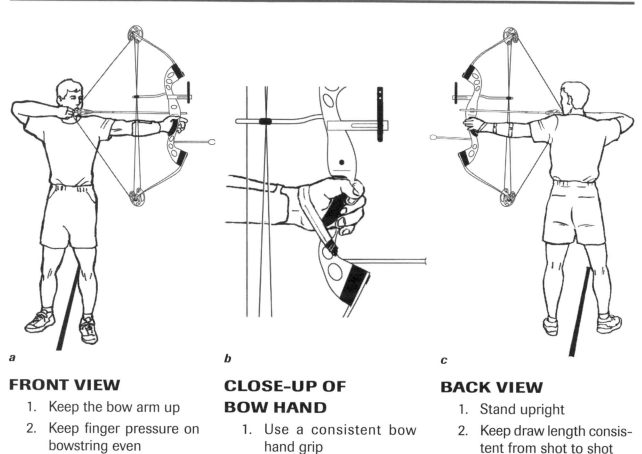

a

FRONT VIEW

1. Keep the bow arm up
2. Keep finger pressure on bowstring even
3. Use a consistent anchor

b

CLOSE-UP OF BOW HAND

1. Use a consistent bow hand grip

c

BACK VIEW

1. Stand upright
2. Keep draw length consistent from shot to shot

 Misstep

You come out of T-form during the draw, aim, or follow-through.

Correction

Use a bow with a draw weight that you can control without losing T-form. Many flaws in T-form are the result of archers' shooting bows too high in draw weight. Because of the high draw weight, they cannot draw with just the back muscles, so they recruit other muscle groups. Be sure to maintain alignment of the limbs and trunk instead of moving the arm, shoulder, and trunk joints or pushing the bow arm while pulling with the string hand (the push-pull draw). Also avoid an extremely open or closed stance.

Misstep

Your alignment varies from shot to shot.

Correction

Use a consistent anchor position. Align the string and bowsight consistently or use a peep sight if rules allow it.

Technique Analysis Drill 1. Checking Errors in Vertical Alignment

Place a camcorder on a tripod about chest high and 10 feet up the shooting line from your shooting position so that the recording provides the view shown in figure 7.8. If possible, suspend a sheet or canvas with vertical and horizontal lines from a coat rack behind you. Record at least 10 shots. If you do not have access to a camcorder, have a friend take still photographs or observe your shooting. Watch the video and look for errors in body alignment such as those shown in figure 7.9. Compare your alignment to the vertical and horizontal lines on the sheet. Try to correct any errors in alignment as you videotape five additional shots. Repeat this cycle until you shoot with good alignment.

To Increase Difficulty

- Videotape the last 10 shots of a 60-shot practice session. Remember that form tends to break down as you tire, yet the last arrow counts just as much as the first arrow in competition.

Success Check

- Keep shoulders level.
- Stand erect.
- Keep bow arm up.

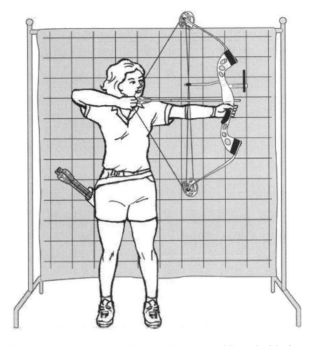

Figure 7.8 Having vertical and horizontal lines behind you will help you identify and correct errors in technique.

a *b*

Figure 7.9 Errors to watch for: *(a)* front shoulder hunched; *(b)* hips sliding, upper body tilted.

Score Your Success

Correct alignment by the fifth recorded shot = 5 points

Correct alignment by the sixth recorded shot = 4 points

Correct alignment by the seventh recorded shot = 3 points

Correct alignment by the eighth recorded shot = 2 points

Correct alignment by the ninth recorded shot = 1 point

Your score_____

Technique Analysis Drill 2. Checking Errors in Horizontal Alignment

Place a camcorder or observer behind you, looking down range. Shoot 10 arrows, and then check with your observer or watch the video. Try to detect errors in alignment that would affect the arrow horizontally, such as an uneven stance or incorrect T-form (figure 7.10). Now try to correct those errors as you videotape five additional shots. Repeat this cycle until you shoot with good alignment.

To Increase Difficulty

- Videotape the last 10 shots of a 60-shot practice session.

Success Check

- Align stance and shoulders toward target.
- Maintain T-form by drawing with back muscles.
- Stand erect.

Figure 7.10 Errors to watch for: *(a)* upper body bent; *(b)* stance misaligned; *(c)* shoulders not aligned to target.

Score Your Success

Correct alignment by the fifth recorded shot = 5 points

Correct alignment by the sixth recorded shot = 4 points

Correct alignment by the seventh recorded shot = 3 points

Correct alignment by the eighth recorded shot = 2 points

Correct alignment by the ninth recorded shot = 1 point

Your score_____

Technique Analysis Drill 3. *Checking Anchor Variations*

Videotape 10 shots as in technique analysis drill 1, except zoom in or move the tripod to record a close-up view of your anchor position and release. Watch the video to detect incorrect anchor positions or variations in your anchor position from shot to shot. Look especially for the flaws shown in figure 7.11. If you find errors in your anchor position, review step 6. If you find variations in your anchor position, develop a mental checklist to remind yourself to position your anchor consistently. Now videotape 10 additional shots to see if you are more consistent.

To Increase Difficulty

- Record your anchor position for 30 shots.

Score Your Success

Correct your anchor position by the fifth recorded shot = 5 points

Correct your anchor position by the sixth recorded shot = 4 points

Correct your anchor position by the seventh recorded shot = 3 points

Correct your anchor position by the eighth recorded shot = 2 points

Correct your anchor position by the ninth recorded shot = 1 point

Your score_____

Success Check

- Touch string to nose.

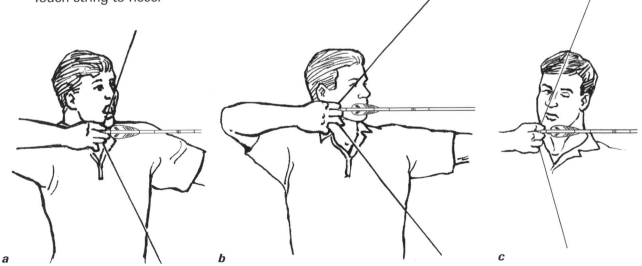

Figure 7.11 Errors to watch for: *(a)* mouth open, anchor lowered; *(b)* string drawn past nose; *(c)* head rotated.

Technique Analysis Drill 4. Checking Errors in Release

Use your video or pictures from technique analysis drill 3, but examine your release. Compare the ideal of relaxing the string fingers (or triggering your mechanical release) and the hand following through over the rear shoulder. Errors might involve plucking the string, creeping, or dropping the elbow of the string arm (figure 7.12). Additional errors might include a dead release or punching a mechanical release.

To Increase Difficulty

• Record your release for 30 shots.

Success Check

• Increase back tension.
• Relax fingers.

Score Your Success

Correct your errors in release by the fifth recorded shot = 5 points

Correct your errors in release by the sixth recorded shot = 4 points

Correct your errors in release by the seventh recorded shot = 3 points

Correct your errors in release by the eighth recorded shot = 2 points

Correct your errors in release by the ninth recorded shot = 1 point

Your score_____

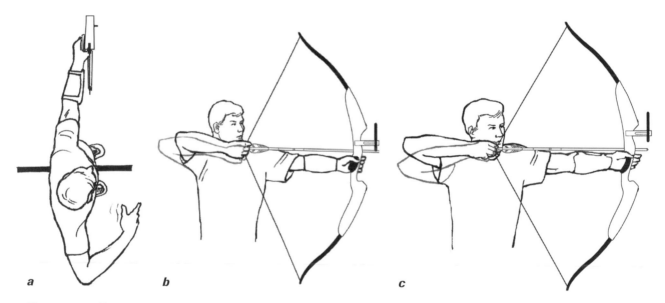

a *b* *c*

Figure 7.12 Errors to watch for: *(a)* plucking the string rather than relaxing the fingers; *(b)* string hand creeping forward before release; *(c)* dropping the elbow of the string arm.

Technique Analysis Drill 5. Checking Errors in Bow Hand

Videotape 10 shots as in technique analysis drill 1, except zoom in or move the tripod to record your bow hand. You could also work with a partner. Watch the video or consult with your partner. The bow should jump forward slightly upon release, and the fingers should remain relaxed. If you find that you grab the bow, heel it, or turn it upon release, as shown in figure 7.13, review step 4 to work on a relaxed bow hand. Also, watch the time period before release to ensure that your

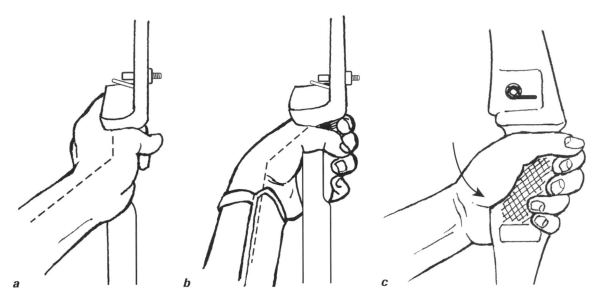

Figure 7.13 Errors to watch for: *(a)* wrist bent back; *(b)* wrist bent forward; *(c)* heeling the bow.

wrist position does not change during the draw and aim. Record 10 additional shots to monitor your improvement.

To Increase Difficulty

- Record the last 10 shots of a 60-shot practice session.

Success Check

- Bow arm and hand are aligned behind handle.
- Fingers are relaxed.

Score Your Success

Correct errors in bow hand by the fifth recorded shot = 5 points

Correct errors in bow hand by the sixth recorded shot = 4 points

Correct errors in bow hand by the seventh recorded shot = 3 points

Correct errors in bow hand by the eighth recorded shot = 2 points

Correct errors in bow hand by the ninth recorded shot = 1 point

Your score_____

Technique Analysis Drill 6. Checking Errors in Draw

Videotape 10 shots as in technique analysis drill 1 and then watch the video, or work with a partner. Analyze your draw. Identify errors such as those pictured in figure 7.14. Ideally, your bow arm is extended throughout the draw, and your draw comes all the way to your anchor position. After you identify any draw errors, videotape 10 additional shots and analyze them. Repeat this cycle until you eliminate your errors.

To Increase Difficulty

- Record the last 10 shots of a 60-shot practice session.

Success Check

- Extend bow arm to target.
- Touch string to nose.

Figure 7.14 Errors to watch for: *(a)* arms not fully drawn; *(b)* bow elbow bent.

Score Your Success

Correct draw errors by the fifth recorded shot = 5 points

Correct draw errors by the sixth recorded shot = 4 points

Correct draw errors by the seventh recorded shot = 3 points

Correct draw errors by the eighth recorded shot = 2 points

Correct draw errors by the ninth recorded shot = 1 point

Your score_____

Technique Analysis Drill 7. *Checking Follow-Through*

Videotape 10 shots as in technique analysis drill 1 and then watch the video, or work with a partner. Analyze your follow-through. Identify errors such as those pictured in figure 7.15. Ideally, your bow arm is extended throughout the draw and follow-through. When you release the bowstring, your head and bow arm should maintain their positions and you should maintain T-form. After you identify any errors in follow-through, videotape 10 additional shots and analyze them. Repeat this cycle until you eliminate your errors.

To Increase Difficulty

- Record the last 10 shots of a 60-shot practice session.

Success Check

- Maintain head position upon release.
- Bow arm extends to target even after release.

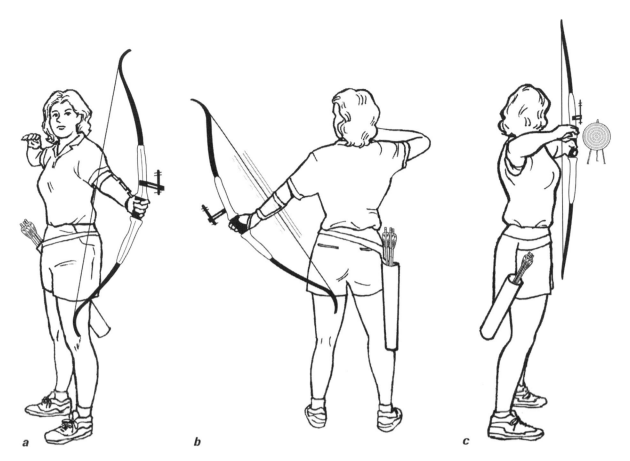

Figure 7.15 Errors to watch for: *(a)* peeking at arrow after release; *(b)* dropping bow arm after release; *(c)* plucking the string.

Score Your Success

Correct errors in follow-through by the fifth recorded shot = 5 points

Correct errors in follow-through by the sixth recorded shot = 4 points

Correct errors in follow-through by the seventh recorded shot = 3 points

Correct errors in follow-through by the eighth recorded shot = 2 points

Correct errors in follow-through by the ninth recorded shot = 1 point

Your score_____

OVERCOMING TARGET PANIC

Target panic is the anticipation of the release of the bowstring, which disrupts a smooth release and follow-through. If archers come to anticipate release, the time between release and some movement of the head, arms, or hands gets shorter and shorter. Eventually, archers with target panic move early enough to influence the release of the bowstring and the flight of the arrow. They can even progress to moving *before* the release!

Target panic varies in severity and frequency, but most archers who shoot long enough eventually have one or more of its symptoms:

- Flinching is any sudden movement immediately before or during the release, often of the bow arm, that affects clearance of the arrow as it leaves the bow.

- Punching refers to jerking a mechanical release to release the bowstring.

- Plucking the bowstring or creeping forward toward the target when using a finger release is a sign of target panic.

- Snap shooting means releasing immediately when the sight aperture crosses the bull's-eye and before the sight has settled on the bull's-eye. This tendency might progress so that release occurs even before the sight aperture gets to the bull's-eye.

- Freezing is the inability to move the sight aperture from a spot off the bull's-eye to the bull's-eye (or, in hunting, to the kill zone). Freezing can also refer to the inability to release even when the aperture is settled in the bull's-eye or the inability to move the arrow through the clicker, a device that promotes an increase in back tension (see step 10).

Remember, you can have more than one symptom of target panic. As the symptoms progress, you might struggle to shoot well. Shooting then becomes a frustration and can cause you to stop enjoying the sport. More than any other single reason, target panic probably causes many archers to leave the sport.

One cause of target panic might be trying to control every aspect of the shot, especially trying to make the release happen at a particular time, when you should be devoting attention to aiming. It is a classic case of not being able to do two things at once or do them well. Through repetitive practice, athletes progress from conscious control of every aspect of a skill to an automatic stage. Well-practiced movements are carried out subconsciously. For example, you do not have to think about alternately swinging your legs and planting your feet when you walk. Archers ideally devote conscious attention to aiming and relegate execution of the release to the subconscious. When archers let their conscious attention switch back to *making* the release happen *now,* over time they begin anticipating the release, and then target panic develops.

Your goal as a new archer should be to consciously control your stance, draw, and anchor. Once you are anchored and you are in the position you want to be in, commit to executing the shot (figure 7.16). Begin to increase your back tension, then switch your attention to aiming; focus on the exact center of the target and trust your body to take the sight aperture there. It takes 3 to 4 seconds to develop sufficient back tension to release, so continue to focus on the center of the target and let your release occur as a natural consequence of increasing back tension.

Figure 7.16 | Subconscious Release

1. Assume stance and nock arrow
2. Release or fingers are on string
3. Set bow hand
4. Draw to anchor
5. Check position; if OK, commit to shot
6. Begin increasing back tension
7. Aim
8. Allow release explosion to occur
9. Maintain position to the follow-through

Misstep

On the release, you move (flinch, creep, pluck, punch). You freeze the sight aperture off the bull's-eye or you release when the aperture first approaches the bull's-eye without settling.

Correction

Practice shots with your conscious attention on aiming only. Try rotational aiming as described in target panic drill 1. If you cannot overcome target panic this way, reprogram your shot (see target panic drills 2 and 3).

Pellerite (2001) suggests archers with target panic reprogram a subconscious release through two practice phases designed to rebuild the shot sequence. The first phase involves practicing on a blank bale or target butt at a short distance (5 yards), that is, with no target of any kind. This type of practice also can be done with a bow simulator. During this time you must suspend participation in all tournaments or leagues. There should be no shooting at a target! Target panic drill 2 is based on this phase of reprogramming.

The second phase of the Pellerite program is equally important. It serves as a bridge back to shooting at a target. It begins with shooting at a very short distance to a large target and progresses very gradually back to a longer distance and smaller target. Target panic drill 3 is based on this phase. It is important to refrain from using shortcuts; go back to the previous yardage for three days if any symptom of target panic returns.

Pellerite, B. 2001. *Idiot proof archery*. Gahanna, OH: Robinhood Video Productions.

Target Panic Drill 1. *Rotational Aiming*

Place a handful of dot stickers randomly on a target face. Being careful to execute your shot sequence, draw and aim at one of the stickers from 5 to 10 yards away. Hold 4 to 6 seconds and then let down. Rest, then draw again and aim at another sticker. Continue until you have aimed at each of the stickers. The more you repeat this drill, the better, especially when you first see symptoms of target panic. If you have target panic, you would benefit from doing this drill 30 to 60 times a day for three weeks.

Success Check

- Draw, anchor, and check position.
- Focus on the target.
- Aim.

Score Your Success

Aim at each sticker three times ("ends") = 3 points

Aim at each sticker twice = 2 points

Aim at each sticker once = 1 point

Your score_____

Target Panic Drill 2. *Blank Bale Program*

This drill is based on the first phase of Pellerite's reprogramming. Take your equipment to shoot at a bale or target butt with no target face from a distance of 5 yards. Shoot 30 to 60 shots per day for a minimum of 21 days. Shoot with your eyes open. Be sure to execute your shot sequence correctly (that is, make good shots even though you are not scoring).

Success Check

- Check position; if OK, commit to shot.
- Increase back tension.

Score Your Success

Complete the blank bale program = 10 points

Your score_____

Target Panic Drill 3. *Bridge Program*

This drill is based on the second phase of Pellerite's reprogramming. Place a 9-inch paper plate on the target butt. From a distance of 5 yards, shoot 30 to 60 shots per day for at least three days. Don't worry about hitting the middle of the plate. Shoot one arrow at a time, pulling that arrow after the shot. Next, move back 2 1/2 yards and decrease the size of the paper plate by 1 inch. Shoot another 30 to 60 shots per day for at least three days. Continue this pattern until you reach 20 yards. If at any time a symptom of target panic returns, move back to the previous yardage and repeat the three days of practice.

Success Check

- Commit to shot.
- Increase back tension.
- Aim and let release occur.

Score Your Success

Complete the bridge program = 10 points

Your score_____

SUCCESS SUMMARY
OF IMPROVING ACCURACY

Errors in technique affect horizontal accuracy, vertical accuracy, or both. You can avoid horizontal deviations in your shots (also called 3 o'clock and 9 o'clock errors) by maintaining bow and string alignment. Watch for these causes of horizontal errors:

- Canting the bow
- Moving the bow sideways on release
- Breaking your bow wrist on release
- Holding the bow to the side of the center of the handle
- Misaligning the bowstring with the sight aperture
- Taking a stance that is not aligned to the target

You can avoid vertical deviations in your shots (also called 12 o'clock and 6 o'clock errors) by keeping T-form, keeping your draw length consistent, and following through. Possible causes of 12 o'clock vertical errors are raising the bow arm upon release, opening the mouth and therefore lowering your anchor, and overdrawing. Possible causes of 6 o'clock errors include dropping the bow arm, creeping, and not coming to a full draw. Diagonal errors, such as 8 o'clock or 4 o'clock errors, can indicate that you are making multiple technique errors that are affecting both horizontal and vertical accuracy.

Repeat the drills in this step periodically. Detecting and correcting your errors early can minimize the chance that they will become bad habits. Enter your score for each drill in order to monitor your progress. Add up your scores to rate your total success. If you have 27 or more points, go on to the next step. If not, repeat some of the drills to earn additional points.

Arrow Pattern Drills

1. Analysis of Arrow Pattern		___ out of 4
2. Analysis of Arrow Pattern From a Distance		___ out of 4
3. Checking Aiming Errors		___ out of 3

Technique Analysis Drills

1. Checking Errors in Vertical Alignment		___ out of 5
2. Checking Errors in Horizontal Alignment		___ out of 5
3. Checking Anchor Variations		___ out of 5
4. Checking Errors in Release		___ out of 5
5. Checking Errors in Bow Hand		___ out of 5
6. Checking Errors in Draw		___ out of 5
7. Checking Follow-Through		___ out of 5

Target Panic Drills

1. Rotational Aiming		___ out of 3
2. Blank Bale Program		___ out of 10
3. Bridge Program		___ out of 10

Total   ___ *out of 69*

With the completion of this step, you have covered the basic techniques of shooting. If you have been practicing and becoming a more proficient shooter, it may be time to maximize the contribution of your equipment setup to your scoring. One way to do this is to upgrade your equipment. Better equipment is generally more consistent and more forgiving of errors in technique. Another way that equipment can help you score better is through proper adjustment to provide smoother arrow flight. Smoother flight also is more forgiving of errors in technique. In step 8, you will learn what you should look for in upgrading your equipment and then how to adjust it so that it makes the best contribution possible to your score. You also will consider what you need to do to keep your equipment in good working order.

Upgrading, Tuning, and Maintaining Equipment

What percentage of accurate shooting is due to the archer and what percentage is due to equipment? This question would keep any two archers in debate for a long time, especially if they tried to attach exact numerical percentages to each. In general, though, if every archer had a good set of matched arrows, a beginning archer's technique would have more impact on accuracy than his equipment would; a skilled archer would benefit relatively more from equipment that is adjusted for her technique; and an expert archer has such good technique that he could shoot accurately with almost any contemporary archery setup. Archers at all levels depend on their equipment, but particularly at this point in your climb up the steps to success, you can benefit from good equipment adjusted for your technique.

In this step, we consider three aspects of archery equipment. First we review upgrades you can make to your equipment. Perhaps you have been refining your archery technique with basic equipment but now realize you would like to pursue archery activities more seriously. You need to know what equipment to upgrade and how to be a critical consumer of archery accessories. Second, we cover the process of adjusting, or tuning, your archery equipment so that it operates efficiently, given your unique body structure and technique. Finally, we cover the maintenance you should perform to keep your equipment in good working order.

UPGRADING EQUIPMENT

You know the saying "You get what you pay for." Why is this true in archery? Equipment that's made of good materials and has the latest technological advances performs more consistently. Just as shooting form should be consistent, archery equipment must be consistent. At the same time it is important to be a critical consumer and recognize when and if an equipment purchase benefits shooting performance. Someone will always be willing to sell you the latest magic bow that can't miss its mark. Remember that form is the biggest factor in the beginning and intermediate phases of learning to shoot.

Arrows

Good arrows are so important to accurate shooting that it is often said that if you give a skilled archer a choice between high-quality arrows and

103

a basic bow or basic arrows and a high-quality bow, the archer would choose high-quality arrows and a basic bow. Good arrows are the foundation of an equipment setup that maximizes scoring. A set of good arrows should be your first equipment upgrade. The best arrows are those that are consistent in the degree to which they bend when stressed a specified amount. This bendability is called *spine*.

To see why spine is so important, you must understand how an arrow clears the bow when you release the bowstring. First consider what happens to the bowstring when a finger shooter releases it. Even with the cleanest release, the bowstring rolls off the archer's fingertips and finger tab, sending it slightly in toward the archer as it moves forward. It then rebounds away from the archer, and then moves slightly toward the archer as it reaches brace height. The string, being attached to the limbs, reaches its limit of forward movement and reverses direction, moving slightly away and then oscillating at brace height (figure 8.1).

The arrow is attached to the bowstring at release, so the nock end of the arrow moves

toward the archer with the bowstring. At the same time, the full forward force of the bow's stored energy is transferred through the string to the arrow. The point end of the arrow, resting against the bow, pushes against the bow. The bow resists this push. The arrow center is free to bend between the two pressure points. It first bends slightly to the right of a direct line to the target (figure 8.2). As the arrow continues forward, the center of the shaft bends to the left in an equal and opposite reaction to the first bend. The shaft is bending around the bow handle at this point. Just as the fletching approaches the bow handle, the shaft bends to the right once more and moves the fletching away from the arrow rest and bow handle. In effect, the arrow bends around the bow without touching it. This action is referred to as the *archer's paradox*. The arrow continues toward the target, alternately bending right and left in decreasing amounts until it straightens out about 10 yards in front of the bow and flies on line to the target.

In light of how arrows clear the bow, arrows must have two qualities. First, the spine must be just right for your draw length and bow weight so that the arrow fletching clears the bow handle without contact. Second, every arrow you shoot must have the same spine. Arrows do not group unless their spines are identical, no matter how good your form is.

When an archer shoots with a mechanical release, the deflection of the string to the side is negligible, so the arrow bends vertically rather than horizontally. The alternate bending or cycling of the arrow is still significant in matching arrow shafts to equipment. The arrow's fletching must still clear the arrow rest and handle riser without contact. Therefore, release shooters also need consistent arrows that are matched to their equipment setup.

Choosing Arrow Shafts

For serious archers, aluminum, carbon, or aluminum-carbon are the arrows of choice. You can be very selective in matching arrow spine to draw length and weight with these shafts. If you would like to compete, you should upgrade to arrows designed for your type of competition.

Archers shooting in outdoor target events with long distances, such as Olympic-style

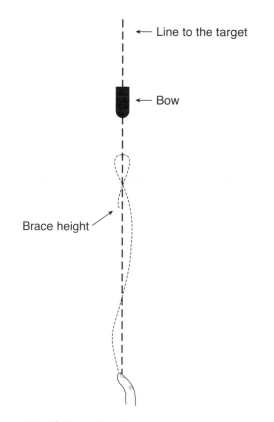

Figure 8.1 String path after release.

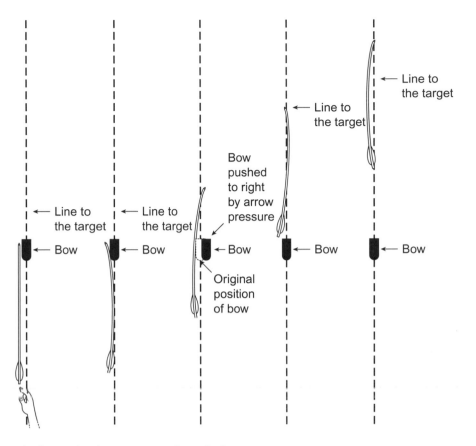

Figure 8.2 The archer's paradox: how an arrow clears the bow.

events, use aluminum carbon arrows. These arrows are made of strong carbon fiber bonded to an aluminum core tube. The shaft is barreled, the middle being a little less than 1/4 inch in diameter while the ends are just over 1/8 inch in diameter. The result is a lighter (less than 3/4 ounce), stiffer arrow that is faster (140 to 145 miles per hour) than aluminum and minimizes cross-wind effects. Because the shaft is light, smaller fletching can be used to stabilize it, helping to minimize contact with the arrow rest or handle riser.

Some target archers select all-carbon arrows. Carbon is more easily damaged than aluminum when it strikes a hard object or other arrows. Carbon arrows must be consistently inspected for damage since they shatter when they fail, creating sharp splinters. They must be discarded when damaged.

Many 3-D target shooters and release shooters who shoot at multispot targets (one arrow in each end per each minitarget) prefer large-diameter arrows. Such arrows are more likely to cut the lines on a target and score at the higher value. Fat shafts are available in carbon, making them relatively light despite their diameter. Since multiple arrows are usually not shot at the same target, damage to the carbon is minimized.

Aluminum arrows are still the choice for many target archers and hunters. Aluminum shafts are available in several alloys. The more expensive varieties are the strongest and do not bend on impact as easily as others. Aluminum arrows generally are durable and easy to maintain and they can withstand more impact from other arrows than carbon shafts can. If bent, aluminum arrows can be straightened. For indoor shooting at short distances and when many arrows are shot at one bull's-eye, aluminum shafts are a good choice.

Hunters have the same range of choices in arrow shafts as target archers do. As the number of setups for hunting bows has increased, the number of possibilities in arrows has also increased. Overdraws especially increase the choices since they allow for shorter arrows. Hunters can shoot relatively short and light arrows, given the weight of a broadhead, or longer and bigger shafts, or combinations in between.

High-quality arrows usually provide archers with many choices of nock and tip styles (figure 8.3). Today, many arrows, especially carbon and aluminum carbon arrows, use nock inserts. An advantage of inserts over the tapered end of an aluminum shaft is the precise alignment of a nock that can be obtained with an insert. The insert also minimizes shaft damage from rear impact of another arrow. Wooden and fiberglass arrows do not allow for this range of choices.

Tips are sometimes mounted directly into the shaft and sometimes mounted on an insert (figure 8.4). Arrow manufacturers recommend a range of tip weights. The archer then decides on a weight within that range. Some tips are break-off styles that allow archers to easily change the tip weight. If you shoot light poundage and long distances, or both, you should start with a lighter tip weight. Tungsten tips are denser than stainless steel tips; tungsten tips shift the weight of the arrow forward, something that is advantageous in windy conditions. Remember that all your arrows need to be the same weight and identical in weight distribution. Some archers adjust the percentage of an arrow's total weight that is in the front half of the arrow. This weight distribution shapes an arrow's trajectory. At shorter distances and indoors, this adjustment is not significant, so only archers shooting very long distances need to attend to any front-of-center adjustments. Tip weight is the chief means of adjusting this distribution. Again, wooden and fiberglass shafts do not allow for various tip styles.

Selecting Arrow Size

In addition to having arrows that are uniform in spine and weight, you need arrows matched to

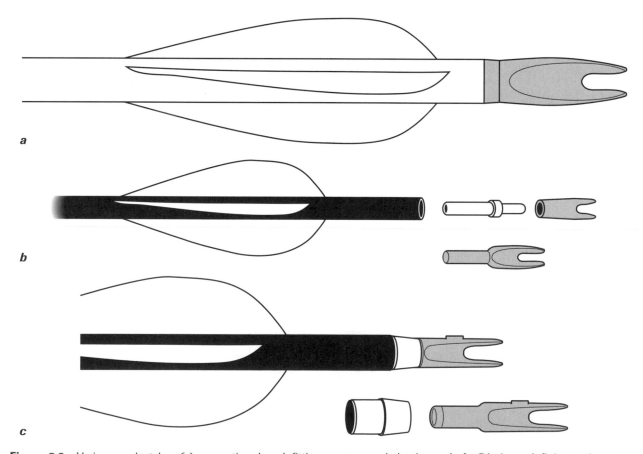

Figure 8.3 Various nock styles: *(a)* conventional nock fitting over tapered aluminum shaft; *(b)* pin nock fitting an insert or "G" nock fitting directly into an aluminum-carbon shaft; *(c)* super nock fitting a UNI bushing or insert.

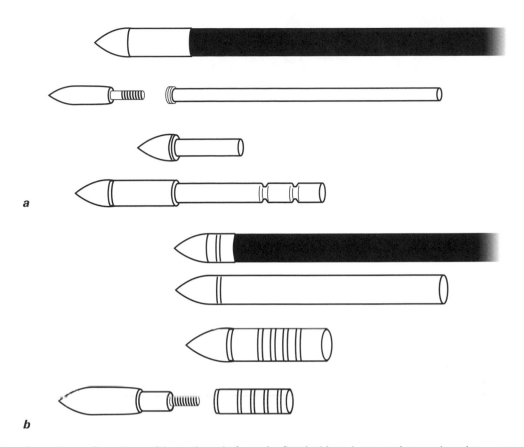

Figure 8.4 Arrow tip configurations: *(a)* a carbon shaft can be fitted with an insert and screw-in point, a one-piece point, or a stainless steel break-off point; *(b)* an aluminum shaft can be fitted with various points or an insert and screw-in point.

your draw length and to the bow's draw weight, which also reflects your draw length. To select the best arrow size for you and your equipment, you need to know several things. First, you need to know how arrows are sized and marked for that size. Then, you need to know how to read an arrow spine chart.

The size of an arrow shaft is printed on the side of the shaft. Arrows are tubes. They vary in diameter as well as in wall thickness. Both diameter and wall thickness determine spine. Table 8.1 is a guide to reading arrow shaft sizes. As you can see, aluminum arrow shafts are labeled with a four-digit number. The first two numbers indicate the outside shaft diameter, measured in 64ths of an inch. The second two numbers give the thickness of the aluminum tube wall, measured in thousandths of an inch. For example, an 1813 shaft is 18/64 of an inch in diameter and 13/1000 of an inch in wall thickness. Generally, a stiffer arrow is recommended as bow draw weight increases and a heavier arrow is recommended as arrow length increases.

Arrow manufacturers provide arrow spine charts listing one or more shaft sizes and types for a given bow draw weight and arrow length. You can obtain one of these charts from the manufacturer or from an archery pro shop. They are also available on the manufacturer's Web site. Some manufacturers even allow you to enter your personal information on the Web site to obtain a list of recommended shaft sizes. Keep in mind that such tables provide only a guideline. Sometimes the unique qualities of bow and archer result in an arrow selection other than the recommended one, but unless you have a specific reason for varying, stick with the sizes recommended.

Let's consider how you select your arrow size from an arrow spine chart. First you need to know the length of arrow you require. To determine arrow length, add 1/2 to 3/4 inch to your draw length or draw an extra long arrow and have someone mark 1 inch in front of the farthest point forward of where the arrow contacts the arrow rest. If you are using a clicker (see

107

Table 8.1 Arrow Shaft Sizes

Type of arrow	Shaft marking	Key
Aluminum	Four-digit number	First two digits: shaft diameter in nearest 64th of an inch Second two digits: wall thickness in thousandths of an inch
Carbon	Three-digit or four-digit number	Deflection in thousandths of an inch (spine) of a 28-inch shaft
Aluminum-carbon	Hyphenated three-digit number (such as 3-60) followed by a second three-digit or four-digit number	Number before hyphen: relative thickness of carbon fiber Number after hyphen: core tube diameter in thousandths of an inch Second number is spine (see carbon)
Aluminum-carbon	Two three-digit or four-digit numbers	First number is diameter and thickness of aluminum core tube, as with aluminum Second number is the spine, as with carbon

step 10), keep in mind that your arrow length must allow for use of the clicker. The clicker must strike the handle riser to make a sound, so arrows must be cut so that the clicker is on the arrow tip at full draw. Some handle risers can be fitted with extensions for the clicker to allow a slightly longer arrow length. Bowhunters sometimes need extra arrow length to accommodate a broadhead (see step 11).

Some bows, especially compounds, feature handle risers that place the arrow rest as close to the archer as possible. This allows the archer to use a shorter and therefore lighter arrow than would otherwise be the case. Before this feature was incorporated into some bow designs, some archers mounted attachments called *overdraws* to their bows in order to use a shorter arrow. With bows of this design or with overdraw attachments, archers should determine their arrow length from drawing a long arrow and marking 1 inch in front of the rest rather than adding to draw length, especially if the preference is to shoot a short and light arrow.

Table 8.2 is a small portion of an Easton arrow selection chart. Here, we are just looking at the recommendations for a recurve bow

Table 8.2 Condensed Aluminum Arrow Spine Chart

Compound bow weight*	27-inch arrow	28-inch arrow	29-inch arrow	Recurve bow weight
45 to 50 pounds	T4	T5	T6	36 to 40 pounds
50 to 55 pounds	T5	T6	T7	41 to 45 pounds
55 to 60 pounds	T6	T7	T8	46 to 50 pounds

* Includes release aid and soft cam. Calculated peak bow weight.

T4		T5		T6		T7		T8	
Size	Alloy model	Size	Alloy model	Size	Alloy model	Size	Alloy model	Size	Alloy model
1912	X7	2012	X7	2112	X7	2212	75	2212	X7
2012	X7	2013	75	2013	75	2114	X7, 75	2213	X7, 75
1913	75	1914	X7	2014	X7	2016	75	2114	X7, 75
1914	X7	1916	75	1916	75			2115	75

or compound bow with a specific type of cam and only at aluminum arrows. A complete chart would include compound bows with other types of cams and carbon and aluminum-carbon arrows as well. The columns of the chart are arrow lengths and the rows are draw weights.

Depending on which bow you use, you can locate the row corresponding to your draw weight and then read across to arrow length. In the box at the cross-section of draw weight and arrow length is a reference to a group of arrow sizes. For example, if you are shooting a recurve bow with a draw weight of 38 pounds and your arrows need to be 27 inches long, you would read along the first row to the 27-inch arrow column. This tells you to choose one of the shaft sizes in group T4. Below the chart, you can see that group T4 includes shaft sizes 1912, 2012, 1913, and 1914.

It is typical to have a choice of several sizes and aluminum alloys. In this example, all of the shafts are available in the X7 alloy model except for 1913, which is available in the 75 model. The price of the arrows depends in part on the alloy you choose. A complete chart also provides choices for carbon and aluminum-carbon arrows. Recall you can obtain a complete chart from the arrow manufacturer, the manufacturer's Web site, or an archery pro shop.

You can see from the arrow selection chart that generally a stiffer arrow is recommended as bow draw weight increases and a heavier arrow is recommended as arrow length increases. There is a risk of bow breakage if arrows are too light for a bow, so you should also check charts for the minimum recommended arrow weight for your type of bow and poundage.

Selecting Arrow Accessories

Once you have selected your arrow shaft, you then must decide what type of nock, tip, and fletching to use. All modern nocks should be snap-on nocks. A snap-on nock lightly holds the arrow on the bowstring and minimizes the chances of a dry-fire (releasing the string with the arrow having slipped off). However, the nock should not be too tight, especially with light-poundage bows. Test nocks by holding your bow horizontally and snapping an arrow onto the string so that it hangs down. Tap the string an inch or two from the arrow. The arrow

should fall off. If it does not, change the nock size or the thickness of the center serving on your bowstring.

As long as you have a well-fitted nock, what type you use is both a matter of preference and how tightly you shoot your arrows. When you become skilled enough to shoot tight groups of arrows, you can expect to hit arrows in the target face with subsequent shots more often, breaking more nocks.

Most archers experiment to find the best tip weight. A heavier tip results in heavier arrow weight, but it is usually more effective than a lighter tip in crosswind conditions. A heavier tip also makes an arrow stiffer in spine. Archers sometimes adjust arrow tip weight as part of the tuning process that we will consider later.

You also must decide whether to shoot arrows fletched with feathers or plastic vanes as well as what size of fletching to use. These decisions often hinge on whether you anticipate shooting indoors or outdoors. Many archers fletch their arrows with feathers for indoor shooting and vanes for outdoor shooting to take advantage of the strengths of each type of fletching.

Feathers are lighter and can better compensate for shooting flaws such as a poor release. Slight contact between feathers and the arrow rest or bow window does not usually affect arrow flight as significantly as the same contact by plastic vanes. On the other hand, feathers are affected by rain and wind. Vanes are thinner and smoother than feathers and do not slow down an arrow as rapidly as feathers do. Being uniformly produced, they typically yield better arrow groupings at longer distances.

Archers using mechanical release aids typically use vanes for indoor and outdoor shooting. Because the arrow does not bend very much with mechanical release of the string, the forgiveness of feathers can be sacrificed for the consistency of vanes. Also, small vanes are sufficient for stabilizing the arrow in release shooting, and it is easier to obtain good arrow clearance of the bow and arrow rest with small vanes.

Generally, the larger and heavier the arrow, the larger the fletching needed. Arrows with broadheads require larger fletching than arrows with target tips require. Archers generally use the smallest-sized fletching that can stabilize their arrows quickly. Because large fletching increases arrow weight, you do not want to use unnecessarily large fletching.

Many archers like to mount their fletching on the arrow shaft at a small angle rather than aligning it precisely along the shaft's center line. The oncoming wind causes the arrow in flight to spin around its long axis, providing stability. This spinning also slows down the arrow—the greater the spin is, the slower the arrow flies. If you decide to angle the fletching and you are shooting feathers, be sure to offset the feathers so that the oncoming air contacts the rough side of the feather. Others mount their fletching straight on the shaft, preferring speed over the spinning effect. Later, we will cover how to fletch your own arrows.

Upgrading Arrows

1. Determine draw length.
2. Determine arrow length.
3. Determine draw weight.
4. Select arrow size from an arrow spine chart.
5. Choose tip weight.
6. Choose fletching.

Misstep

The arrows you are shooting have mixed types and sizes of fletching.

Correction

Feathers and vanes differ in weight, as do feathers or vanes of different sizes. No matter how good your technique is, you will not achieve good arrow grouping with arrows of differing weights.

Arrow Selection Drill. *Reading an Arrow Spine Chart*

Practice reading the arrow spine chart in table 8.2. For each combination of draw weight and arrow length, indicate the arrow size you should choose for the aluminum alloy indicated. Answers are on page 137.

1. Recurve bow with a draw weight of 46 to 50 pounds, 28-inch arrow

   X7 alloy model sizes _____

   75 alloy model sizes _____

2. Compound bow with a release aid, peak bow weight of 50 to 55 pounds, 29-inch arrow

   X7 alloy model sizes _____

   75 alloy model sizes _____

3. Compound bow with a release aid, peak bow weight of 45 to 50 pounds, 27-inch arrow

   X7 alloy model sizes _____

   75 alloy model sizes _____

Success Check

* Find arrow length and read down.
* Find bow weight and read across.

Score Your Success

Identify all six sets of arrows correctly = 6 points

Identify five sets of arrows correctly = 5 points

Identify three or four sets of arrows correctly = 3 points

Identify one or two sets of arrows correctly = 1 point

Your score_____

Bows

If you are serious about participating in some form of archery, you should have your own bow, matched to you for draw weight and for bow or draw length. Also, the bow can be tuned specifically for you. A good general rule is to buy the best bow you can afford that is commensurate with your interest in the sport.

An important consideration when purchasing a bow is to look for a bow that is center shot. A center-shot bow has a bow window cut into the handle, which allows the drawn arrow to sit at a point close to or at the centerline of the limbs. A bow without a window puts the arrow in a position in which it is pointed significantly to the side. Even allowing for the effect of the archer's paradox with the arrow bending around the bow, an archer with a bow without a window must aim so that he or she allows the arrow to fly off center. A center-shot bow overcomes this problem. An arrow of appropriate spine can compensate for the slight offset from center caused by the archer's paradox.

Center-shot bows must be wooden bows that are laminated (usually with layers of fiberglass on the face and back of the bow) or must be bows with metal handle risers. A simple wooden bow would not be strong enough if a bow window were cut into the handle. Most good bows today have metal handle risers, often made of magnesium or aluminum alloys to be strong enough to withstand the forces to which they are subjected in shooting even when cut exactly center shot (figure 13 in The Sport of Archery, page xxi). You can find both recurve and compound bows with metal handle risers.

A recent innovation in handle risers is a cutout design (figure 10.11a, page 166). Such designs minimize the effect of wind since the wind can flow through rather than push the riser broadside when held at full draw. They also allow the riser to be lighter in weight yet able to absorb the shock and vibration that accompany the release.

Bows with metal handle risers have detachable limbs made of a variety of materials. Most have a wooden or foam core and layers of fiberglass or carbon, or both, on each side. Higher-quality limbs can be multilaminated. The quality of bow limbs is more important for an archer who uses a recurve bow since the limbs alone determine the speed of the shot and the stability and smoothness of the bow. If you decide to upgrade to a quality recurve bow, it is likely that the more you spend for limbs, the better quality you will get. Yet there is no need to spend more than your performance level warrants. Until your shooting is very good and your scores are very high, the most expensive set of limbs will not improve your score over a moderately priced set.

One thing a good recurve bow affords you is the opportunity to fit the bow closely to your size and strength. For example, a riser might be available in two lengths, such as 23 inches and 25 inches. Limbs then might be available in three lengths. So, a 68-inch bow might be a shorter riser with long limbs or a longer riser with medium-length limbs. You can then get a combination of poundage and cast ideal for you. Bows with detachable limbs allow you to replace the limbs without having to purchase an entirely new bow should you decide to upgrade your limbs or the older limbs become damaged. Recurve bows can be taken apart for easy transportation, too; for this reason they are frequently called *take-down bows*.

Compound bows are usually left assembled, but the advantage of a compound bow's metal riser and limb construction is that you can adjust the angle of the limbs by turning the limb bolt. Adjusting this angle allows you to adjust the draw weight within a specified range of a compound bow.

Many types of compound bows are available today. They vary in handle, eccentric, and limb design. The first compounds were called *four-wheelers*. In addition to the two eccentrics at the limb tips, they had pulleys mounted at midlimb to route the cables. These four-wheelers were replaced by two-wheel compounds. One-cam and two-cam compounds have added to the choices. A recent trend has been to use short (measured axle to axle) compounds with short brace heights.

Compound bow handles can be straight, reflex, or deflex (figure 8.5). The reflex handle places the grip behind the limb's fulcrum points, where the limbs attach to the handle riser. The advantage of this design is that the nock of the

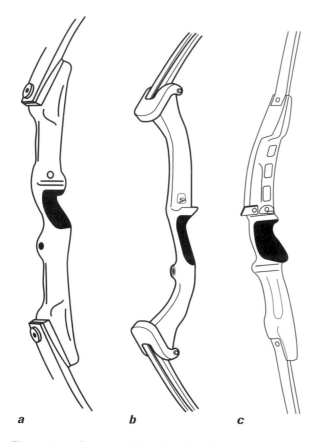

a   b   c

Figure 8.5 Compound bow handles: *(a)* straight; *(b)* reflex; *(c)* deflex.

arrow stays on the string until it is approximately 7 inches from the handle, imparting more energy to the arrow and increasing arrow speed. There has been a definite trend toward this design, especially in bows designed for hunting.

The deflex handle has a grip farther away from the bowstring than the other designs have. It is stable to aim and accurate, but it shoots a slower arrow than the other designs.

Wheel design, especially size and shape, affects how much the limbs of a compound bow flex when the bow is drawn and unflex when the bowstring is released. Round eccentric wheels provide a smooth feel as you draw the bow through its peak weight and into the valley of the force-draw curve (figure 8.6). Cam-shaped wheels result in the bow being at or near its peak weight over a greater distance in the draw stroke so that more energy is stored in the bow limbs. This energy propels the arrow at higher speeds. Eccentric wheels can be cam shaped on one or both sides; the two-sided or full cams

yield the highest speeds. Full-cam bows should be efficient, transferring at least 70 percent of the energy stored in the limbs during the draw to the arrow. Otherwise, they do not give you very much speed for the draw weight required.

Cams (figure 8.7) are very common on hunting bows. The longer period of near-peak weight and quick drop into the valley during the draw make the cam eccentric wheel less comfortable than the smooth, round eccentric for target shooting, where the number of arrows shot is greater. As you can see from the force-draw curve in figure 8.6, cams tend to have a point of maximum let-off rather than a valley.

The choice between cams and round eccentrics for target archery has largely become a matter of preference. Some archers like the feel of pulling against the stops with a cam since the draw weight increases very rapidly past the valley. They choose to shoot a cam bow even for target competition, but they must have the strength and endurance to pull through the long peak weight for the number of arrows to be shot in competition. Differently designed cams make for greater or lesser differences between cam and round eccentrics.

Whereas early compound bows provided 50 percent or less drop between the peak weight and the holding weight, today's compounds typically provide 65 to 80 percent let-off. Cams tend to allow for more let-off than round eccentrics. The eccentric wheels and cams on today's compound bows offer archers a wide range of adjustment. Some cams have 4 to 5 inches of adjustment in draw length and anywhere from 10 to 30 pounds of adjustment in peak weight.

It is important to recognize that many bow manufacturers and archers have put an emphasis on speed and many new innovations are designed to increase speed. Sometimes speed is achieved at the expense of forgiveness. The fast bow can be very critical and accentuate any errors in form or mistakes upon release. In other cases, speed is achieved, but relatively great strength and endurance are required for executing a shot. This can be difficult for target shooting. Many scoring records for compound bows were set with bows that would be considered slow in comparison to what is available today. When choosing a bow, remember that

Force

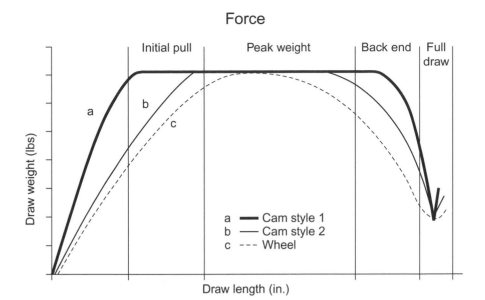

Figure 8.6 A force-draw curve for compound bows. Curves *a* and *b* are two styles of cams; the bow is at or near peak weight for a greater portion of the draw and decreases abruptly near full draw. Curve *c* is a round eccentric (axle off-center) wheel; draw weight increases gradually to a peak, decreases gradually, and provides a valley of approximately an inch or so with minimal holding weight at full draw when matched to an archer's draw length.

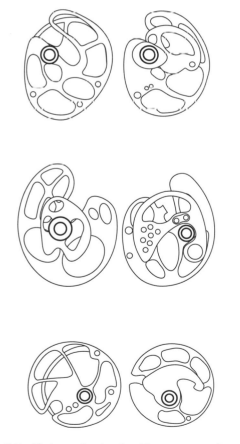

Figure 8.7 Various wheel styles. The top two pairs are cams and the bottom pair is round. All are eccentric (that is, the axle is off center).

faster does not always translate into better. A bow that you can shoot accurately is far more valuable to you than one that is the fastest on the market but is difficult for you to shoot.

Arrow Rests

For relatively little cost, you can add to the accuracy of shooting by upgrading your arrow rest, particularly if you have been shooting off the bow shelf itself. You must first decide whether to upgrade to a shoot-around rest or a shoot-through rest. Finger shooters most often use shoot-around rests, and release shooters most often use shoot-through rests.

If you decide on a shoot-around rest, the ideal combination is a collapsible arm on which the arrow rests and a plunger button (figure 11b in The Sport of Archery, page xx). When a finger shooter releases the string, the tip end of the arrow pushes against the bow since the nock end, which is attached to the bowstring, has deflected to the side. The cushion plunger gives as the arrow pushes. When tuning your equipment, you can adjust the tension on the plunger for the amount of give (figure 8.8). You can also adjust arrow alignment by how far out of the handle riser the plunger protrudes. The

113

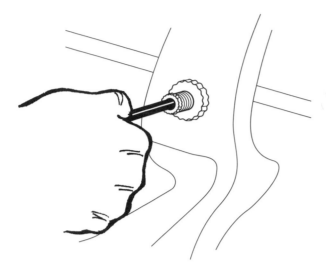

Figure 8.8 Adjusting the plunger tension.

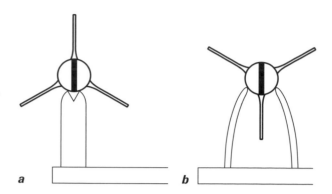

Figure 8.9 Shoot-through rests: *(a)* the index or cock feather is straight up; *(b)* the index feather is straight down.

collapsible arm should be spring loaded. In case the fletching does contact the arm, the arm will collapse instead of remaining rigid, minimizing the effect of the contact. It then springs back into position for your next shot.

An alternative shoot-around rest is a spring, the end of which forms the arm the arrow sits on (figure 11a in The Sport of Archery, page xx). You can adjust the amount of give by choosing a heavier or lighter spring, but obviously you cannot have as many variations as with a cushion plunger. This type of rest, though, is more durable than the collapsible arm and cushion plunger and so is preferred by some archers, including hunters.

Shoot-through rests come in a variety of styles. They can be combined with an overdraw shelf so that the archer can use a shorter and lighter arrow (figure 15 in The Sport of Archery, page xxiii). With some styles, the arrow sits on two arms that are rather close together. The index or cock feather or vane then is placed straight up. An alternative is to have the two arms wide apart and to orient the arrow so that the index vane is straight down (figure 8.9). Remember, nocks have to be mounted for the desired orientation. Also make sure that the arms are stiff enough to support your arrow but

flexible enough to give when the arrow pushes against the arms at release.

Drop-away rests are a newer innovation in shoot-through rests. The arms are designed to collapse downward as the arrow clears the bow to ensure that there is no contact. Some models are triggered by the cables moving forward when the bowstring is released (figure 8.10). These models add to the expense of the bow, but they allow for a clean exit of the arrow from the bow.

If you have used this opportunity to upgrade your equipment or have decided to continue shooting with the equipment you have, you can now adjust your equipment so that you get the best possible performance from your equipment.

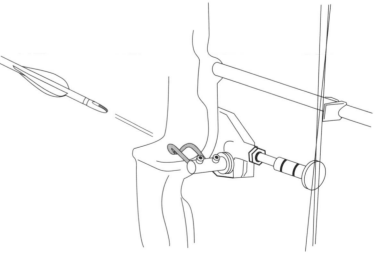

Figure 8.10 A drop-away rest. The rest drops down when the cables contact the plunger on the arrow rest assembly so that there is no contact with the arrow fletching as the arrow clears the bow handle.

TUNING EQUIPMENT

Archers want an equipment setup that gives them the very best possible result considering their technique and performance on a given day. An equipment setup is most helpful to an archer when it is forgiving (that is, when it compensates for a mistake to produce the best possible result at the target). An arrow that is poorly shot with properly tuned equipment might result in 7 points out of a possible 10, for example, instead of 2 points. In archery, the process of adjusting equipment to the particular size, build, strength, and technique of an archer is called *tuning*. You will learn how to tune archery equipment according to various techniques and over several stages of tuning precision.

State-of-the-art equipment is complex and can be adjusted in many ways. While it is always possible for an archer to get help when tuning his or her equipment, it is ideal for every archer to understand how and why specific equipment adjustments affect shooting. This knowledge also keeps archers from spending unnecessary money or time on something touted to be the latest, "can't miss, everyone must have it" gizmo that actually will not change results one bit.

You are most likely to achieve your tightest arrow groups with smooth arrow flight. The more cleanly your bow launches your arrows, the less arrows porpoise (wobble up and down, as in figure 8.11 a) or fishtail (wobble side to side, as in figure 8.11 b) in flight. Smooth-flying arrows travel faster, minimizing the time during which any mistake on your part can affect the arrow. Ideally, tuning achieves good clearance for the arrow as it leaves the bow and eliminates all porpoising and fishtailing of arrows in flight.

The combination of settings that achieve this goal is unique to you and your equipment. By tuning your equipment yourself, you can be assured that your equipment maximizes your performance, and you can make timely adjustments to your equipment as needed. Expert archers can probably shoot bull's-eyes with matched arrows that fishtail or porpoise simply because they would shoot each arrow exactly the same way. This is demonstrated by shooting machines that launch arrows from out-of-tune equipment! Most of us, though, are not machines and not expert archers, so we benefit from tuning our equipment to minimize the effects of any mistake.

a

b

Figure 8.11 *(a)* An arrow porpoising in flight. *(b)* An arrow fishtailing in flight.

You might hear archers talk about tuning their *bows,* but in fact tuning involves adjustments to an archer's *bow, arrow rest, and arrows.* Tuning is accomplished in a specific order of steps so that you adjust some things first and then move on to finer adjustments (fine-tuning or microtuning). There are sometimes differences in the tuning process for recurve versus compound bows and for finger shooters versus mechanical-release shooters. We begin with the initial necessary adjustments to the bow itself, both recurve and compounds bows.

Making Initial Bow Adjustments

You must make several determinations as the first steps in tuning your equipment. These determinations include the bow's draw weight, the bow's string height, and the bow's tiller (the perpendicular distance between the string and each limb, measured where the limb attaches to the handle riser); your draw length, the size of the arrow shaft, fletching type and size, and tip weight; and the stabilizer setup. Changes in any of these factors could make it necessary to

retune the bow. Some of these factors are more pertinent for recurve bows than for compound bows, and others are more pertinent for compound bows than for recurve bows.

Recurve Bows

First determine your bow's draw weight and your arrow length to choose an arrow size. You need to determine your draw length in order to determine your arrow length. If you have not checked your draw length recently, recheck it before purchasing arrows and tuning your bow to them (see step 1, fitting drill 2, page 3). Your form is probably more consistent now than it was when you began. A common error is for archers to set up their equipment for a draw length that is too long for them. This can gradually lead to form flaws, such as leaning back.

Most bow shops have a scale that gives the draw weight of a bow at any draw length (figure 8.12). Bows are labeled for draw weight at a standard draw length, but you should make sure the label is correct and the appropriate adjustment is made for draw lengths longer or shorter than the standard.

Figure 8.12   Recurve Bow Adjustments

1. Install accessories
2. Recheck your draw length
3. Determine draw weight at your draw length
4. Set tiller
5. Set brace height

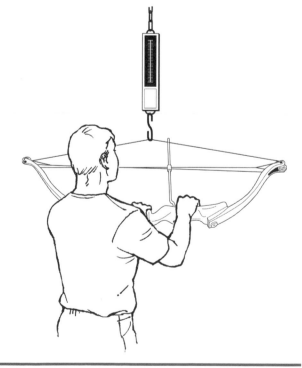

You should also set the tiller on a bow with removable limbs according to the manufacturer's specifications (figure 8.13, page 118). The tiller is the perpendicular distance between the string and each limb at the point the limb attaches to the handle riser. You adjust the tiller by turning the bolt that attaches the limb to the handle riser.

The string, or brace, height of a recurve bow (the distance between the bow's pivot point and the string) must be set before tuning. The bowstring's length fixes the string height. For straight-limb bows, you should use a string length that results in a string height of 6 to 8 inches. For recurve bows, the string height should be slightly over 8 inches (table 8.3). Manufacturers typically specify a string height for their quality recurve bows. You can adjust the string height from this starting point. If the manufacturer gives a range of brace heights, experiment with the shorter heights first.

Table 8.3   Recommended Brace Heights and Ranges for Recurve Bows

Recurve bow length (inches)	Suggested starting height (inches)	Height range (inches)
64	8 1/4 to 8 1/2	7 3/4 to 9
66	8 3/8 to 8 5/8	8 to 9 1/4
68	8 1/2 to 8 3/4	8 1/4 to 9 1/2
70	8 5/8 to 8 7/8	8 1/2 to 9 3/4

The sound of the bow upon release is often a good indicator of the ideal string height for a given bow and archer. The string height that results in the quietest action is the ideal one. You can make slight changes in string height by twisting or untwisting the bowstring. Obviously, twisting the bowstring shortens its length and increases the string height. The twists should always be in the same direction as the center serving. Never remove all the twists from a bowstring. It should have 6 to 10 twists to keep it round and without flat spots that plane in the air upon release and slow its speed. On the other

hand, the increased friction of too many twists increases the likelihood of string breakage.

Before tuning, install any accessories you plan to use, such as stabilizers, a bowsight, a clicker (draw check), and a kisser button. Changes in accessories, especially those that can affect arrow clearance or weight of the bowstring, can affect the tuning.

Compound Bows

You must follow several steps before tuning a compound bow. Some steps are similar to those involved in setting up a recurve bow; others are unique.

First, have your compound bow set for your draw length. This procedure should have been done at the pro shop when you purchased your bow. Just as with recurve bows, this is a good time to double-check your draw length since your form is probably more consistent now than when you began shooting. Using a bow with too long a draw length for you can lead to form flaws. You can follow the instructions that came with the bow to change the draw length yourself, but this procedure requires unscrewing the limb bolts to take all the tension off the cables. A pro shop has a bow press that enables instantaneous adjustment of the draw length.

Next, adjust and tighten the cable guard if your bow is equipped with an adjustable guard. The cable guard holds the cables away from the nocked arrow so that the bowstring and arrow can pass freely upon release. Set the cable guard to route the cables just out of the way but no farther than necessary. On some compound bows, changes in the position of the cable guard slightly affect the draw length, which is why you need to make this adjustment before tuning your bow.

Compound bows have a range of draw weights. Before setting the desired draw weight, you must adjust the tiller of a compound bow (figure 8.13). The tiller is the perpendicular distance between the string and each limb measured from where the limb attaches to the handle riser. Manufacturers often recommend the tiller settings for their bows, but most compound bows are meant to shoot with the same top and bottom tiller. You can measure the tiller with a bow square or metal tape.

Figure 8.13 | Compound Bow Adjustments

1. Install accessories
2. Recheck your draw length
3. Set draw length
4. Set cable guard
5. Set tiller
6. Set draw weight
7. Set brace height
8. Set wheel and cam rollover

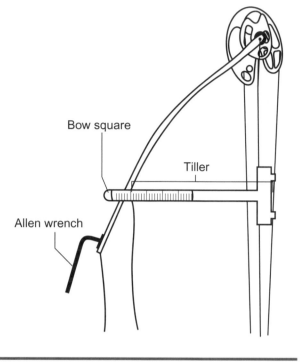

Misstep

Your bow's draw weight or draw length is not set for you.

Correction

If you are shooting a compound bow, determine your draw length and set the bow for that draw length. For either type of bow, choose a draw weight and set it so that you are shooting the most pounds you can handle, maintaining good form for an entire shooting round. Ill-fitted bows encourage form flaws.

To change the tiller, use an Allen wrench to turn the limb bolt clockwise to lengthen the tiller or counterclockwise to shorten it. On compound bows, the exact tiller measurements are not as important as setting them and checking periodically to be sure that they remain the same.

After you set the tiller on your compound bow, you can measure the draw weight with a scale and adjust the poundage by turning the limb bolts with an Allen wrench. The draw weight should be the weight you can shoot with good form over the course of a shooting round.

A clockwise turn increases the poundage. Be sure to adjust the top and bottom bolts an equal number of turns to maintain the tiller ratio.

Manufacturers also specify the brace height for a compound bow. You can adjust this height by using the same methods used for recurve bows. Remember that changing the brace height of a compound bow affects its draw weight and draw length.

As with a recurve bow, you should install all accessories on your compound bow before tuning it. These accessories include stabilizers, a bowsight, a draw check, a kisser button, a peep sight, and any cable keepers that hold the cables close to one another.

Finally, if you are shooting a two-wheel or cam compound bow, you should check to see that the wheels and cams are synchronized. Assuming your normal stance, come to full draw and have someone check to see if the bowstring comes off the wheels at the same point on each wheel, within 1/16 of an inch. If the wheels are not synchronized, follow the manufacturer's procedures for adjusting them. Once they are synchronized, you can mark the wheels in order to check from time to time that their alignment remains the same.

Preliminary Adjustment Drill 1. *Settings*

Your bow must be prepared for tuning, just as for shooting. Consider the bow you are now using. Record your draw length and weight and your preliminary bow settings.

Draw length:_____

Draw weight:_____

Bow's tiller measurements:
  top_____ bottom_____

Bow's brace height: _____

Accessories installed:_____

Success Check

- Measure carefully.
- Record accurately.

Score Your Success

Begin a log of your settings = 3 points

Your score_____

Setting Bow Alignment

The next step in the tuning process is to adjust the horizontal and vertical orientations of the nocked arrow for proper arrow alignment. Later in the fine-tuning process, you will make fine corrections for alignment and adjust the tension of the cushion plunger if you are using one. At this point, you will make larger adjustments for how the arrow is oriented when nocked.

Select your arrow rest and install it before tuning your bow. If you are using a finger release, it is best to use an arrow rest in combination with a cushion plunger because the plunger allows both for movement of the pressure point in and out and for independent adjustment of the spring tension. With a cushion plunger, adjust the arrow rest support arm so that the center of the arrow shaft is at the center of the cushion plunger button when the shaft rests on the support arm. If you decide to use a spring rest, you will not be able to adjust as finely as with a cushion plunger, but adjustments are still possible in the tuning process.

If you are using a mechanical release, a shoot-through type of rest, sometimes called a launcher rest, is best. This rest consists of a V or two arms on which the arrow rests (figure 8.14). Be sure that the type you are using provides good vane clearance (figure 8.15). The launcher is made to depress when the bowstring is released and the arrow flexes to push down on it. The amount of tension on the arm should be just enough to keep the arm from sagging at full draw. If it is too stiff, the arm might pop back up too soon after the arrow's initial push, contacting the fletched end of the arrow before it clears the bow.

Horizontal Adjustment

Your first step in preliminary alignment is to horizontally align the nocked arrow as it sits in the bow. When an arrow bends, it oscillates around two points, or nodes (figure 8.16). Ideally, the two nodes are aligned to the target when the arrow starts forward upon release. This preliminary adjustment estimates the best horizontal position for the arrow.

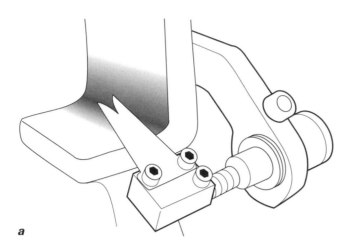
a

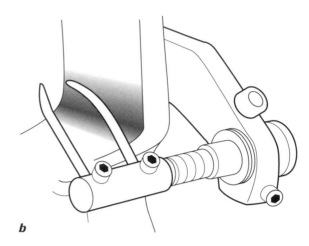
b

Figure 8.14 Two types of shoot-through rests.

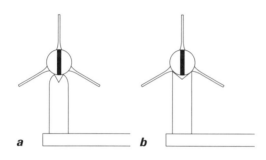
a   b

Figure 8.15 Shoot-through rests must provide good vane clearance: *(a)* good vane clearance; *(b)* poor vane clearance.

When you sight down the arrow to align it, you must have the bowstring centered on the bow. On a recurve bow, the bowstring is aligned with the center of the bow limbs, so it is relatively easy to center the sight of the bowstring on the limbs. But on a compound bow, the bowstring is offset to the outside because of the eccentric pulleys or cams. If you are tuning a compound bow, place a piece of masking tape across the top and bottom limbs near the handle riser. Mark the actual center of the limb and then place a second mark 3/16 of an inch to the left of it (for a right-handed bow). Use this second mark to center the bowstring.

The most desirable starting position for an arrow depends on the type of equipment and release you are using. If you are shooting a finger release with a recurve bow and have a cushion plunger, you can screw the plunger in or out so that it protrudes from the handle riser a lesser or greater amount. Nock an arrow and hold the bow away from you. Align the bowstring with the center of the bow limbs. Adjust the cushion plunger in or out until you see the tip of the arrow just outside the bowstring, pointing away from the handle riser, about 1/16 to 1/8 of an inch (figure 8.17a).

If you are shooting a finger release with a compound bow and have a cushion plunger, you can follow the same procedure, but be sure you align the bowstring with the second mark you made on the masking tape (figure 8.17b).

If you are using a mechanical release with a compound bow, nock an arrow and hold the bow away from you. Align the bowstring with the second mark you made on the masking tape. Adjust the launcher assembly left or right so that the arrow tip is directly in line with the bowstring (figure 8.17c).

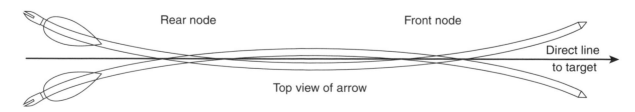

Rear node   Front node   Direct line to target

Top view of arrow

Figure 8.16 On release of the bowstring, the arrow bends, oscillating around two points called nodes.

| Figure 8.17 | Horizontal Preliminary Alignments |

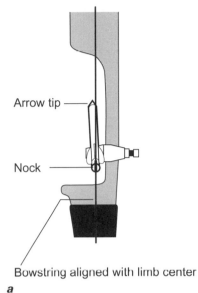

Arrow tip

Nock

Bowstring aligned with limb center

a

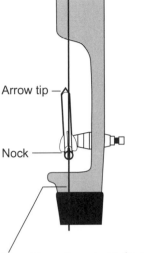

Arrow tip

Nock

Bowstring aligned with 3/16 inch mark

b

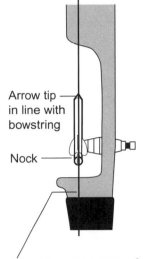

Arrow tip
in line with
bowstring

Nock

Bowstring aligned with 3/16 inch mark

c

RECURVE BOW, FINGER RELEASE

1. Arrow tip is 1/8 to 3/16 inch outside bowstring
2. Bowstring is aligned with limb center

COMPOUND BOW, FINGER RELEASE

1. Arrow tip is 1/8 inch outside bowstring
2. Bowstring is aligned with 3/16-inch mark

COMPOUND BOW, MECHANICAL RELEASE

1. Arrow tip is directly aligned
2. Bowstring is aligned with 3/16-inch mark

Why are the settings different for finger and mechanical releases? When you release the bowstring from your fingers, the bowstring with the rear of the arrow attached will deflect slightly left if you are a right-handed archer. The front of the arrow pushes against the cushion plunger, which gives in, so that the arrow's nodes are aligned to the target as the arrow starts forward. With a mechanical release, the arrow bends vertically but not horizontally upon release, so you want the arrow's nodes aligned as the arrow sits in the bow. Remember, these alignments are starting points. You will make further adjustments in the fine-tuning process.

Vertical Adjustment

The next phase in preliminary alignment is to position the nock locator on the bowstring so that the arrow nock is approximately 1/2 inch above the line forming a perfect 90-degree angle with the string (figure 8.18) for a finger release and 1/4 inch above the line for a mechanical release. Ideally, you should use a clamp-on nock locator. It should be clamped on firmly but not tightly at this time. In fine-tuning, you can thread the locator up or down to make a fine adjustment, and then tightly clamp it down. Be careful not to clamp down the nock locator too tightly and cut the bowstring's strands, especially if your bowstring is made of a delicate material such as Kevlar.

Figure 8.18 | Vertical Preliminary Alignment

1. Arrow is 1/2 inch above 90-degree line for a finger release
2. Arrow is 1/4 inch above 90-degree line for a mechanical release

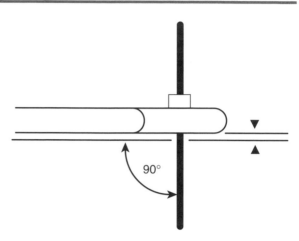

Preliminary Adjustment Drill 2. *Clearance Test*

Even though you will next fine-tune your equipment, it is interesting to note whether your arrows are clearing the bow without the fletching contacting the handle riser or rest. Put some talcum powder on the fletching of one of your arrows. Shoot your arrow and then examine your bow and rest for any evidence that the fletching touched.

Success Check

• If your fletching is making contact, proceed to fine-tuning and repeat the clearance test after fine-tuning.

Score Your Success

Conducting a clearance test = 2 points

Your score_____

Fine-Tuning Arrow Orientation

There are two phases of fine-tuning arrow orientation, one for the horizontal orientation of the arrow and one for the vertical orientation of the arrow. The methods for fine-tuning vary slightly depending on whether you use a finger release or a mechanical release aid. Remember, when tuning, ignore bad shots. Make decisions only on well-executed shots. You will be able to fine-tune only if your technique is good enough to produce arrow groups. If it is not, work on your form and return to fine-tuning at a later time.

Horizontal Fine-Tuning

If you use a finger release with either a recurve or a compound bow, turn an indoor target face over and place one or two strips of black tape vertically down the center of the target. Strips should be about 1 inch wide. Shoot an arrow from 15 or 20 yards, aiming at the black line at the top of the target. Shoot five additional arrows, aiming at the black line but spacing arrows vertically. Take note of the width of the group. Now move your rest (plunger button or spring rest) a small amount in or out and repeat an end of six arrows. If the width of the group is narrower, continue moving the rest in that direction and shoot more ends, noting the width of the group until the group gets wider. Note the rest position that provided the narrowest group, then go back to your starting position and move the rest in the opposite direction. Follow the same procedure to see if you can find a better setting, one that gives an even narrower group.

Put your rest at the position that produces the narrowest group.

If you use a mechanical release, fine-tune your horizontal alignment by using the walk-back method. Put a new target face at the top of the target butt and set your sight for 20 yards. Shoot three arrows from 30 yards with your 20-yard setting. Now shoot three more arrows from 35 yards. Continue walking back in 5-yard increments until your arrows are landing at the bottom of the target butt. If your groups land farther left as you move back, move your rest (launcher arm assembly) slightly to the right if you shoot right-handed and repeat the walk-back. Continue until the arrows line up directly below the bull's-eye. If your groups land farther right, move your rest slightly to the left. Again, continue until your arrows fall in a straight line. Be careful not to cant your bow or torque your bow handle when tuning. Both of these flaws produce a diagonal line of arrows as shooting distance increases.

Fine-Tuning Steps

1. Shoot at your preliminary setting.
2. Adjust in one direction to find the best setting.
3. Return to your preliminary setting and adjust in the opposite direction to determine whether a better setting can be found.

Vertical Fine-Tuning

To fine-tune your nock locator setting, prepare a target with a black line, as when doing horizontal fine-tuning. This time place the target on the target butt with the line running horizontally. Shoot six arrows from 15 or 20 yards and note the vertical spread of the arrow group. Do not worry about left or right movement; just spread your shots across the target. Your only concern is the vertical spread. Move your nock locator slightly up or down and shoot again. Keep going in this manner as long as the vertical spread decreases. Stop when your group increases in vertical spread. Note the point at which you shot the narrowest group, then go back to your starting point and go the other direction. Look for the setting that produces the narrowest spread.

Fine-Tuning Drill 1. *Horizontal*

Choose one of the methods to fine-tune your horizontal setting, depending on whether you shoot with a finger or mechanical release.

If you shoot with a finger release, note the width at your preliminary setting. Move the plunger out and note the width of the first, second, and third group of arrows you shoot. Move the plunger in and note the width of the first, second, and third group of arrows you shoot.

If you shoot with a mechanical release, mark your groups on figure 8.19. Note the distance the button or launcher rest is from the handle riser for the narrowest group.

Success Check

• Note whether group is wider or narrower.
• Use the position yielding the narrowest group.

Score Your Success

Determine horizontal setting from fine-tuning = 3 points

Your score_____

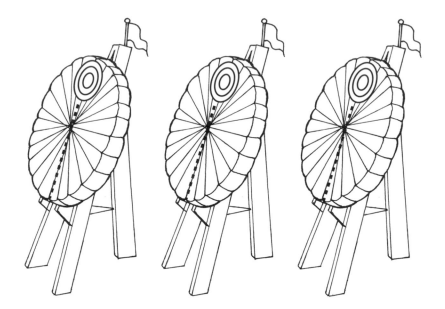

Figure 8.19 Mark your arrow groups. Use the setting that produces arrow groups along the dotted line straight down the target butt rather than settings producing a diagonal line of arrow groups.

Fine-Tuning Drill 2. *Vertical*

Adjust your nock locator setting, recording the vertical spread of your groups as you proceed.

Move the nock locator up. Note the vertical spread of your arrows for the first, second, and third group you shoot.

Move the nock locator down. Note the vertical spread of your arrows for the first, second, and third group you shoot.

Note the distance of the nock locator above the perfect right-angle intersection for the narrowest vertical group.

Success Check

- Note the vertical spread.
- Use the setting producing the narrowest group.

Score Your Success

Determine nock locator position by fine-tuning = 3 points

Your score_____

Testing Fine-Tuning

You can use several methods to test fine-tuning. Every archer tends to prefer one over the others, depending on the method that gives him or her the best result. The methods included here are the bare-shaft and paper-tuning methods. In this section, you will have an opportunity to experiment with the two methods and determine which you prefer. These methods are described for right-handed shooters. If you shoot left-handed, transpose the directions for left and right.

Bare-Shaft Method

For bare-shaft testing, you will need three fletched arrows and two or three identical arrows without fletching. Some archers like to add a little tape to the rear of their unfletched shafts so that they weigh the same as their fletched arrows.

The first step is to test for porpoising of the arrow in flight (figure 8.20a), which means the nock end of the arrow appears to move up and down in flight. Shoot three fletched arrows to a target from 10 to 15 yards. Then shoot two or three unfletched arrows that are identically aimed. If the unfletched shafts hit higher on the target than the fletched shafts, move the nock locator slightly up on the bowstring. If the unfletched shafts hit lower than the fletched shafts, move the nock locator slightly down. After an adjustment, repeat this process until the fletched and unfletched shafts hit at the same height on the target. You must correct porpoising before moving to the next step.

The second phase in bare-shaft tuning is a check for fishtailing (figure 8.20b), which means the nock end of the arrow appears to move from side to side in flight. Repeat the procedure used in testing for porpoising. If the unfletched shafts land to the left of the fletched shafts, your arrow reaction is too stiff. If the unfletched shafts land to the right of the fletched shafts, your arrow reaction is too weak. Consult table 8.4 for corrections.

After each adjustment, repeat the process until you can bring the unfletched shafts within at least 4 inches of the fletched shafts at a distance of 15 yards. If you cannot make further adjustments to bring the unfletched shafts within 4 inches, you may have to change the size of your arrow shaft to achieve good arrow flight. Some right-handed release shooters prefer to have their bare shafts strike low and left of their fletched arrows, believing that an arrow that clears the bow slightly nock high and left is more forgiving.

The final check in bare-shaft tuning is a check for proper clearance of the arrow through the arrow rest and bow window (figure 8.20c). This step is important if you are using lightweight arrows such as carbon shafts. Sprinkle talcum powder on the arrow rest and bow window or spray both the fletched end of the arrow and the arrow rest assembly with dry-spray deodorant.

Figure 8.20 — Bare-Shaft Tuning

PORPOISING
1. Shoot three fletched arrows
2. Shoot three bare arrow shafts
3. If bare shafts strike high, move nock locator up
4. If bare shafts plane up, move nock locator up
5. If bare shafts strike low, move nock locator down
6. If bare shafts plane down, move nock locator down
7. When bare shafts are within 4 inches of fletched shafts, proceed to next stage

FISHTAILING
1. Shoot three fletched arrows
2. Shoot three bare shafts
3. If bare shafts land left, arrow reaction is too stiff
4. If bare shafts land right, arrow reaction is too weak
5. If bare shafts are within 4 inches of fletched shafts, proceed to next stage

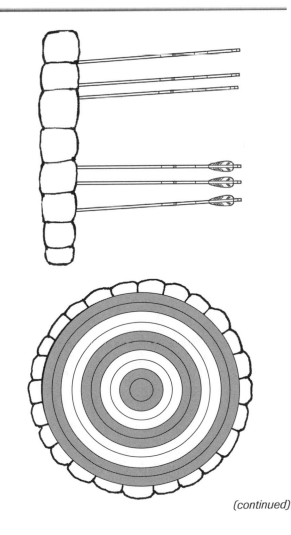

a

b

Figure 8.20   *(continued)*

CLEARANCE

1. Sprinkle arrow rest and bow window with talcum powder
2. Shoot arrow
3. Inspect bow for contact
4. Inspect arrow for contact
5. If contact is visible, make corrections for minnowing

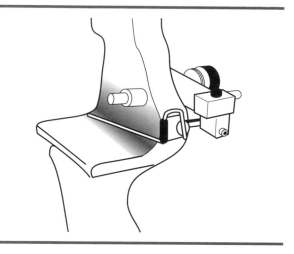

c

Shoot an arrow and examine the bow. You will be able to identify places where the arrow fletching strikes the arrow rest or bow window. Arrows that strike the arrow rest or bow usually move side to side in flight, similar to fishtailing but with quicker, smaller movements. This action is called minnowing. Consult table 8.4 for ways to correct minnowing.

Table 8.4   Adjustment for Tuning Results

Finding	Adjustment
Arrow reaction is too stiff	Decrease the spring tension on the cushion plunger Use a weaker spring rest Slightly increase the draw weight of your bow if it is adjustable Use a heavier arrow point Use a lighter bowstring Use a weaker arrow shaft With a compound bow, move the cushion plunger in For release shooters, move the arrow rest left; check for arrow clearance of the cables and cable guard
Arrow reaction is too weak	Increase the spring tension of the cushion plunger Use a stiffer (heavier) spring rest Decrease the bow's draw weight, if it is adjustable Use a lighter arrow point If you do not have a cushion plunger, move the pressure point out With a compound bow, move the cushion plunger or pressure point out Use a stiffer arrow shaft For release shooters, move the arrow rest to the right
Arrow contacts rest on bow window and minnows in flight	Rotate the arrow nock very slightly Trim the arrow rest support arm so that it does not protrude beyond the arrow shaft Use lower-profile fletching Move the cushion plunger or pressure point farther out and return your bow for fishtailing Make sure the bowstring is not catching on something, such as a shirt pocket or sleeve
Arrow minnows even after corrections have been made	Change your arrow shaft size Change the weight of your bowstring; decrease strands if the arrow reaction is stiff Change your bowstring's center serving; a heavier serving causes stiffer arrow reaction Change your arrow tip weight and include the insert if you use one; try a heavier point plus insert weight if your arrow reaction is too stiff Adjust your bow's brace height

Some archers use only one bare shaft when they tune. If you attempt to do so, be sure you base your adjustments on bare-shaft shots that are well aimed and well executed. You will spend considerably more time tuning your bow if you make unnecessary or incorrect adjustments after a poorly executed shot with a bare shaft.

Paper-Tuning Method

Paper-tuning has been very successful with compound bows. To do a paper test, you need a large picture frame that can be hung 2 yards in front of a target butt at shoulder height. Tape newspaper onto the frame, then shoot arrows through the paper and use the pattern of the tear to help you make tuning adjustments. Finger shooters should shoot from a distance of 8 to 10 yards, and release shooters should shoot from 4 to 5 yards from the frame for paper-tuning.

Before paper-tuning, check for proper clearance of the fletching as it passes the arrow rest and handle riser. As described in the section on bare-shaft tuning, sprinkle talcum powder or apply dry-spray deodorant on the arrow fletching, the arrow rest, and handle riser (figure 8.20c). Shoot an arrow and then look for evidence that the fletching contacted the arrow rest or handle riser. Slight contact can sometimes be corrected by rotating the arrow nock. Severe contact can result from a nock that fits too tightly on the string or from an arrow that is too stiff. Torquing the bowstring with the draw fingers can also cause this problem. Experiment with nock size and hand position. If these changes do not correct the problem, you may need to change arrow sizes.

As with the bare-shaft tuning method, the first adjustment is for porpoising. Shoot several fletched arrows through the paper. The ideal tear pattern is a perfect hole or a hole that shows the arrow went through slightly nock high or slightly nock high and left if you are a right-handed archer (figure 8.21a). If the hole indicates the arrow went through the paper with the nock 3/4 inch or more high, move the nock locator down. If the arrow goes through the paper nock down, move the nock locator up. It is perfectly acceptable for the arrow to be slightly nock high, as much as 1/2 inch, at this point in arrow flight because this means the arrow is probably not hitting the rest as it passes the handle riser. A tear up to 1 inch high may be acceptable for carbon or aluminum-carbon arrows. If you cannot correct a higher tear by moving your nocking point, you might still have clearance problems. If you use a mechanical release, your arrow shaft could be too weak, so you could try a stiffer shaft, a more flexible or lighter-tension shoot-through arrow rest, or a lower peak draw weight on your bow.

The next adjustment is for fishtailing. If a right-handed archer's shots tear holes with the nock left (figure 8.21b), the arrow reaction is too weak. If a right-handed archer shoots arrows that tear holes with the nock right, the arrow reaction is too stiff. Consult table 8.4 for corrections.

Figure 8.21 | Paper-Tuning

PORPOISING

1. Shoot several fletched arrows through paper
2. Examine for ideal tear pattern
3. If tear shows nock is high or low, move nock locator
4. Recheck; if you can't correct it, recheck clearance

a

FISHTAILING

1. Shoot several fletched arrows through paper
2. If tear shows nock is left, correct for weak arrow reaction
3. If nock is right, correct for stiff arrow reaction

b

As with the other methods of tuning, make adjustments in small increments and shoot several arrows through the paper afterward to check the effect of your adjustment. The ideal pattern is a perfect hole or a hole slightly nock high and left for a right-handed shooter and nock high and right for a left-handed shooter. If you shoot a compound bow and cannot correct high or low tears by fine-tuning, check the synchronization of your bow's eccentric wheels or cams.

Testing Drill 1. *Porpoising Test*

Use one of the testing methods described in this step to test for porpoising. Sketch either the paper tear if you paper-tested or the impact pattern if you used the bare-shaft method. Describe any adjustments you made on the basis of your test.

Success Check

- Rely on well-executed shots.

Score Your Success

Successfully test for porpoising and make indicated adjustments = 3 points

Your score_____

Testing Drill 2. *Fishtailing Test*

Assume that you have corrected for porpoising. Use one of the testing methods to test for fishtailing. Sketch either the tear pattern if you paper-tuned or the impact pattern if you used the bare-shaft method. Describe any adjustments you made on the basis of your test.

Success Check

- Rely on well-executed shots.

Score Your Success

Successfully test for fishtailing and make indicated adjustments = 3 points

Your score_____

Microtuning

The ultimate test to use to check your tuning is to shoot arrows to see that they group well. Occasionally, archers find that the tuning setup that produces the best groups is not the one that produces the most smoothly flying arrows and vice versa. Shoot ends of 8 to 10 arrows from the longest distance you plan to shoot in competition. If your arrows do not group, you might want to make further, but very fine, adjustments.

If your groups spread vertically, you can make a 1/32-inch adjustment in your nocking point. If an adjustment increases the size of your groups, return to the starting point and move in the other direction. If your groups improve and then open up with further adjustment, you probably went too far. Go back to your best setting.

If your groups spread horizontally and you use a compound bow, make 1/32-inch in-and-out adjustments of the cushion plunger. Finger shooters who use compound bows can then make 1/8-turn adjustments in the cushion plunger tension. Recurve bow shooters should make only 1/8-turn adjustments in the cushion plunger tension. Move up 20 yards and make your left-to-right impact adjustments again, continuing to a shooting distance of 20 yards.

A kisser button or peep sight may need minor adjustments in its position after tuning. The need for these adjustments is a result of changes in the position of the nocking point in the fine-tuning process and the resulting changes in the position of your hand or release aid on the string.

As you can see, tuning requires time and patience. You must be willing to experiment and find out what effect an adjustment has on arrow flight. Try to make one adjustment at a time, shooting after each change. You will be rewarded in the end by knowing that your equipment is contributing the utmost to your scoring accuracy.

Microtuning Drill. Obtaining New Sight Settings

Once you have tuned your bow to your satisfaction, obtain a set of sight settings for the distances you commonly shoot. Many of the adjustments you made in tuning might have influenced your sight settings. Record your sight settings in table 8.5.

Success Check

- Rely on well-executed shots.

Score Your Success

Obtain new sight settings = 10 points

Your score_____

Table 8.5   New Sight Settings

Yardage	New sight setting
15 yards	
20 yards	
25 yards	
30 yards	
35 yards	
40 yards	
45 yards	
50 yards	
55 yards	
60 yards	

MAINTAINING EQUIPMENT

Over months of shooting, you will need to keep your bow in good working order, maintain your arrows, and sometimes replace parts and accessories. You can save money by doing the simpler maintenance yourself and leaving the maintenance requiring special tools and expertise to the staff of a pro shop. For example, you can often purchase a dozen nocks for the price that a pro shop charges to replace one nock.

You also learn more about your equipment when you maintain it yourself. You can see how changing a setup affects shooting. Then you can begin to customize your equipment to match your shooting style. Once you are comfortable with adjusting and maintaining your equipment, you will find that these tasks are an especially rewarding part of archery.

Maintaining Arrows

If your form is consistent enough for you to shoot groups, arrows will group if they are exactly matched. You can replace nocks, replace tips, replace fletching, and care for your shafts yourself, but be sure to do it with precision. In this section, we cover some of the maintenance you can do yourself, but you should also check for any specific procedures the arrow manufacturer recommends. A general precaution is to heed the manufacturer's recommendation about the amount of heat you can apply to arrow shafts and about the type of adhesive you can use with specific shafts and components.

Nocks

Archers who shoot tight arrow groups often break the plastic nocks on the ends of their arrows. It is worthwhile to purchase replacement nocks in bulk quantities and replace your own nocks. Straight nocks are important to shooting accuracy. A nock misaligned by a few thousandths of an inch can send an arrow 6 inches off its mark at 40 yards. The procedure for replacing a nock depends in part on the type of shaft used.

Aluminum shafts are typically tapered at the nock end. Nocks are simply glued onto the taper. Nocks vary in size according to the size of the arrow shaft. Table 8.6 lists the appropriate size to purchase for your arrows.

To replace a nock, carefully heat the old nock over a candle. (Do not place the arrow in

Table 8.6   Replacement Nock and Insert Sizes

Aluminum shafts, conventional nocks		Universal nock installation (UNI) system	
Shaft size	Recommended nock size (inches)	Shaft size	Recommended insert
1413 to 1518	7/32	Smaller than 2012	Standard UNI insert
1614 to 1816	1/4	2012 and larger	Super UNI insert
1818 to 2016	9/32		
2018 to 2219	5/16		
2317 to 2419	11/32		

an open flame.) When the nock begins to melt, remove it with pliers. Wipe the nock area with lacquer thinner or methylethylketone (MEK) to clean the area for a good bond. Avoid touching the area because your fingers will deposit oil on the shaft.

Archery suppliers sell a fletching cement appropriate for bonding nocks and fletching to aluminum shafts. Place a drop of such fletching cement on the taper. Rotate the shaft as you spread the cement evenly around the arrow with your finger. Place the new nock on the arrow and turn the nock several times counterclockwise to further spread the cement. Rotate the nock clockwise with a slight downward pressure and align it at a right angle to the index feather (figure 8.22 a and b). Wipe off any excess cement oozing from under the nock.

Place the arrow on a table with the index feather up. If the nock is on properly, you should not see either side of the nock when you look directly down on it from above. Adjust the nock if necessary before the cement sets. This is the standard nock position. Some archers, though, rotate their nocks slightly to achieve feather or vane clearance of the bow if they do not get the effect they desire with the standard position. Note that earlier we saw how archers using shoot-through rests oriented the arrow with the index vane either straight up or straight down when nocked. If you are using this type of rest, be sure to adjust your nock accordingly.

Another test of nock straightness (figure 8.22c) is to roll the shaft on a smooth table with the fletching hanging off the table. Watch the nock to make sure its rotation doesn't have a wobbly appearance. You can also test nock straightness by resting the shaft on the finger-

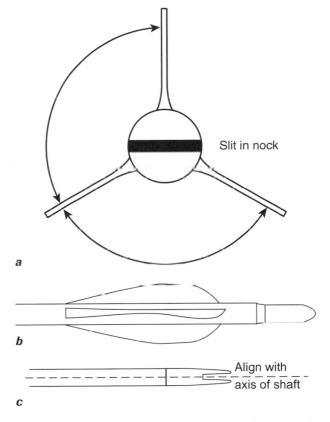

Figure 8.22   Arrow nock: *(a)* cross-section; *(b)* mounted on shaft; *(c)* aligned with axis of shaft.

nails of your thumb and middle finger with the arrow point on the palm of your other hand and blowing against the fletching. The arrow will spin, so you can watch for any wobbling of the nock. Adjust the nock if necessary before the cement sets. Stand the arrow up to allow the cement to dry.

Aluminum shafts can also use the universal nock installation (UNI) system (figure 8.3c, page 106). This system features a tapered insert (bushing) into which a plastic nock is inserted flush against the bushing for good alignment. There are two sizes of inserts (table 8.6) and consequently one size nock to fit each. The nocks may come in various string groove sizes, though, to best fit different bowstring thicknesses. The installation guidelines outlined in the following section are for aluminum-carbon shafts.

A third possibility is aluminum shafts that feature a parallel tapered section at the nock end. This swage is a standard diameter for many shaft sizes and allows for an insert-type nock to be installed directly into the shaft without an insert.

Aluminum-carbon shafts. Some aluminum-carbon shafts accept the UNI system bushing. An advantage of this system is that the plastic nock can be replaced if broken while the brushing remains. The plastic nocks can actually be installed without adhesive. They can be pushed into the bushing by hand with a nock tool. Some archers prefer to use an adhesive, but only a light removable glue or rubber cement should be used.

A UNI insert or bushing is installed with a hot-melt adhesive stick available from archery suppliers and also used for arrow tips. Clean the inside of the shaft with a cotton swab and 91 percent isopropyl alcohol and then let it dry. The bushing should be twisted on a sharpened pencil to hold it. Heat the glue stick over a small gas flame and apply a small ring of adhesive inside the shaft. Heat the bushing just enough to melt a coating of adhesive from the adhesive stick around the bushing shank. Lightly reheat the bushing and insert it into the shaft. Wipe off excess glue and allow the adhesive to set before removing the pencil.

Cracked nocks can be twisted off the bushing with pliers. If the nock is broken flush with the bushing, twist a small screw into the plastic and grasp the screw with pliers to remove the broken nock.

Carbon shafts. Carbon shafts sometimes use overnocks. These nocks fit over the outside of the shaft. They can be twisted onto the shaft without an adhesive or with a small amount of rubber cement. Broken nocks can be removed with pliers. Wipe the shaft with 91 percent isopropyl alcohol before installing the new nock.

An alternative is to permanently install a nock outsert. An epoxy is used for gluing the outsert onto the carbon shaft and then an insert-type nock can be installed without adhesive or with rubber cement.

Arrow Tips and Inserts

It is not difficult to replace tips and inserts, but you should be careful not to overheat shafts and to use only recommended adhesives.

Aluminum shafts. To remove an old point or insert, heat the shaft over a small gas flame just enough to melt the old adhesive. Pull the tip or insert out with pliers. Leave the tip screwed into the insert in order to grip it with the pliers. To replace the new tip or insert, clean the inside of the shaft with 91 percent isopropyl alcohol. Heat the end of the shaft just enough to melt a ring of hot-melt adhesive inside the shaft. Grip the point or point and insert with pliers. Heat the end of the shaft slightly and insert the tip or insert about 1/4 inch. Heat the exposed part of the tip or insert shank so that you can rotate it over the hot-melt adhesive stick to apply a thin layer of adhesive (figure 8.23). While the adhesive is fluid, push the tip or insert into the shaft until it seats against the shaft. Wipe off excess adhesive before it dries.

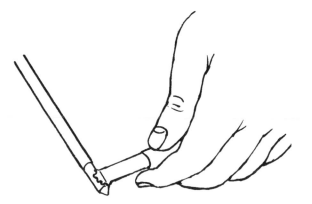

Figure 8.23   Melt a layer of cement on the entire point shaft.

Aluminum-carbon shafts. To install tips and inserts in aluminum-carbon shafts, follow the same procedures as with aluminum shafts, but be cautious in using heat with these shafts. When possible, heat the tip rather than the shaft.

Carbon shafts. Arrow tips and inserts are installed in all-carbon shafts with epoxy such as a flexible, two-part 24-hour epoxy. Fast-drying epoxies are sometimes brittle. Use a cotton-tipped applicator to wipe the tip or insert shank and the inside of the shaft with 91 percent isopropyl alcohol. Let them dry and then place a small ring of epoxy into the end of the shaft and around the point or insert shank. Rotate the shaft while slowly inserting the point or insert and continue several more rotations once the tip or insert is seated so that the inside of the shaft is thoroughly coated with epoxy. Wipe off any excess epoxy and stand the shaft perfectly vertical for the cure time. Once installed with epoxy, arrow tips and inserts cannot be removed from a carbon shaft.

Fletching

With time and use, the fletching on your shafts can wear. Certainly, contact with the arrow rest or bow window can cause feathers to fray. Both feathers and vanes can be damaged when struck by other arrows. You might enjoy fletching your own shafts, although this is certainly something you can have done at a pro shop. You need to have a fletching jig (figure 8.24), so it might only be worth fletching yourself if you do it frequently or do it for others in your family. The fletching process varies with the type of shaft.

Aluminum shafts. To remove old vanes or feathers, scrape them and any excess glue off the shaft with a dull knife. Clean the shaft with MEK or lacquer thinner and then wipe the shaft with 91 percent isopropyl alcohol. You can refletch the arrow shaft when it dries. If you are fletching with vanes, you can also wipe the base of each vane with MEK or lacquer thinner. Avoid handling the base of a feather or cleaned vane. Oils from your fingers could prevent a good bond.

Be sure to use a fletching cement intended for this purpose. Insert the vane or feather into the clamp of your fletching jig. The rear of the vane or feather should be 1 to 1 1/4 inch from the bottom of the nock groove. Apply a thin line of cement the length of the feather or vane and then insert the clamp into the jig so that the entire length of the fletching makes contact with the arrow shaft. Let the cement dry for the length of time recommended, then open the clamp and remove it so that you can rotate the jig to the next position. Repeat the process with the next feather or vane. When finished, apply a drop of cement at each end of each feather or vane to minimize the chances that it will be ripped off if the arrow completely penetrates a target.

Many archers mount plastic vanes straight, that is, parallel to the long axis of the arrow. Feathers, on the other hand, are always mounted at a slight angle, and some archers prefer to do this with plastic vanes as well.

Feathers come from either the right or left wing of a turkey. The underside of the feather is rougher than the top side. The underside is the side of the fletching you want to expose to the oncoming air as the arrow flies. You can tell if you have right- or left-wing feathers by holding them on a shaft and looking down the shaft from the nock end. See how the catch lip of the feather matches figure 8.25.

If you have left-wing arrows, you should offset them slightly so that the oncoming air meets the underside of the feather. The arrow will rotate counterclockwise in flight after it clears the bow, providing a stable flight. Mount a right-wing feather at the opposite angle. A right-wing arrow will rotate the arrow clockwise in flight.

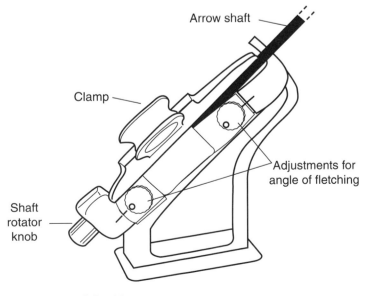

Arrow shaft

Clamp

Adjustments for angle of fletching

Shaft rotator knob

Figure 8.24 A fletching jig.

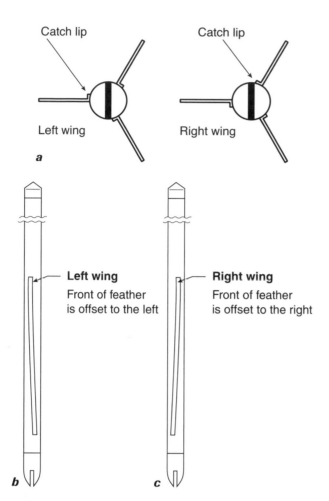

a

Left wing
Front of feather
is offset to the left

Right wing
Front of feather
is offset to the right

b   *c*

Figure 8.25 *(a)* Viewing from the nock end, note the location of the catch lip to determine if your feathers are from the left wing or right wing. *(b)* Left-wing feathers are mounted with the front of the feather to the left; *(c)* right-wing feathers are mounted with the front of the feather to the right.

It makes no difference whether you use left- or right-wing feathers, but you want to use the same wing on an arrow and probably on your entire set of arrows. Fletching jigs can be set to mount feathers at this slight offset. Remember that you do not need a large angle and that the

entire length of the feather must be in contact with the arrow shaft.

You can choose from a wide range of fletching options. Vanes are cheaper and weatherproof, but advocates of feathers believe that feathers are faster, lighter, and more forgiving.

It makes little difference whether feathers are round shaped or shield shaped. As a starting point, lightweight arrows can be stabilized with three 4-inch feathers, and arrows with broadheads attached can be stabilized with three 5-inch feathers.

Archers who use vanes probably select a size somewhat smaller than the feather they might otherwise use. Archers who shoot long distances, such as in Olympic-style shoots, often use spin-wing vanes. These are very light Mylar vanes that are curled (figure 8.26). They provide minimum drag and high spin rates for this style of shooting. Spin-wing vanes are attached with double-sided tape rather than an adhesive.

Fletch colors are a personal preference, except that it is a tradition to use a different color for the cock or index feather than the hen feathers to minimize the chances that arrows are nocked backward. Most archers make it a habit to fletch the cock feather first. Beginners will likely do well to begin with three 4-inch feathers. Once you gain more experience, you can experiment with different combinations to find the one that gives good arrow clearance and arrow grouping.

Aluminum-carbon and carbon shafts. Generally the process for fletching aluminum-carbon and carbon shafts is similar to that for aluminum shafts, but you must pay particular attention to the materials used for cleaning shafts and to the adhesives used. Use only those recommended for these shafts and for this purpose. For example, superglues provide a good bond with carbon, but it might be impossible to remove

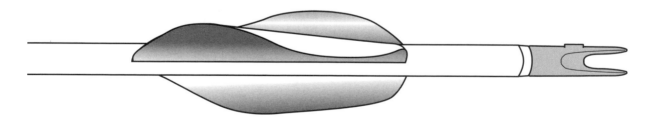

Figure 8.26 Spin-wing vanes.

fletching attached with a superglue without ruining the carbon shaft.

To remove old fletching attached with an instant adhesive, peel off fletching with a dull knife. Be careful not to scrape so deeply as to damage the carbon fibers. You should be able to pull off old fletching attached with a standard fletching cement. Wipe the fletching area with lacquer thinner; be sure to keep it away from the nock and any size markings or logos. Use 91 percent isopropyl alcohol for a final wipe and let the shaft air-dry. Do not touch the area to be fletched after cleaning. Try to fletch within 8 hours of cleaning the fletching area or repeat the cleaning process.

If you are fletching plastic vanes, wipe the base of each vane with MEK or lacquer thinner unless the manufacturer says this is unnecessary. Avoid touching the base with your fingers after cleaning. Be sure to use an adhesive made for the carbon surface of the shaft and follow the same process to fletch as described for aluminum shafts.

Aluminum Arrows

Straight arrows are as important to shooting accuracy as straight nocks. You can straighten aluminum shafts on any of several commercial straighteners if the shafts are not too severely bent. Most pro shops make a straightener available to their customers.

Arrow straighteners have two adjustable blocks, each of which has two ball-bearing wheels. The arrow rests in the trough created by the two wheels (figure 8.27). For slight bends, leave the blocks at the ends of the straightener. For sharp bends or bends near the end of the shaft, move the blocks closer together. Raise the plunger and place the arrow underneath it and in the trough of each block. Starting at the point end, rotate the arrow with your index finger, being sure to position your finger on the arrow directly over the wheels in either one of the blocks. Repeat, moving the arrow through the straightener until you reach the fletched end.

If at any point the needle on the straightener's dial swings more than two lines, the arrow should be straightened. Find the place on the arrow shaft that yields the most needle deflection by rotating the arrow until the needle swings the greatest amount in the clockwise direction. The peak of the bend is now uppermost. Press down on the straightening lever. Rotate the arrow to see whether the bend has been removed. If it hasn't, repeat the process. When the needle

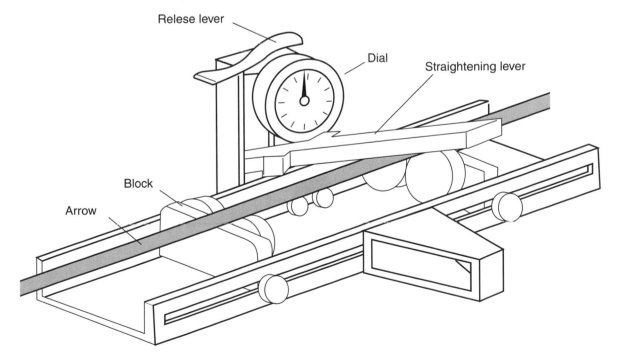

Figure 8.27 An arrow straightener.

deflection remains within the two lines on the dial, the arrow is straightened.

Arrow straightness is important, so you should check your arrows frequently. To check your arrows when you are away from a straightener or are on the range after scoring, put the fingernails of your thumb and middle finger together. Rest the arrow shaft on your fingernails below the fletching with the arrow point resting in your other palm. Blow on the fletching. If the shaft jumps on your fingernails rather than spinning smoothly, the shaft might have a bend.

Carbon Shafts

When carbon shafts enter a target mat, the heat generated as friction slows the arrow and can cause particles from the target mat to bond to the carbon surface. This can make it difficult to remove the arrow from the target. You can avoid this by periodically putting a coat of hard paste wax on the point end of the shaft or even rubbing a bar of soap on the point end. You also can wipe the point end of the shaft with a rag coated in silicone wax. When pulling arrows, use an arrow puller or rubber sheet like a jar opener.

Check carbon shafts for cracks and damage before shooting and after every shot. Carbon shafts are more susceptible to cracking than other arrow shafts if they hit a hard object. To check for damage, hold the arrow at each end. Bend it an inch or two away from you and listen for cracking noises. Repeat four to six times as you rotate the shaft until you have gone around the entire arrow. If you hear or feel cracking, the arrow is damaged. You should also twist the shaft in both directions as you hold each end. If it twists easily or relaxes, it is damaged. Do not shoot a damaged arrow. It could splinter on release and injure you or someone around you.

Maintaining a Bow

Most bows will shoot well for years if properly maintained. One key to maintaining a bow is remembering that laminated bows and limbs have layers of materials that are bonded together. Extreme heat, such as that in a closed car on a hot, sunny day, can affect the adhesives

used in manufacturing a bow. Prolonged exposure to moisture can affect them as well. Never lay a bow in damp grass. If you shoot a bow in the rain, wipe it dry when you finish shooting. You can help protect the bow by waxing it frequently with a special bow wax or other wax. Solid fiberglass bows can withstand heat and moisture better than laminated bows, but you should still avoid extremes.

Store bows in a case that lies flat or is hung vertically. In these positions, neither limb takes more pressure than the other. Standing a bow in a corner eventually weakens the lower limb. Recurve and straight-limb bows should be unstrung for any month that they will not be shot. Storing them in the relaxed position helps maintain their strength. Stringing and unstringing a bow with a bowstringer is better than doing it by hand because bowstringers put equal tension on both limbs and do not twist the limbs.

Compound bows should remain strung. Their limbs are not under as much tension as those of a strung recurve or straight-limb bow because the eccentric pulley does much of the work. If you are going to store your compound bow for a long time, however, you should unscrew the limb bolts in order to reduce the poundage.

You may also need to lubricate your compound bow periodically. Usually the bow manufacturer gives specific instructions on what parts need lubrication (some may be sealed or self-lubricating), how to do this, and what lubricant to use. Most pro shops also provide this service. You also need to have the cables on a compound bow replaced periodically. Archers shooting four or more times per week often replace their cables about every 18 months.

Bowstrings deserve your attention. Breaking a string can cost you points in competition because the arrow might not score well or at all. Waxing your bowstrings frequently with a bowstring wax minimizes fraying and wards off moisture. Waxed strings are also less likely to tangle when not in use. Compound bow archers should wax the string and cables on a regular basis. To wax a string, rub the wax on the string once or twice, and then run your fingers up and down the string for a few minutes to distribute the wax evenly.

You don't have to wax the serving on a bowstring. You should, however, replace the serving if it is loose. If the serving begins to fray during a tournament or shooting session, you can tie it off temporarily and replace it later.

Tournament archers always carry one or more backup strings with them. Because new strings stretch slightly when they are first put on a bow, the well-prepared archer breaks in backup strings by shooting them for a practice session or two. Tournament archers often keep a log of the number of shots they have taken with a string so that they can replace it before it is likely to break.

You must replace arrow rests periodically because they become worn or broken. To maintain good equipment performance, make sure the new rest is in the right place. If your bow is equipped with a cushion plunger, adjust the height of the new rest so that the center of your arrow shaft contacts the center of the cushion plunger. Adjust your arrow rest in the forward or backward direction so that the arrow contacts the rest below the cushion plunger.

If your bow does not have a cushion plunger, install an arrow rest that has a pressure point made of a flexible material such as plastic. Place the arrow rest so that the pressure point is directly above the pivot point of the bow. Deviating from this point either forward or backward usually magnifies the effect of poor bow hand position and torque caused by the bow hand.

Maintaining Drill. *Replacing a Nock*

Obtain an aluminum arrow without a nock and a nock of the appropriate size for that arrow shaft size (table 8.6, page 131). Obtain a tube of fletching cement and install the nock as directed. Allow the adhesive to dry, then test the straightness of your nock. Place the shaft on a table with the fletched end extending off the table. Roll the arrow back and forth on the table and examine the nock. If it does not have a wobbly appearance, it is ready to be used. If the nock does appear to wobble, the nock is crooked. Remove the nock and reinstall it.

Success Check

- Align the nock with the axis of the shaft.

Score Your Success

Properly installed nock on the first try = 3 points

Properly installed nock on the second try = 2 points

Your score_____

Answer Key

Arrow Selection Drill. *Reading an Arrow Spine Chart*

1. X7 alloy model sizes 2114; 75 alloy model sizes 2212, 2114, 2016

2. X7 alloy model sizes 2114; 75 alloy model sizes 2212, 2114, 2016

3. X7 alloy model sizes 1912, 2012, 1914; 75 alloy model sizes 1913

SUCCESS SUMMARY OF UPGRADING, TUNING, AND MAINTAINING EQUIPMENT

In archery, success depends on equipment as well as form. Archers must have confidence that their equipment will produce the best score possible, given their performance on a given shot on a given day. Archers want equipment that is durable, consistent, and forgiving. At the same time and because archery involves so much equipment of various types, someone is always willing to sell you the latest innovation. Learn to be a critical consumer. Identify the advantages and disadvantages of new equipment and decide whether any new equipment is likely to make a difference in your score.

Whatever equipment you are able to afford, you can make sure it is set up and adjusted to your benefit. Tuning is a sequence of activities.

It requires time and patience. Tuning your own equipment teaches you how various equipment settings interact with technique and affect results. Use this knowledge to make good judgments when choosing accessories such as an arrow rest.

Finally, be sure to keep your equipment in good working order. Good maintenance also ensures you will get the most from your equipment. Many of the drills in this step gave you practice in upgrading, tuning, and maintaining your equipment. Record your progress in the drills and total your score. If you earned at least 25 points, you can move to the next step. If you scored less than 25 points, repeat some of the tuning drills to earn additional points.

Arrow Selection Drill

   1. Reading an Arrow Spine Chart   ___ out of 6

Preliminary Adjustment Drills

   1. Settings   ___ out of 3

   2. Clearance Test   ___ out of 2

Fine-Tuning Drills

   1. Horizontal   ___ out of 3

   2. Vertical   ___ out of 3

Testing Drills

   1. Porpoising Test   ___ out of 3

   2. Fishtailing Test   ___ out of 3

Microtuning Drill

   1. Obtaining New Sight Settings   ___ out of 10

Maintaining Drill

   1. Replacing a Nock   ___ out of 3

Total   *___ out of 36*

In the preceding steps you worked on your technique; in this step you've worked on upgrading and tuning your equipment. If you are getting the most from your equipment and you have been refining your technique, your scores should be improving. Now you might be wondering what distinguishes elite performers from all the other archers. Certainly dedicated practice is a large part of the difference, but solid mental skills are another important contribution. In fact, among elite performers with similar equipment and form, mental skills could be the major difference between finishing first and finishing last! It is never too early to acquire and practice good mental skills. Aside from helping you to be successful, strong mental skills increase your enjoyment of archery.

Sharpening Mental Skills

Athletes from many sports talk about performing in the zone. When they do, they are referring to a time or contest in which their performance was superior and success came almost without thought or effort. Their concentration was extremely focused, even to the point that objects appeared larger than normal or actions seemed as if they were in slow motion. Experiencing the zone while shooting archery is truly an incredible experience. The bull's-eye seems so large that it is hard to miss. The bow feels light. Drawing the bow is effortless.

Performance in the zone is rare. Most athletes would be fortunate to experience it once in their careers. Athletes cannot make themselves perform in the zone, but they can prepare themselves mentally as well as physically to perform. With good mental preparation, athletes open the

door to superior performance. They create the conditions that almost always result in success and occasionally result in a once-in-a-lifetime performance. In this step, you will learn how to take a positive mental approach to shooting archery.

As you have learned, the movements involved in archery are relatively simple. Most participants can develop good shooting form if they have an interest in doing so. What often distinguishes elite performers from good performers is their mental approach to shooting. You can enhance your performance by learning to focus on the important aspects of shooting and blocking out unnecessary or distracting thoughts. In this step we focus on these mental skills: managing anxiety, focusing attention, and building confidence.

MANAGING ANXIETY

Sport psychologists often describe an optimal level of anxiety for skill performance. This optimal level reflects the fact that being overly anxious can detract from peak performance but being totally relaxed can detract from peak performance as well, since a lethargic athlete might not be as alert and attentive as required. An intermediate level of anxiety is optimal. This

optimal zone does not fall at an absolute level of anxiety. Rather, it can be somewhat higher or lower depending on the nature of the task. It also might be slightly higher or lower for different people on the same task.

Research on shooting tells us that the optimal level of anxiety in archery is probably lower than that for most other sports. Archers must be calm and steady, make only a fine movement to release, and maintain the follow-through position. They also must replicate their shot setups as exactly as possible over and over again.

Each person's optimal level of anxiety is different, but overall a low level of anxiety is necessary for accurate shooting. It is natural to be nervous when shooting competitively or shooting game, but archers must learn to attain this relatively low optimal zone of anxiety.

Shooting is a rather strange mixture of tension and relaxation when compared to most sport skills. You must hold upward of 25 pounds of force while you hold the bow steady. At the same time, the act of releasing is a small movement, and you must maintain a completely relaxed bow hand throughout the shot, release, and follow-through. You must learn to be selective about which parts of the body are under tension and which are relaxed. The points noted in figure 9.1 include cues to help you relax your bow hand and draw hand. You can add these to your personal mental checklist, especially if you tend to grip your bow or wrap your fingers around the bowstring tightly. You also can practice relaxing specific parts of your body so that you can more easily relax your bow hand and draw hand on cue.

Figure 9.1　Staying Relaxed

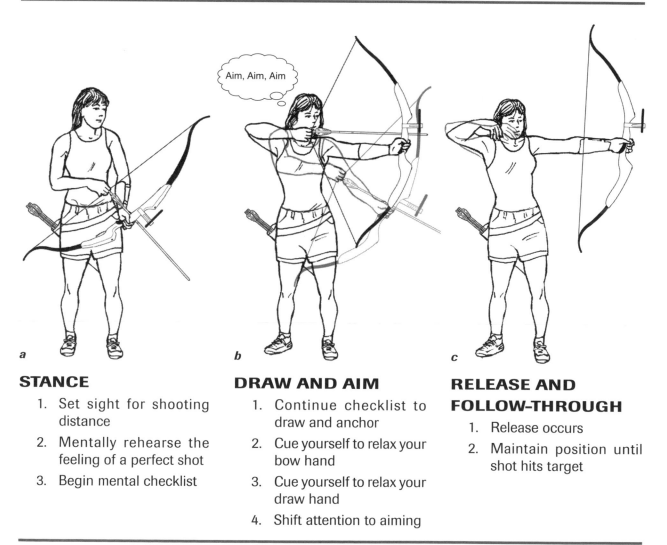

STANCE

1. Set sight for shooting distance
2. Mentally rehearse the feeling of a perfect shot
3. Begin mental checklist

DRAW AND AIM

1. Continue checklist to draw and anchor
2. Cue yourself to relax your bow hand
3. Cue yourself to relax your draw hand
4. Shift attention to aiming

RELEASE AND FOLLOW-THROUGH

1. Release occurs
2. Maintain position until shot hits target

Misstep

You get so nervous shooting that your performance in competition is below that in practice.

Correction

Learn to expect that you will be nervous, but focus on the task at hand. Practice relaxation techniques and associate a cue with your relaxed state. Use the cue when you feel nervous, then focus on the task of shooting.

You might find it more difficult to maintain relaxation under certain situations. Often when archers really want to shoot well, they tend to tighten their hands so that the bowsight is forced into the bull's-eye. This action is self-defeating because a tight bow hand will cause bow torque and a tight draw hand will work against a smooth release.

If you shoot archery competitively or hunt, you are likely to experience nervousness. This nervousness comes with competition in most sports. It shows that you care about the outcome. However, you will not be moving about to relieve some of the nervous energy. In archery, you do not run, you do not hit a ball, and you do not throw a ball. Instead, you must relax and hold steady! Accept the fact that you will be nervous but need to give your attention to executing every shot. One archer, commenting on his performance just after he had won a national championship, said that he always got nervous in important competitions but he simply refused to focus on being nervous and instead focused on executing his shots.

Many archers visualize shooting in the situation that makes them nervous. They visualize being at the shooting range with others watching, standing in front of the target, holding their equipment, nocking an arrow, setting up the shot, aiming, releasing, and following through. They mentally practice (cue) relaxing during their shots so that the process comes more easily when they are in the actual setting.

Although most people have the challenge of being nervous and needing to relax, sometimes it is necessary for archers to raise their level of alertness. Remember, the optimal level is an intermediate one! Mental imagery often helps archers prepare and center themselves on the tasks at hand if they are lethargic or unfocused as the time to compete approaches.

The more you compete or hunt, the better you should become at identifying your own optimal level of alertness. Learn to recognize when you are too laid back and need to center yourself or get up for competition. Learn to recognize when you are too anxious and need to relax. Your optimal level might be different from another archer's optimal level, so you should learn to manage your own level to achieve the state that will allow you to perform your best.

Relaxation Drill 1. *Hand and Arm Relaxation Routine*

Practice this drill in a quiet place where you can sit or lie down. Go through the following steps:

1. Extend your right wrist. Hold for 10 seconds, then relax. Repeat.

2. Flex your right wrist. Hold for 10 seconds, then relax. Repeat.

3. Repeat extending and flexing with your left wrist.

4. Extend and flex your right wrist as in steps 1 and 2 but with half as much tension on your hold.

5. Extend and flex your left wrist as in step 3 but with half as much tension on your hold.

6. Extend and flex your right wrist with just enough tension that you feel the hold.

7. Extend and flex your left wrist with just enough tension that you feel the hold.

8. Bend (flex) at your right elbow. Hold for 10 seconds, then relax. Repeat. Repeat with your left elbow.

9. Flex your right elbow and then your left elbow with half as much tension.

10. Flex your right elbow and then your left elbow with barely enough tension to feel.

11. Clench your fist and tighten your right arm. Hold for 10 seconds, then relax. Repeat.

12. Clench your fist and tighten your left arm.

To Increase Difficulty

- Add the legs and feet.
- Add the trunk.

Success Check

- Think about only one body part at a time.

Score Your Success

Complete the entire routine = 3 points

Complete part of the routine = 1 point

Your score_____

Relaxation Drill 2. *Visualization*

Practice this exercise in a quiet place where you can sit or lie comfortably. You can play quiet music if you like. Close your eyes. Imagine you are lying on a warm, sunny beach. Imagine how the sand and sun feel. Then imagine the sound of the ocean. Add more and more detail to your mental picture. Or imagine being in any location that you consider relaxing. Associate a label with your image, such as *beach.* The more you practice this visualization, the more likely just recalling the label will be relaxing!

To Increase Difficulty

- Play relaxing music compatible with your imagined location.

Success Check

- Put your mind in the imagined environment.

Score Your Success

Achieve a totally relaxed state = 3 points

Achieve a slightly relaxed state = 1 point

Your score_____

FOCUSING ATTENTION

The previous steps to success emphasize the need to repeat as exactly as possible every aspect of putting a shot together. This repetition requires concentration. Letting the mind wander to other things and forgetting a critical aspect of shooting form will cause errors. Following your mental checklist in every detail on every shot maximizes the number of good shots you make. Of course, your checklist may need updating from time to time. Yet your ability to concentrate on putting a shot together by moving through the list is related to your success. The secret to archery is learning how to make the perfect shot and then repeating it over and over again.

It is easy to say that concentration is the key to good shooting. What is difficult is knowing which aspects of putting a shot together need your attention. This information changes as you acquire more skills. You may recall that some of the early steps include details about preparing a shot that were later dropped. With practice, these preparations became second nature. As archers acquire skill, they trim their checklists of items needing conscious attention to a minimum so that they can devote more of their attention to aiming.

Successful shooters have been studied with the use of tools such as the electroencephalograph

(EEG) and heart rate monitors. The EEG measures electrical activity in the brain. Good archery performance is associated with lower levels of brain activity, indicating that movements are carried out automatically. Skilled shooters have little conscious regulation of the release movement. Heart rate during the shot also has been studied. Experienced shooters' heart rates decelerate just before release. This is thought to indicate their focus on something external to themselves—a focus on aiming. Successful shooters also report that their total focus is on aiming when they shoot well, allowing the release to happen when the time is right rather than attempting to make it happen. They free themselves of any thoughts or worry about their form, technique, equipment, or even the release of the bowstring.

Ideally, you should give your conscious attention on every shot to the items on your checklist up until the time you are ready to aim (figure 9.2). Consider your stance, bow hand position, draw hand position, anchor, leveling, and so on. If everything feels right, aim. All of your concentration must now be devoted to aiming. Your concentration should be so intense that you seem to burn a hole in the middle of the bull's-eye. Nothing interferes with the aiming process.

Figure 9.2 — Focusing Attention

a *b* *c*

STANCE

1. Set sight for shooting distance
2. Mentally rehearse the feeling of a perfect shot
3. Begin mental checklist

DRAW AND AIM

1. Continue checklist to draw and anchor
2. Cue yourself to relax the hands
3. If setup feels right, shift attention to aiming
4. Aim at bull's-eye, mentally repeating, *Aim, aim, aim*

RELEASE AND FOLLOW-THROUGH

1. Release occurs
2. Maintain concentration on bull's-eye

Misstep

You think about other things while you shoot.

Correction

Practice concentrating outside of archery sessions. While shooting, focus your attention on your mental checklist.

Misstep

You think about form while you should be aiming.

Correction

When you arrive at the aiming step in your mental checklist, shift attention completely to aiming. It may help to repeat a verbal cue to yourself over and over, such as *Aim, aim, aim.*

The physical aspects of the release should be turned over to your subconscious. You must trust that if there is any indication that the shot is not right, you can assume conscious control and let the shot down. Otherwise, your subconscious will take care of making the release happen at the right time. You do not have to worry about when to make the release happen. The zone described by some athletes probably reflects their intense concentration on their goal, such as aiming at the bull's-eye in archery and the turning over of the physical execution of their skills to their subconscious.

Mental imagery can help you improve your attentional focus. If you tend to let your mind wander to things other than archery, visualize shooting an entire end. Every time your mind wanders to another topic, bring your attention back to the image of shooting. You can do something similar if you tend to think about your form rather than aiming once your shot is set up. Visualize shooting an end. During the visualization of each shot, proceed through your personal mental checklist. When it is time, imagine the bull's-eye and your sight settling in the bull's-eye before the release. If your attention wanders to anything other than aiming, bring it back to focus on the bull's-eye.

Concentration Drill 1. *Concentration Grid*

You can practice your concentration outside archery practices with a concentration grid (figure 9.3). A concentration grid is a 10-by-10 grid filled with scrambled two-digit numbers starting with 00. Starting with 11, find the next number in order and put a slash (/) through it. See how many numbers you can put a slash through in one minute.

To Increase Difficulty

- Extend the time to 90 seconds and double the numbers you need in order to earn points.

Success Check

- Focus on the grid.
- Push other thoughts away.

85	61	55	84	27	51	78	59	52	13
57	29	33	28	60	92	04	97	90	31
86	18	70	32	96	65	39	80	77	49
46	88	00	76	87	71	95	98	81	01
42	62	34	48	82	89	47	35	17	10
94	69	56	44	67	93	11	07	43	72
14	91	02	53	79	05	22	54	74	58
66	20	40	06	68	99	75	26	15	41
45	83	24	50	09	64	08	38	30	36
19	12	63	03	73	21	23	16	37	25

Figure 9.3 Concentration grid.

Score Your Success

25 or more numbers slashed in one minute = 4 points

21 to 24 numbers slashed in one minute = 3 points

16 to 20 numbers slashed in one minute = 2 points

10 to 15 numbers slashed in one minute = 1 point

Your score_____

Concentration Drill 2. *Verbal Cue Drill*

Shoot two ends of six arrows each from any distance you choose. Prepare your shot to the point of aiming. When you are ready to aim, say to yourself, *Aim, aim, aim,* until the release occurs.

To Increase Difficulty

- Bring a friend along to watch you shoot.
- Have the friend talk while you are aiming.

Success Check

- Proceed through checklist.
- Refocus if your mind wanders.

Score Your Success

Complete 10-12 repetitions with focus on the bull's-eye at release = 4 points

Complete 7 to 9 repetitions with focus on the bull's-eye at release = 3 points

Complete 4 to 6 repetitions with focus on the bull's-eye at release = 2 points

Your score_____

BUILDING CONFIDENCE

For an arrow to hit the center of the bull's-eye, you must believe it will hit the center of the bull's-eye. You must have confidence that every one of the arrows shot has the potential to be a bull's-eye. Remember, success in archery competition comes not from shooting one bull's-eye but from scoring high when all the arrows that have been shot are totaled. Successful archers report having this positive expectation during a peak performance.

It is very easy in archery to blame the equipment for your mistakes. The action in archery is so small that it is easy to convince yourself that the equipment is responsible for the outcome, whether good or bad. Archers who lack confidence in their shooting and their ability to execute good shots often blame their failure on their equipment. Continuing to blame the equipment stands in the way of developing confidence in shooting.

As you perfect your form and practice, you will build confidence. You will believe that you control every shot. Think of the saying "Success breeds success." In archery, success in practice builds confidence and breeds success in competition or in hunting.

What undermines confidence? A common problem with archers is trying to please others with their shooting. Many archers want to live up to someone else's expectations, even on those days when, try as they might, nothing seems to work well. The only person you need to please is yourself. If you make a mistake, don't spend your time trying to explain it away to everyone around you. Accept it, and go on.

When archers make a mistake, they often begin to expect that they'll make that mistake again. They talk about and think about making that mistake. They undermine their confidence. If you find yourself verbalizing a negative statement about your shooting, either aloud or to yourself, turn it around to a positive statement. For example, if you find yourself saying, "Oh, no, it's windy, and the last time I shot in the wind I scored terribly," turn this statement around. Say, "The wind will give me a chance to improve over my last score on a windy day." This helps you develop a positive expectation and, over time, confidence in your shooting.

Some archers undermine their confidence when they set unrealistically high goals for themselves. For example, an archer who has been shooting 270 on a 300 round consistently for the past several weeks might go to a tournament wanting to shoot 280. If the 280 happens, great. But is it realistic to expect to shoot above average in the tournament? Of course not! Most likely this archer is destined to come back from every tournament disappointed and discouraged when anything but a personal best is shot. If the goal had been to shoot 270 and the archer achieved that goal,

he or she would be building rather than undermining confidence.

John Williams, an Olympic gold medalist, recommends setting scoring goals conservatively. Even in practice, if you set what is really the minimum score you would ever want to shoot on a given round, your chances of feeling confident and positive after every practice session are good. Setting the minimum goal makes you work to achieve at least that level. Most often, you will score above it and in your mind you will be that many points up rather than points down. When you set a very high scoring goal and fail to reach it, you have a negative mind-set, even if your score was a very good one.

Mentally rehearse shooting a bull's-eye by imagining each of the points listed in figure 9.4. Sit or lie down in a comfortable position with your eyes closed. You can visualize from an internal perspective or an external one (seeing yourself on television, for example) as you prefer.

Figure 9.4   Mentally Rehearsing a Bull's-Eye

1. See yourself take your stance and nock an arrow
2. Imagine yourself standing tall
3. See yourself taking your bow hand grip and raising the bow
4. See yourself setting your draw hand hook or your release aid
5. Feel yourself drawing and setting your anchor
6. See yourself aligning the bow, string, sight, and target and aiming
7. Imagine the release
8. See the arrow hit the bull's-eye
9. See yourself maintaining your follow-through position

Misstep

You verbalize negative statements about your shooting.

Correction

Stop the statement immediately and formulate a positive statement on the same topic.

Misstep

You hold a visual image of a bad shot and keep seeing it over and over.

Correction

Stop imagining the bad shot. Mentally rehearse a perfect shot that lands in the middle of the bull's-eye.

Confidence Drill 1. *Mental Rehearsal*

At a regular practice session, shoot three ends as you normally do. After any shot you consider a mistake, mentally rehearse the feel of a good shot and see the arrow hitting the bull's-eye before you take your next shot.

Success Check

• Proceed through your mental checklist.

Score Your Success

Improve your score 5 points or more over three ends with mentally rehearsed shots = 3 points

Improve your score 1 to 4 points over three ends with mentally rehearsed shots = 2 points

Your score_____

Confidence Drill 2. *Imagery Practice*

Sit quietly with your eyes closed. Practice using imagery by trying to see every detail of a close friend. Make the image as vivid as possible, almost as if you were seeing this friend on television. When you can do this exercise well, picture your bow, including every detail possible. Then picture yourself performing with the bow. See every detail and hear the sounds that accompany shooting. Feel your muscles as they tense or relax. Note that you can picture your performance from the outside as if you were seeing yourself on television or from the inside as it feels to perform.

Success Check

• See more and more detail.
• Stay relaxed.

Score Your Success

8 minutes of imagery practice = 4 points

6 minutes of imagery practice = 3 points

4 minutes of imagery practice = 2 points

Your score_____

Confidence Drill 3. *Thought Stopping*

In this drill, you turn negative statements about archery performance into positive statements. For each negative statement in table 9.1, write a positive counterpart. Verbalize these statements. Then write several negative statements you find yourself saying and create positive counterstatements. Say the positive statements aloud several times.

Success Check

• Think positively.

Table 9.1 Turning Negative Statements Into Positive Statements

Negative statement	Reformulated positive statement
It is so windy, I cannot keep the arrows on the target	
I can't shoot well from 40 yards	
I'm afraid I'll miss the whole target	

Score Your Success

Write five positive statements about your archery performance = 2 points

Write three positive statements about your archery performance = 1 point

Your score_____

Confidence Drill 4. *Goal Setting*

Athletes often overlook setting goals for performance on several levels. For example, you can set goals for the very near future or the distant future. Considering your recent archery performance, write goals for the time lines listed in table 9.2. Also, set a target date for achieving your long-term goals.

Score Your Success

Establish goals in four time frames = 3 points

Establish goals in three time frames = 2 points

Establish goals in two time frames = 1 point

Your score_____

Success Check

• Keep goals realistic.

Table 9.2 Setting Goals

Time frame	Goal	Target date
Next practice		
Short term		
Intermediate		
Long term		

SUCCESS SUMMARY
OF SHARPENING MENTAL SKILLS

Archers can be successful by establishing good form and repeating that good form on every shot. As with so many sports, though, often little separates archers in physical skills and equipment. A good mental approach takes on increasing importance.

Strong mental skills help archers achieve success and long-lasting enjoyment of the sport. Good mental skills are no more accidental than good shooting skills. Both must be practiced. The time spent practicing good mental skills will return to you in years of archery enjoyment. Your goals and expectations will be realistic, and you will stay relaxed and feel competent when shooting.

For each of the drills in this step, you can earn points to chart your progress. Enter your scores and add them up to rate your total success in applying mental skills. If you earned at least 16 points, move to the next step. If you earned less than 16 points, repeat some of the drills before moving on.

Relaxation Drills

1. Hand and Arm Relaxation Routine — ___ out of 3

2. Visualization — ___ out of 3

Concentration Drills

1. Concentration Grid — ___ out of 4

2. Verbal Cue Drill — ___ out of 4

Confidence Drills

1. Mental Rehearsal — ___ out of 3

2. Imagery Practice — ___ out of 4

3. Thought Stopping — ___ out of 2

4. Goal Setting — ___ out of 3

Total — ___ *out of 26*

The movements in archery are small, fine movements. Most people can learn the movements and good technique with adequate instruction and practice. Continued practice can bring them more scoring success. What often distinguishes archers is the mental approach to shooting. Now that you have acquired both physical and mental skills for archery, it may be time to apply those skills in either competitive target shooting or bowhunting. In the next step, you will read about competing in target archery tournaments, and you can decide whether this archery activity is for you.

Competing in Target Archery

Probably no group was more touched than the archery participants in the opening ceremonies of the 1992 Olympics when an archer lit the Olympic torch with a flaming arrow. That opening ceremony gave them a special memory in addition to a special event in their lives: representing their countries in Olympic competition. Sharing this event with the best archers in the world was probably a long-standing goal for most. Although few archers can have this experience, every archer can come together with others to shoot in tournaments and weekly leagues.

Submitting your skills to the test of a tournament provides a landmark for which you can prepare by bringing your mental and physical skills together. The results also motivate you to continue practicing and striving for new goals. This step will familiarize you with tournament shooting and give you an opportunity to shoot a tournament score, either alone or with a group of archers.

While learning a skill such as archery, most people find it helpful to have clear goals. This is particularly true once you have learned the basics and need further practice and refinement to reach a higher level. Shooting for a score provides a basis for setting goals by score; you can

set your sights on obtaining an appropriately higher score the next time you compete.

Monitoring your scores over time tells you how you are progressing; scoring is a source of feedback on your progress in archery skills. If you improve on your previous scores, it is likely that your form is good and you are on the right track. A drop in score can signal that you have fallen into a bad habit. You can then review your form for the basics and reestablish your form. Archery is the type of sport in which competition is within more than it is against another archer. Yet scores also provide a means of comparing your skill with those of other archers.

Tournaments are the ultimate test of archery skills. They are a good test of your skill in a more public setting than practice sessions. If you can perform well when your score counts, then you can take pride in your archery achievements. Competing in tournaments also is an excellent way to meet other archers and to talk with them about equipment and shooting. Tournaments are held at many levels: local, state, national, and international. Start with local tournaments and work your way up as you gain competitive experience.

Another way to enjoy archery competition is by shooting in an archery league. These are usually weekly competitions organized around teams; each archer has a handicap so that shooters of all levels, both genders, and any equipment classification can compete in the same program. Awards might be given for first-place team, most improved archer, or other distinctions.

To shoot competitively, you need to take several steps. First, you must learn how to score in a tournament. You also must know how to participate according to the rules of archery. You need to know how to shoot in wind and rain at outdoor tournaments and how to handle nerves during tournaments. Finally, you need to know about additional equipment appropriate for tournament shooting. You will review these topics, but remember, too, that your equipment needs to be in good order to allow you to shoot competitively. You should get the best equipment you can afford and then tune your equipment as discussed in step 8.

SCORING IN A TOURNAMENT

The first step toward participating in a tournament is to learn the scoring procedures used in archery. To compare your performance with that of other archers, you must consistently score the arrows shot. Otherwise, you would obtain very different scores if, for example, one time you gave arrows cutting two rings the higher value and another time you gave them the lower value.

You must record the scores the same way as others are recording them, particularly in a tournament with many people shooting. Questions may arise regarding the accuracy of a score at the conclusion of shooting, and the scorecard is the official and permanent record of what really happened (figure 10.1a). Some tournaments break ties by counting the number of hits on the target, the number of bull's-eyes, and so on. All archers must be aware of scoring procedures and must keep score accurately in order to compare their performances.

When shooting in a tournament, each archer is assigned to a target at check-in. Scorecards are either given to the archer or placed at the assigned target. Typically four archers are assigned to a target (figure 10.1b). These archers perform specific scoring duties either by assignment of the tournament officials or by mutual agreement of the archers. One archer serves as target captain and calls out the value of each arrow on the target, archer by archer. If any of the other archers disagree with a call, a tournament official is called to make the final decision on that arrow (figure 10.1c). The tournament official might use a magnifying glass to decide. Two of the remaining archers keep score on independent sets of scorecards. They may cross-check each archer's end score and running score on each end so that discrepancies can be quickly rectified. The fourth archer retrieves any arrows that miss the target and may assist the target captain by checking the scores announced.

Figure 10.1 | Scoring in a Tournament

SCORECARD

1. Obtain scorecard at check-in
2. Obtain target assignment

a

RULES

1. One archer calls arrow values
2. Two archers write scores independently
3. One archer checks scores as announced and retrieves arrows

b

RULES

1. Arrows on lines get higher value
2. Arrows are not touched until scored
3. Highest value is dropped if too many arrows are shot
4. Unshot arrows are lost to score
5. Undecided arrows are called by tournament official

c

The tournament officials usually provide a scorecard that is prepared specifically for the round being shot. Figure 10.2 shows an example. The value of each arrow is entered on the card in the appropriate area, as is the end score and, often, a running score. Although the two archers keeping a score on each target cross-check the scorecards, the archer being scored is responsible for seeing that everything on the card, including addition of the score, is in proper order before the scorecard is turned in at the conclusion of the day's shooting. In some tournaments, an archer can be disqualified for scorecard errors.

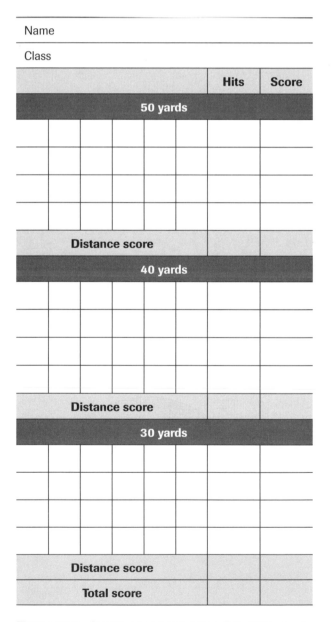

Name

Class

						Hits	Score
50 yards							
Distance score							
40 yards							
Distance score							
30 yards							
Distance score							
Total score							

Figure 10.2 Scorecards prepared for a Columbia round.

When the archer is satisfied that the scorecard is correct, each scorekeeper and the archer signs the card before submitting it.

Each archery governing body and tournament can have specific rules for scoring, but the following guidelines are common to most sets of rules:

1. The traditional target face in archery consists of five concentric scoring zones: gold or yellow, red, blue, black, and white, from the center outward. Each color zone is divided into two equally sized zones by a thin line. This division results in 10 scoring zones of equal width. The innermost zone has a value of 10, the next 9, and so on through the outermost zone, which has a value of 1. The target face can be of various diameters, but the scoring zones must all be of equal width.

2. The lines dividing the scoring zones are considered to be entirely within the higher scoring area. Any arrow touching a dividing line even slightly is therefore assigned the higher value. An exception is a tournament or certain scoring ends designated for inside-out scoring. If an arrow touches a line in this type of scoring, it is considered to be in the lower scoring area. Inside-out scoring is sometimes used as a tiebreaker or in classifications for archers using mechanical releases. The competition in this category can be so close that only finer scoring will determine a winner.

3. Arrows are scored by the positions of the shafts in the target face at the time that archers arrive at the target butt to score the arrows. Arrows sometimes enter the target at an angle or vibrate on impact, tearing into an adjacent scoring ring. These tears are ignored and the arrows are scored as they are sitting in the target face. A subsequent shot arrow can strike an arrow in the target and push it slightly. Again, the arrows are scored as they are sitting in the target face.

4. You are not allowed to touch any of the arrows in the target or the target face itself until all the arrows are scored and any questionable scores are decided by the appropriate official.

5. Arrows that skip into the target after striking the ground receive a score of 0.

6. If an arrow passes through the target face but not the target butt, it can be pushed back through the butt and target face to determine which scoring zone it penetrated.

7. If an arrow passes completely through the target butt or bounces out of the scoring area and is witnessed by another archer or tournament official, it is scored as 7 points unless the procedure in the tournament is to mark the target face at the impact point of each arrow during scoring. In this case, the pass-through or bounce-out arrow is scored according to the hole made in the target face.

8. If you shoot more arrows than the number specified to constitute an end in the round being shot, only the lowest-scoring arrows in the number constituting an end are scored. For example, if an end consists of six arrows and you shoot seven, only the lowest-scoring six arrows are scored.

9. If you do not shoot all the arrows allowed in an end and do not discover this fact before the signal to score or retire from the shooting line, you lose the chance to shoot those arrows and you receive 0 points for them.

10. Any arrows you shoot into a target other than the particular target assigned to you are not scored.

11. An arrow that embeds itself in another arrow and does not therefore reach the target face is scored as the same value as the arrow in which it is embedded.

Some tournaments, including the Olympics, have archers shoot against another archer, and the higher scorer advances to meet the winner of another pair of shooters until eventually a winner is determined. Within each minicompetition, a small number of ends, perhaps two or three, might be shot. Sometimes archers qualify for this head-to-head shooting by competing for total score in a short tournament round, and the scores are used to seed archers for the head-to-head portion. In the case of head-to-head shooting, the actual score is not important. The person with the higher score merely moves on in the tournament, but the scoring rules presented here still apply.

Scoring Drill. *Scoring by End*

Figure 10.3 through figure 10.6 show four targets. Each target has the location of shot arrows marked by dots. Place the value of each arrow in the appropriate space on the scorecard shown in figure 10.7, with the arrows of greater value to the left. Also indicate the number of hits, or arrows striking the target face, as well as the total score for the end and the running score as additional ends are shot. Double-check your score by adding the column of end scores and comparing the result with the running score. The correct complete scorecard is on page 173.

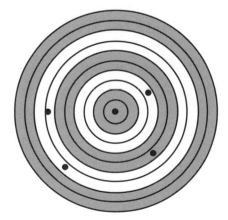

Figure 10.3 End 1: One arrow missed the target.

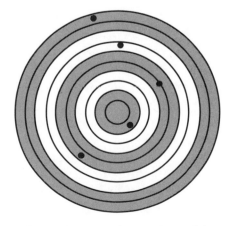

Figure 10.4 End 2: One arrow bounced out of the target and was witnessed by another archer.

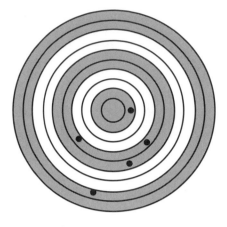

Figure 10.5 End 3: One arrow skipped into the 2 ring after striking the ground and another is embedded in the arrow in the 9 ring.

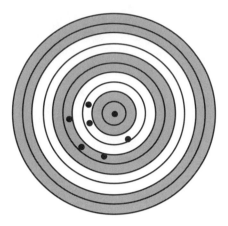

Figure 10.6 End 4: Seven arrows are in the target face.

End	Scorecard						Hits	End score	Running score
1									
2									
3									
4									
Total									

Figure 10.7 Scorecard for the scoring by end drill.

Success Check

- If too many arrows are shot, the highest value is dropped.
- Arrows that bounce out count as 7 points. Arrows that skip in count as 0 points.
- Any arrow embedded in another arrow takes the same value.

Score Your Success

Completely accurate scorecard = 5 points

Complete scorecard with one error = 2 points

Your score_____

SHOOTING IN A TOURNAMENT

Before the day of a tournament, you have several responsibilities. One is to see that all equipment is in safe condition; another responsibility is to ensure that the equipment will provide the best possible shooting efficiency. Inspect your arrows and straighten them if necessary. Prepare a backup bowstring and gather other spare parts such as arrow nocks and arrow rests (figure 10.8a). Inspect the nock locator and serving. Inspect the bowsight and tighten any screws.

Inspect the arrow rest and cushion plunger or spring rest. Take the time to see that the equipment is prepared to perform as expected. Furthermore, you must obtain sight settings for all distances that will be shot in the tournament. In contests that are important to competitors, such as the Olympics, archers typically have two identical bows, set up as identically as possible, in case there is a problem with one bow or any of its parts.

Prepare carefully for outdoor tournaments. In hot and humid weather, you should take the same precautions as any other athlete would. Although archery competition is not as intense as other sport contests, it can last longer, sometimes all day. Bring plenty of water and a hat. Use sunscreen and consider bringing a chair and sun umbrella. You should also prepare for rain. Unless there is lightning, most tournaments continue in light rain.

A tournament official controls the shooting in a tournament with whistle signals. One whistle blast typically indicates that archers on the shooting line can begin shooting. Two blasts signal that archers can cross the shooting line to score. Three or more blasts mean that shooting should cease immediately because an emergency situation exists.

Large tournaments often have multiple shooting lines. Half the archers assigned to a target step up to the line to shoot their ends, and then they retire from the line while the remaining archers shoot, all before any arrows are scored (figure 10.8b). In this case, another single whistle blast is used to indicate the end of shooting for one line and to call the second group to the line. Yet another single blast indicates that the second shooting line can begin shooting.

Tournament officials often establish a time limit for shooting the arrows within an end. The time limit chosen depends on the number of arrows shot in each end, but it is also variable from tournament to tournament. Check to see whether a time limit will be in effect and, if so, how long it will be. Usually a warning signal is given when only 30 seconds remain in the time period.

Figure 10.8 | Shooting in a Tournament

PREPARATION

1. Check equipment for safety and efficiency
2. Gather spare parts for backup
3. Get sight settings for needed distances
4. Prepare food, drink, and clothing

a

PROCEDURES DURING SHOOTING

1. Follow signals of tournament official
2. Retire from line when finished shooting
3. Manage your time to shoot all arrows if time is limited
4. Raise bow if equipment fails
5. Be courteous to other archers

b

If your equipment fails while you are on the shooting line, most tournament rules provide a time period during which you can repair or replace the equipment. If this problem should happen, raise your bow while on the shooting line to signal the tournament official. You will be given an opportunity to shoot missed arrows at a later time, provided you can make the necessary repairs in the time allowed.

Archery tournaments provide an opportunity to make new friends and renew old acquaintances. Between shooting ends, you can visit with other archers or friends or keep to yourself as you prefer. It is common courtesy, however, not to disturb archers who are on the line shooting, either directly or indirectly by talking loudly or creating distractions. You should never talk while on the shooting line, unless it is necessary for the purposes of the tournament. You should also avoid distracting fellow archers on either side of you by moving onto or off of the shooting line while they are at full draw. Among some archers it is traditional to remain on the shooting line until the archer on either side has finished shooting all arrows so that no archer is left on the line alone to finish shooting.

The exact number of arrows shot in a scoring round, the size of the target, and the shooting distances vary from round to round. This variety often adds to the interest of target shooting. Each round provides its own challenge. Examples of the common scoring rounds are given in table 10.1. Though these are the established archery rounds, archers are always free to design their own or modify an established round, provided all participants are made aware of the rules beforehand.

In recent years, the archery governing bodies have used tournament formats that make watching tournaments more exciting for spectators. These formats usually involve one-on-one competition between two archers (match play) for a small number of ends, and the winner advances to shoot against another archer. Sometimes this format is used after a traditional round, and the scores from that round determine seeding positions for the one-on-one competition. Eventually, two archers shoot against each other for the tournament title. Such a format truly increases the excitement of shooting and watching tournament archery.

Table 10.1 Popular Target Rounds

Round	Number of arrows per distance	Size of face	Number of arrows per end	Perfect score	Age group
FITA Outdoor Target Archery round, men	36 at 90 m 36 at 70 m 36 at 50 m 36 at 30 m	122 cm 80 cm	6 (shot 3 and 3)	1440	Adult
FITA Outdoor Target Archery round, women	36 at 70 m 36 at 60 m 36 at 50 m 36 at 30 m	122 cm 80 cm	6 (shot 3 and 3)	1440	Adult

Olympic round, men
  Elimination round
  Finals round
	
	18 at 70 m
	12 at 70 m
		122 cm	
			6
			3
				
				180
				120
					Adult (adapted for youth)

Olympic round, women
  Elimination round
  Finals round
	
	18 at 60 m
	12 at 60 m
		122 cm	
			6
			3
				
				180
				120
					Adult

Olympic rounds, team
  Men
  Women
	9 per archer
	27 per team
	men 70 m
	women 60 m
		122 cm	3 per archer	270	Adult

FITA standard round	36 at 50 m 36 at 30 m	122 cm	3	720	Adult
Metric 900 or FITA 900	30 at 60 m 30 at 50 m 30 at 40 m	122 cm	6 (shot 3 and 3)	900	Adult
Metric Easton 600	20 at 60 m 20 at 50 m 20 at 40 m	122 cm	5	600	Adult
Metric Collegiate 600	20 at 50 m 20 at 40 m 20 at 30 m	122 cm	5	600	Adult
American	30 at 60 yd 30 at 50 yd 30 at 40 yd	48 in., scored 9 to 1	6	810	Adult
Columbia	24 at 50 yd 24 at 40 yd 24 at 30 yd	48 in., scored 9 to 1	6	648	Adult
"720" Collegiate	24 at 50 m 24 at 40 m 24 at 30 m	80 cm	6	720	Adult
Junior Metric 900	30 at 50 m 30 at 40 m 30 at 30 m	122 cm	6	900	12 to 15 years

(continued)

Table 10.1 *(continued)*

Round	Number of arrows per distance	Size of face	Number of arrows per end	Perfect score	Age group
Cadet Metric 900	30 at 40 m 30 at 30 m 30 at 20 m	122 cm	6	900	Under 12 years
Interscholastic Metric	36 at 50 m 36 at 30 m	122 cm 80 cm	6	720	14 to 18 years
Modified Collegiate, boys	20 at 50 m 20 at 40 m 20 at 30 m	122 cm 80 cm	5	600	14 to 18 years
Modified Collegiate, girls	20 at 40 m 20 at 30 m 20 at 20 m	122 cm 80 cm	5	600	14 to 18 years
Junior Metric	36 at 60 m 36 at 50 m 36 at 40 m 36 at 30 m	122 cm 80 cm	6 (shot 3 and 3)	1440	12 to 15 years
Cadet Metric	36 at 45 m 36 at 35 m 36 at 25 m 36 at 15 m	122 cm 80 cm	6 (shot 3 and 3)	1440	Under 12 years
Junior American	30 at 50 yd 30 at 40 yd 30 at 30 yd	48 in., scored 9 to 1	6	810	12 to 15 years
Cadet American	30 at 40 yd 30 at 30 yd 30 at 20 yd	48 in., scored 9 to 1	6	810	Under 12 years
Junior Columbia	24 at 40 yd 24 at 30 yd 24 at 20 yd	48 in., scored 9 to 1	6	648	Under 12 years
18 m FITA Indoor	60 at 18 m	40 cm	3	600	Adult
25 m FITA Indoor	60 at 25 m	60 cm	3	600	Adult
Modified FITA Indoor	30 at 18 m	80 cm	3	300	14 to 18 years
NAA 300 Indoor	60 at 20 yd	16 in., scored 5 to 1	5	300	Adult
Chicago Indoor	96 at 20 yd	16 in., scored 9 to 1	6	864	Adult

Tournament Drill 1. *Modified Metric 900 Round*

Shoot a modification of the Metric 900 round, using the distances of 40, 30, and 20 meters rather than the official Metric 900 distances. Consult table 10.1 to find the target face size and the number of arrows shot at each distance. You can have the option of retrieving and scoring your arrows after shooting six arrows or after shooting three arrows. You can shoot your score alone or with a group of archers. If you shoot with a group, decide who will call the arrow values on a target, who will keep score, and so on. You should also follow the scoring rules listed earlier on pages 156-157. One archer can control the shooting line. Record your score on the scorecard shown in figure 10.9.

To Increase Difficulty

- Shoot from 50, 40, and 30 meters.

Suoooooo Cheok

- Follow the scoring rules.
- Record arrows of highest value first.

Score Your Success

Complete the Modified Metric 900 round — 10 points

Complete two-thirds of the round = 5 points

Your score_____

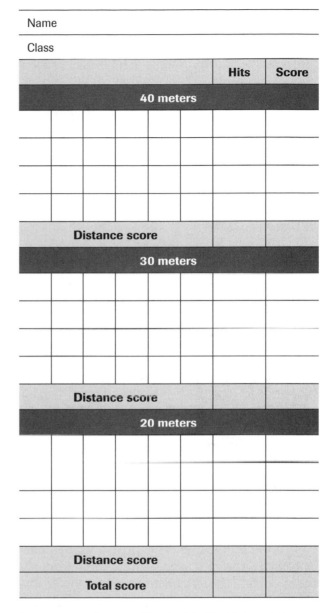

Figure 10.9 Scorecard for the Modified Metric 900 round drill.

Tournament Drill 2. *Interscholastic Metric Round*

Shoot an Interscholastic Metric round from 40 and 30 meters rather than from 50 and 30 meters. Note that you need two different-sized target faces for this round (see table 10.1). Follow the scoring rules. Again, you can shoot alone or with a group. Members of the group should act as target captain, scorer, and tournament officials as mutually decided. Record your scores in the scorecard shown in figure 10.10.

To Increase Difficulty

- Shoot from 50 and 30 meters.

To Decrease Difficulty

- Use the larger target face at both distances.

Success Check

- Have your sight settings beforehand.
- Check your equipment beforehand.
- Use your personal mental checklist.

Score Your Success

Complete the Interscholastic Metric round = 10 points

Complete half of the round = 5 points

Your score_____

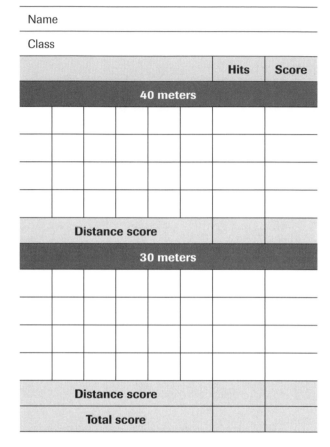

Figure 10.10 Scorecard for the Interscholastic Metric round drill.

Tournament Drill 3. *Head-to-Head Shoot*

Find three other archers and put everyone's name in a hat. Draw out two names; these archers should shoot against each other, as should the remaining two. Shoot four ends of three arrows each. The winners from each pair should then shoot against one another. The remaining archers can determine a third-place finisher.

To Increase Difficulty

- One archer in each pair, as determined by the flip of a coin, starts with a 2-point advantage. The next time you shoot, reverse who gets the point advantage.

To Decrease Difficulty

- If the archers in the group would be in different equipment classifications, determine handicapping points such that you anticipate that everyone has an equal chance of winning.

Success Check

- Relax hands.
- Focus on target and aim.
- Block out other shooters.

Score Your Success

Shoot two tournaments = 10 points

Shoot one tournament = 5 points

Your score_____

SHOOTING IN RAIN AND WIND

Many archery tournaments, especially those held in the warmer months and those featuring long shooting distances, are held outdoors. Naturally, archers hope for sunny, calm weather, but they do not always get their wish. Rain or wind, or both, can affect scoring. Those archers who are able to adapt, though, often gain an advantage over others who let the conditions detract from their performances. Naturally, the scoring might not be as high in inclement weather as in good, but since the conditions are the same for everyone, archers who adapt can be successful.

Archers should not shoot if there is lightning in the area. Standing in open or wooded areas with metal objects is never warranted. If there is no lightning and just rainy conditions, though, most tournaments will go on as scheduled unless the rain is extremely heavy. Plan ahead by taking an outer garment that repels water and will keep you warm if the temperature is cool or cold. Always have a hat to keep the water out of your eyes and off your eyeglasses, if you wear them.

Carry a plastic bag to place over the arrows in your quiver. For outdoor tournaments, many archers use plastic vanes rather than feathers, even if they use feathers indoors. If you do not want to add the weight of vanes, be sure to waterproof your feathers with a spray intended for this use before the outdoor season. Try to keep your finger tab or mechanical release as dry as possible when you are not shooting. Also, have dry towels handy so that you can periodically wipe off your equipment.

Good archery equipment is really very durable. Do what is logical to keep your tackle as dry as possible, but continue shooting as you would in good weather. Stay with your routine and focus on setting up good shots, aiming, and following through. Moisture in the air might cause your arrows to land slightly low, especially at longer distances, so a small correction in your sight settings might be necessary.

Archers who can shoot as routinely as possible in the rain can often score close to their average on a particular round. Don't cancel a practice session just because it is raining. That practice can give you the confidence to shoot well at a rainy tournament!

Shooting in the wind is more problematic than shooting in the rain. The one thing every archer wants to do on every shot is to settle his or her sight around the bull's-eye, and that is the very thing wind works against, especially a crosswind. The wind affects both the arrow in flight and your ability to hold steady. The effect is more pronounced at longer shooting distances. You need specific strategies for shooting in windy conditions.

First, consider your equipment. If you have not yet purchased a bow but plan to shoot outdoors, look for handle risers with cutouts that allow the wind to pass through (figure 10.11a). This reduces the wind resistance when holding on target. A heavier bow is easier to hold steady in the wind than a lighter one. Some archers carry heavier weights for their V-bar stabilizers or extra weights to add to the back of the bow, just in case it is windy. If you adopt this strategy, be sure the total weight is still one you can handle (that is, that the extra weight does not, regardless of the wind, cause you to shake). It is wise to practice with the extra weight from time to time in good conditions.

Second, consider your aiming strategy. Some archers like to deal with a crosswind by aiming at 9 o'clock or 3 o'clock, depending on the wind direction, and letting the wind carry their arrows into the bull's-eye (figure 10.11b). Before trying this strategy, practice in the wind several times to learn how far off to aim for a given shooting distance and the strength of the wind. Take notes on what works so that you have a basis for what to do at a tournament.

Many archers find it difficult to aim off center because this strategy counters the natural tendency to center things. They prefer to adjust their bow sights horizontally, that is, make a windage adjustment, to compensate for the drift of their shots due to the wind. This is effective in a constant rather than gusty wind. An alternative strategy is to cant the bow to compensate for the wind and continue to aim at the center of the target (figure 10.11c). Again, if you decide to use this strategy,

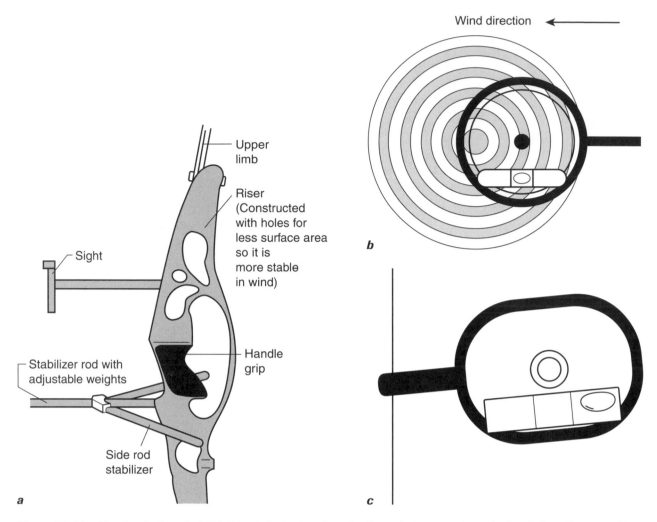

Figure 10.11 Shooting in the wind: *(a)* Cutouts in the bow handle allow wind to pass through; *(b)* aiming off center; *(c)* canting the bow and attached sight aperture to compensate for wind.

practice in the wind several times to determine how much cant works for a given wind velocity and a given shooting distance. Probably the amount of cant will range from 3 to 5 inches or 5 to 15 degrees. If you use an aiming aperture with a level, you can use the bubble to keep track of the cant.

Third, monitor your timing when you shoot in a crosswind. Try to use nearly the same timing you use in ideal conditions. If you tend to get your shots set up and off in 7 to 8 seconds, extending much beyond this in windy conditions will probably be self-defeating. You would be better to let down once you have gone a few seconds beyond normal to set up your shot once again. Obviously, you will need to consider any time limits that are in effect for the tournament.

If the wind is gusty, you can begin your shot sequence as a gust starts to lessen so that you are aiming during a lull.

Recognize that when you shoot in a crosswind, your aim will not be as steady as it is on a calm day. Attempting to force your bow arm to be still in a brisk wind increases the tension in your bow arm and hand, breaking down your follow-through. A better strategy is to stay relaxed and to continue focusing on the center of the target.

If the wind is along the direction of shooting rather than a crosswind, it might not be as difficult to aim. You might find that a tailwind results in high arrows and a headwind results in low arrows. A crosswind might also cause slightly lower arrows. Again, when you have an opportunity to practice in these conditions, note how much adjustment of your sight aperture is needed for a given wind strength and shooting distance.

Practice to find out how particular strategies for shooting in the wind affect your shots, but be careful. An excessive amount of shooting in a crosswind can work in reverse. This might lend itself to anticipating the release, causing release shooters to punch the release or finger shooters to pluck the bowstring.

Keys for Shooting in the Wind

1. Assume stance.
2. Set bow and draw hands (or mechanical release).
3. Draw to anchor.
4. Find aiming spot on target or cant bow.
5. Increase back tension.
6. Focus on aiming spot.
7. Allow release explosion to occur.
8. Follow through.

Wind Drill 1. *Aiming Off Center*

On a windy day with a crosswind, practice aiming off center so that you learn how far to aim off center for a given wind speed. Shoot two ends at 20, 30, and 40 yards. Aim at 9 o'clock or 3 o'clock, depending on the wind direction. On the first end, pick a place to aim. For example, if you are using a five-color target, aim at the line between the red and blue rings. On the second end, adjust if your arrows aren't landing around the bull's-eye. Using the targets shown in figures 10.12 through 10.14, one for each distance, mark each of your arrows. Below each target, record where you aimed and make a note about the wind strength, such as "strong wind" or "light wind." Note what adjustment was required as you moved to longer shooting distances. According to this information, write your strategy for the next time you shoot in a wind of this strength. (For example, "In a strong wind, aim at _____ from 20 yards.")

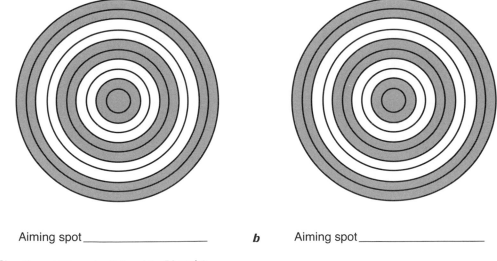

a   Aiming spot_____   *b*   Aiming spot_____

Figure 10.12   Shooting at 20 yards: *(a)* end 1; *(b)* end 2.

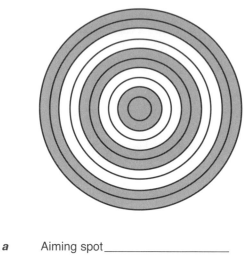

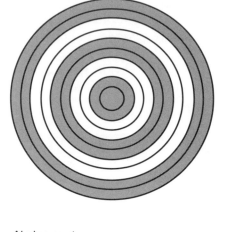

a   Aiming spot_____   *b*   Aiming spot_____

Figure 10.13   Shooting at 30 yards: *(a)* end 1; *(b)* end 2.

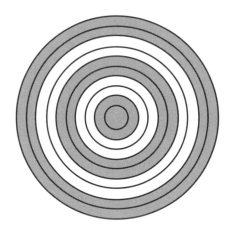

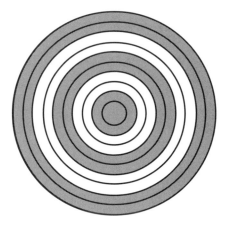

a   Aiming spot_____   *b*   Aiming spot_____

Figure 10.14   Shooting at 40 yards: *(a)* end 1; *(b)* end 2.

Success Check

- Aim at your aiming spot.
- Keep bow arm relaxed.
- Shoot in a normal time frame.

Score Your Success

Determine a complete strategy for shooting in the wind by aiming off center = 10 points

Your score_____

Wind Drill 2.   *Canting the Bow*

On a calm day, shoot two ends at 20, 30, and 40 yards. On the first end, cant your bow slightly to the right and record where your arrows land on the targets shown in figure 10.15. On the next end from the same distance, cant your bow more and note where your arrows land. Since you are shooting on a calm day, expect the arrows to land off center. Repeat for each distance, recording your results on figures 10.16 and 10.17. Note how far off center the arrows land for the amount of cant. When finished, write out a strategy for shooting in a moderate wind and a strategy for shooting in a stiff wind.

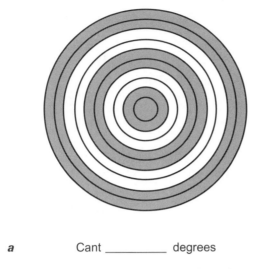

a   Cant _____ degrees   *b*   Cant _____ degrees

Figure 10.15   Shooting at 20 yards: *(a)* end 1; *(b)* end 2.

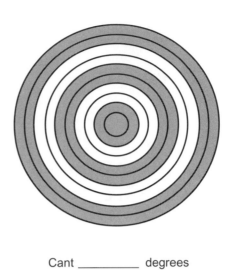

a   Cant _____ degrees   *b*   Cant _____ degrees

Figure 10.16   Shooting at 30 yards: *(a)* end 1; *(b)* end 2.

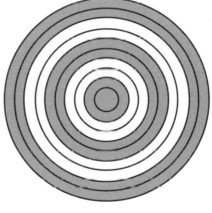

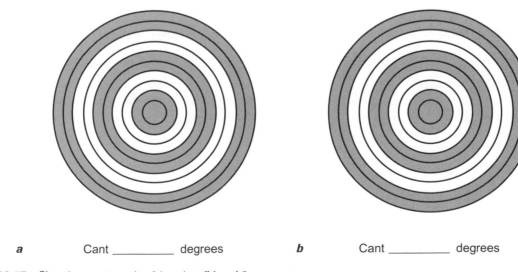

a   Cant _____ degrees   *b*   Cant _____ degrees

Figure 10.17   Shooting at 40 yards: *(a)* end 1; *(b)* end 2.

Success Check

- Aim at the bull's-eye.
- Keep bow arm relaxed.
- Follow through without watching the arrow.

Determine a plan for compensating for moderate and stiff winds = 10 points

Your score_____

ADVANCED ACCESSORIES FOR TOURNAMENT SHOOTING

As archers become more serious about their shooting and decide to enter tournaments on a regular basis, they usually add more equipment accessories. Some of these are specific to certain shooting classifications and others are not. We will review some of the accessories here, but remember that you can acquire some of these as needed. Avoid falling into the trap of thinking that you can do well *only* if you buy an additional piece of equipment!

If you are shooting with a finger release, you might consider adding a device called a clicker (figure 10.18). The clicker is a piece of spring steel about 1/4 inch wide and 3 inches long. It is mounted in the sight window of the handle riser. The upper end is anchored and the lower end is free, extending to a point in front of the arrow rest. When you nock the arrow, the arrow is placed under the clicker, that is, between the clicker and the handle riser. The position of the clicker is adjusted so that when you reach full draw, the clicker just begins to slide down the arrow tip. When you are satisfied the shot is set up, you increase back tension. As back tension increases, the draw hand moves the bowstring and the arrow back so that eventually the arrow slides out from under the clicker. The clicker slaps the handle riser and makes a noise, hence its name. You release only on the sound of the clicker. Archers generally watch the clicker to see that the length of the draw is sufficient to place the clicker on the start of the slope of the arrow tip. After that, visual focus switches to aiming.

The clicker facilitates the use of back tension, plus it discourages anticipation of the release because the archer is never quite sure when back tension will have increased enough

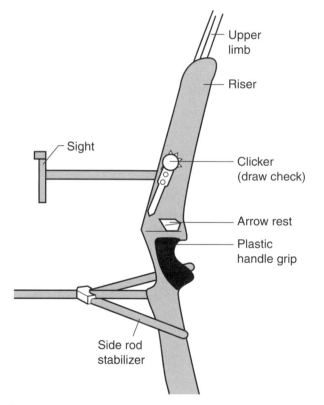

Figure 10.18 The clicker.

to slide the arrow from under the clicker. For finger shooters, these are important advantages in setting up consistent and well-executed shots. Most Olympic-style shooters use clickers. Finger shooters in bowhunter classifications might not be allowed to use clickers.

Another advantage to using a clicker is an identical draw length on every shot. Draw length doesn't vary, so the thrust imparted to the arrow doesn't vary even slightly on any shot. In fact, it is not clear whether the clicker was invented as a draw check or as a cure for snapshooting. For the long distances—70 to

90 meters—shot with recurve bows in Olympic-style shooting, standardizing draw length is important to accurate shooting. Clicker shooters find it advantageous to make sure the draw elbow is high, slightly above nose level, to facilitate using the back muscles in drawing through the clicker.

Many tournament shooters use a sight aperture that is actually a magnifying scope (figure 10.11b, page 166). This makes the target picture bigger and can facilitate aiming. Typically, a level is built into these scopes. Be sure you can use a magnifying scope in your equipment classification. Olympic-style classifications do not allow them.

Magnifying-scope apertures come in a variety of strengths, or magnifications. It is not necessarily the case that more is better. While six-times and eight-times magnifications can fill the sight picture entirely with the bull's-eye or the inner ring (sometimes called the X ring) of the bull's-eye, they also accentuate the perceived movement of the bow arm. No one can hold the bow arm perfectly still, so the natural oscillation of the sight aperture through a scope can seem so great that archers eventually try to muscle the bow arm into a dead stop in the very center of the bull's-eye. This is counterproductive. Since an archer cannot hold the arm perfectly still, the tendency is to begin anticipating when the sight aperture will cross the very center of the bull's-eye, and punching a mechanical release or plucking the bowstring soon follows.

If you decide to try a magnifying-scope sight aperture, a good strategy is to begin with a small magnification and perhaps a version with an open circle etched on the lens rather than a dot or crosshairs. The open circle facilitates a focus on the center of the target and follows the archer's natural tendency to center things.

Figure 10.19 Tripod-mounted telescope, positioned so the archer can check to see where each arrow lands when shooting long distances.

Many tournament archers eventually invest in a good pair of binoculars or a tripod-mounted telescope (figure 10.19). At long distances, archers can check where their arrows are landing in order to make small sight adjustments.

Many archers have two bows identically set up for important tournaments. Even if you do not have two bows, you might want to purchase extra arrows and a backup finger tab or mechanical release. Arrows should be fitted to your bow, draw length, and shooting weight. The finger tab or mechanical release you use probably reflects your personal preference. So it is unlikely you would shoot very well if you had to borrow someone else's arrows, tab, or release! If you are paying an entry fee to shoot in a tournament, the purchase of some backup equipment can be a good investment in ensuring you can finish any tournament you start.

Tournament Equipment Drill. *Magnifying Scope*

Borrow a magnifying-scope sight aperture from a fellow archer. Use the scope to shoot two ends from 20 yards. Remember to focus on aiming at the bull's-eye. Note the power of the scope.

On a scale of 1 to 6, indicate how much greater you perceived your bow arm movement to be with the scope than without the scope (figure 10.20).

No additional
movement

| 1 | 2 | 3 | 4 | 5 | 6 |

Much more
movement

Figure 10.20 Rating scale for a magnifying scope.

Success Check

• Keep bow arm and hand relaxed.
• Allow sight to settle without trying to stop all movement.

Score Your Success

Successfully shoot two ends with a scope = 3 points

Your score_____

SHOOTING WITH TOURNAMENT NERVES

In step 9, we discussed the ideal anxiety level for shooting archery, a relatively low level compared to that for many other sports and activities. We also discussed the ideal of focusing attention on aiming once the shot is set up and ready to be executed. Here, we just briefly expand the discussion to deal specifically with tournament pressure.

Tournaments are not the same as shooting practice or even shooting in a weekly league. You might pay an entry fee for a tournament. Others know you are entered and will ask you how you did. There might be spectators at the tournament. The results might be posted or printed in a newsletter or magazine. Because you are nervous, your bow arm probably won't be as steady as it is in practice. It is easy to see how you would be tempted to control your shooting in a tournament, even if you have practiced for hours by focusing on aiming and letting your subconscious execute the shot. So, you switch from a sole focus on aiming to a state of trying to attend to everything, including the symptoms of nervousness. The key to performing well,

though, is trusting that your subconscious can execute shots while you focus on aiming.

It is important to practice tournament shooting. The more tournaments you shoot, the more you are practicing tournament shooting. If you have trouble shooting well in a tournament, look for ways to practice tournament shooting without actually being in a tournament. Find ways that you can increase the anxiety level of shooting.

Try using imagery to create a tournament atmosphere. Join fellow archers to make your own competitions. Designate a trophy that circulates among the group. As one person wins the trophy, assign everyone else handicap points for the rematch. The handicap points could simply be the difference between the winner's score and the nonwinning archer's score or the difference minus 1 or 2 points. Incorporate some head-to-head competition to practice the format.

Remember that if you are successful in creating shooting conditions with a higher anxiety level, you also have an opportunity to apply the mental skills discussed in step 9.

Tournament Nerves Drill 1. *Pressure Shooting*

Archers often place extra pressure on themselves in head-to-head shooting by focusing on the other archer's success, especially in tournament formats in which the archers shoot arrows alternately. A good practice for head-to-head shooting is to write the various values of 12 shot arrows on small pieces of paper. Make the total value of the 12 shots equal to your average score for 12 arrows. Now shoot four ends of three arrows each, but before each shot, pull out a piece of paper and read the number. Imagine that this number is the value of the arrow just shot by your opponent.

To Increase Difficulty

- Write higher arrow values on the 12 papers.

Success Check

- Use your personal checklist.
- Block out distracting thoughts.
- Set up your shot.
- Focus on aiming.

Score Your Success

Shoot your average or higher on the 12 arrows = 6 points

Shoot within 1 point of your average = 4 points

Shoot within 2 points of your average = 2 points

Your score_____

Tournament Nerves Drill 2. *Time Pressure*

Many tournaments establish a length of time during which archers must shoot all the arrows in an end. To prepare for the pressure of shooting against a clock, practice shooting six three-arrow ends in 2 1/2 minutes each.

To Increase Difficulty

- Shoot with a 2-minute time limit.

Success Check

- Relax hands.
- Focus on aiming.
- Maintain your timing.

Score Your Success

Shoot all 18 arrows within the time limit = 6 points

Shoot 17 arrows within the time limit = 4 points

Shoot 16 arrows within the time limit = 2 points

Your score_____

Answer Key

Scoring Drill. *Scoring by End*

Compare your scorecard from figure 10.7 to the correct, completed scorecard shown in figure 10.21.

End	Scorecard						Hits	End score	Running score
1	10	7	5	4	3	0	5	29	29
2	9	7	6	5	4	1	6	32	61
3	9	9	6	6	5	0	5	35	96
4	8	8	8	6	6	6	6	42	138
Total							22	138	

Figure 10.21 Correct completed scorecard.

SUCCESS SUMMARY
OF SHOOTING COMPETITIVELY

A natural progression for archers is to begin shooting in weekly leagues or local tournaments and later move to larger tournaments. Tournaments are a good test of your skills as well as your ability to shoot under pressure.

Prepare for competition by having your equipment in good order and having all of the equipment necessary, including spares of some equipment. Know the rules of scoring and the format of a tournament before you go to the event, and have sight settings for all distances to be shot, including strategies for adjusting for the conditions on the day of the tournament. Practice in situations in which the anxiety level

is higher than it would otherwise be in a practice session. Confidence is an important part of successful shooting, and solid preparation should make any archer more confident.

For each of the drills in this step, record the points earned to chart your preparedness for tournament shooting. If you earned at least 37 points, you are well on your way to shooting in target archery tournaments. You can also move on to the next step to try shooting activities related to bowhunting. If you earned fewer than 37 points or you want to prepare for an actual tournament, repeat the tournament drills to earn additional points.

Scoring Drill

1. Scoring by End	___ out of 5

Tournament Drills

1. Modified Metric 900 Round	___ out of 10
2. Interscholastic Metric Round	___ out of 10
3. Head-to-Head Shoot	___ out of 10

Wind Drills

1. Aiming Off Center	___ out of 10
2. Canting the Bow	___ out of 10

Tournament Equipment Drill

1. Magnifying Scope	___ out of 3

Tournament Nerves Drills

1. Pressure Shooting	___ out of 6
2. Time Pressure	___ out of 6
Total	**___ out of 70**

Shooting in tournaments is a way to put your archery skills to the test. Your focus should be more on how you do in relation to your practice scores, your previous tournament, or your personal best and less on how you compare to others. Yet, how you place in a tournament also tells you how close you are to achieving the scores shot by the most proficient archers. This can motivate you to continue your practice routines and return to more competitions.

Some archers do not enjoy target shooting as much as they enjoy hunting or some of the archery activities modeled after hunting conditions. Target archers also enjoy the change of pace that some of bowhunting activities afford. In step 11, you can see how archery equipment is adapted for hunting and learn some of the factors that come into play when shooting in field conditions.

Bowhunting

It's early morning in the woods. The sun is coming up. The fall air is cool. Birds are beginning to sing. A lone bowhunter waits in a tree stand. A doe comes over the rise. The hunter's heart begins to pound. *Set bow hand,* the bowhunter thinks. *Set fingers.* The doe turns away, down the far path. *No problem. There's always next week.*

Archers who bowhunt enjoy it for many reasons. Probably all of them like the challenge of hunting, but some also like being in and around nature. They enjoy the peacefulness of the forest, perhaps because it is a contrast to their daily lives. Some appreciate the opportunity to observe wildlife. They look forward to hunting days all year long.

Humans have bowhunted for centuries, first out of necessity, but now for the challenge of hunting and to participate in a natural cycle of checks and balances on the world's animal population. Bowhunters enjoy preparing for bowhunting, testing their skills at judging distance, and executing one perfect shot when the right moment comes. Many have their game meat processed for food and feel part of an age-old tradition. They help control the size of game herds, many of whom have lost their natural predators and would otherwise suffer the disease and starvation that accompany overpopulation.

Bowhunters also enjoy being in the woods, away from the fast pace and pressure of daily life.

Bowhunting is far from a one-weekend-a-year hobby. Bowhunters must spend countless hours preparing their equipment and practicing for that one, all-important shot. Fortunately, there are several enjoyable ways to practice for bowhunting. Some archers make bowhunting a year-round activity by participating in indoor tournaments for archers with bowhunting equipment, in field archery events, and in 3-D target shoots. In fact, 3-D target shooting has become a circuit enjoyed by archers who specialize in it.

The basic archery shot remains the same whether you are shooting at a paper target or at live game. When you execute the fundamentals of a shot well, you are more likely to experience success. A bowhunter who thinks one shot can be made at the critical moment without hours of repetitive practice and preparation asks for failure. The preparation required for successful bowhunting is just as great as for target competition. While the basic technique for the shot remains the same across all forms of archery, bowhunting requires some adaptations to the conditions under which you hunt. They are not as predictable as in target archery, and you usually get only one chance to hit your mark!

Generally, bowhunting equipment must be more durable than target equipment. Bowhunting equipment is used outdoors in the elements and the equipment must be carried, sometimes over rough terrain. You must dress for the elements and still be able to execute a clean shot. Adaptation to an uneven stance is often needed, in contrast to straddling a line on a flat floor. You might shoot from a tree stand (see figure 3 in The Sport of Archery, page xiii) or a kneeling position. You must judge the distance to your target so that you know which sight setting to use without being fooled by the terrain or lighting conditions. The equipment setup must provide adequate penetration of game. Shots must be executed relatively quickly compared to those for target shooting. In this step, we look at these various aspects of hunting with a bow.

CHOOSING HUNTING EQUIPMENT

A typical bowhunting setup consists of a compound bow, often with cam-shaped wheels and an overdraw, a short stabilizer, and a hunting bowsight (figure 11.1). Bowhunting changed dramatically with the advent of the compound bow. The compound has become the bow of choice for hunters, although some archers enjoy traditional hunting days on which hunters are restricted to traditional bows.

As a rule, the compound bow allows you to shoot at a higher poundage than with a recurve bow, resulting in a faster arrow with less arc. This makes judging distance slightly less critical and hunting more humane by producing fewer wounds without a kill. The compound bow makes it easier for smaller archers, children, and people with disabilities to hunt. The compound bow is also shorter and easier to carry through the woods or shoot from a tree stand.

Compound bows have evolved greatly over the years since their inception. Generally, the trend has been toward faster bows that shoot shorter arrows. Cams have replaced round eccentric wheels on either the lower limb or on both limbs of hunting bows; bows are shorter tip to tip; overdraws (moving the arrow rest closer to the archer), either as a feature of the bow's design or an attachment, are common.

As with many aspects of archery equipment, there is often a trade-off between speed and accuracy. Cam-shaped wheels provide you with more arrow speed than round eccentrics, but they tend not to be as smooth. Because hunters shoot fewer arrows than target archers, many trade smoothness for speed. The overdraw makes it possible for you to use a shorter, lighter, and therefore faster arrow. Small errors of the bow hand upon release of the shot, though, are magnified when you use an overdraw. Again, many hunters trade precision for speed when using the overdraw. Compound bows are now so specialized for a category of archery that most archers competing in target tournaments and hunting-type events have different bows for each. They maximize the best features of a particular bow for its intended use.

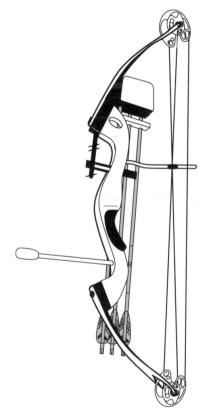

Figure 11.1   A hunting bow.

Selecting a Hunting Bow

1. Choose a recurve or compound bow. If you choose a compound bow, choose a wheel type.
2. Choose the type of bowsight.
3. Choose the type of stabilizer.
4. Choose the type of arrow rest.
5. Choose the type of release.

It is easy for hunters to be convinced by advertisements that more is better when it comes to arrow speed. Remember, though, that if you cannot consistently shoot an arrow into an area the size of a kill zone from the distance you hunt, you are not likely to be a successful hunter. It makes little difference how fast your arrow sails past a deer! When choosing a hunting bow, do not assume that the fastest bow is always the best bow, but rather look for a combination of speed and accuracy that will allow you success, especially if the bow is primarily for hunting.

Hunters use a stabilizer that is shorter than that on a typical target bow. This arrangement provides the benefits of a stabilizer without making the equipment setup too cumbersome to carry in the woods. Recall that you can achieve the same torque-dampening effect by using a heavier weight on a short stabilizer as you would by using a lighter weight on a longer stabilizer. Since hunters do not shoot as many arrows as target archers, this is a reasonable tradeoff. Hunting sights are not extended very far from the bow for the same reason. Hunting sights typically have four or five pin apertures that you can set for various, usually even, distances. A common setup would be for 10, 20, 30, 40, and 50 yards. When you have an odd-distance shot, such as 25 yards, align the bowsight so that 20- and 30-yard pins are approximately equidistant around the kill zone. If you estimate your shooting distance to be 22 yards, you could aim your 20-yard pin slightly above the kill zone. You can see why it is advantageous to hunt with higher poundage, faster arrows, and therefore a lower trajectory. In fact, some archers with high-poundage bows and fast arrow speed need only one or two pins on their bowsights.

Bowhunters often use a quiver mounted on the side of the bow when they hunt with broadheads. Arrows are then handy, but the setup is still compact. The hunting quiver has a hood to shield the broadheads mounted on the arrows. We address arrows and broadheads in more detail later, but one thing all broadheads have in common is their sharpness. They must be handled with extreme care in order not to cut either the archer or the bowstring! Never climb or walk the woods with an arrow or broadhead in hand because you might fall on the broadhead.

Some bowhunters like to shoot with their fingers and others prefer a release aid. When deciding which you will use, consider how quickly you can set up your shot. Hunting does not provide the luxury of time that target shooting does. If it takes too long to set a mechanical release, you might miss your opportunity. Some hunters use releases that are quickly set. These release aids would probably not be the best for precision target shooting, but they are acceptable for hunting. For example, releases triggered by back tension are probably preferable for target shooting. Caliper releases that can be clipped onto the bowstring, though, can be set very quickly. Many archers choose these for hunting, especially models with a wrist strap. Not only does the strap prevent misplacing the release, but it also allows hunters to draw with a relaxed hand and fingers.

In earlier discussions, we acknowledged the tendency for release shooters to punch the release. Hunters, just like target shooters, can counter this tendency by adjusting the release to a heavy tension of 3 to 4 pounds and a very short travel of the trigger. This allows a bowhunter to squeeze the trigger with the finger with about half the pressure required and use back tension to produce the remaining force. This minimizes anticipation and punching the release.

Hunters make other adaptations in their equipment setup because hunting equipment must be more durable and stand up to extremes in temperature and moisture. You may consider using a heavier but less flexible arrow rest than target archers use, or you might use a shooting glove rather than a finger tab. Most hunting equipment comes in a dark color or a camouflage pattern. Some bowhunters like to paint their own camouflage patterns on their equipment.

CHOOSING HUNTING ARROWS

Traditionally, hunters have chosen larger, heavier aluminum shafts for their hunting arrows. Part of this choice is for durability, part to accommodate heavy broadheads, and part to get good penetration. Today, bowhunters have a range of choices for hunting arrow shafts. Many bowhunters have achieved success with shorter, lighter carbon shafts used with overdraws and sometimes with expandable broadheads. These lighter arrows can travel at higher speeds and thus provide good penetration.

Hunting shafts available to bowhunters today include aluminum, carbon fiber bonded to an aluminum-core tube, wrapped carbon, and carbon composite. Charts to help you select the appropriate size of hunting shaft are available, just as those for target arrows, except that additional columns are included for point weight. Table 11.1 is a portion of such a chart. Note that a bowhunter shooting a compound bow and release aid at 48 pounds and needing an arrow length of 27 inches would choose an arrow from group C with a point weight of approximately 75 grains but an arrow from group D with 100-grain points. Each arrow group provides bowhunters considerable choice of shaft type, weight, and diameter.

To determine the correct arrow length for shafts to be shot with broadheads, you must note whether your bow has a broadhead cutout

Table 11.1   Hunting Arrow Shafts

Compound bow release aid Calculated peak bow weight (pounds)				Hunting arrow length (inches)		
Point weight (grains)						
75	100	125	150	26	27	28
45 to 49	42 to 46	39 to 43	36 to 40	C	C	D
50 to 54	47 to 51	44 to 48	41 to 45	C	D	E

Group C		Group D		Group E	
Size	Model	Size	Model	Size	Model
2013	Aluminum	2113	Aluminum	2212	Aluminum
1916	Aluminum	2016	Aluminum	2114	Aluminum
3L-18	Aluminum-carbon	3-18	Aluminum-carbon	2115	Aluminum
600	Carbon	500	Carbon	2018	Aluminum
		520	Carbon	3-28	Aluminum-carbon
				500,460	Carbon
				520	Carbon

sight window. If you're using a bow with a cutout window, your shaft for broadheads should be 1 to 2 inches longer than the point at which the shaft contacts the arrow rest. If it does not, the shaft should be 1 to 2 inches longer than the front of the bow handle. Without a cutout window, a fixed-blade broadhead cannot be drawn past the back of the bow and could bump against the bow if the shaft is too short.

Bowhunters should heed several precautions. First, bow manufacturers recommend a minimum arrow weight based on peak weight of the bow and, if a compound, wheel type. Bowhunters and 3-D shooters should know this minimum weight and choose an arrow shaft and tip that at least meet the minimum. Second, bowhunters who choose carbon shafts must be aware that these shafts damage more easily than aluminum shafts. They should be inspected routinely (see step 8) since a damaged arrow could break on release. They can also shatter when shot into a big game animal. Hunters should check for this possibility, avoiding broken segments and discarding any meat that could contain carbon splinters.

Bowhunters usually practice with heavy or field points that screw into inserts installed on their arrows (figure 11.2). These points are closer in weight to broadheads than are target points. They can be easily replaced by a broadhead when hunting because both points screw into the same insert. Bowhunters can choose traditional two- or multiblade broadheads that are exposed or newer expandable broadheads. Expandable broadheads create less air resistance in flight and are less likely to wind-plane, yet the blades expand on contact. Align the shaft of the broadhead (ferrule) with the arrow shaft. If it is crooked, the arrow may drift on its flight to the target and miss the target.

You still must tune and sight in your broadheads when installing them. A large piece of Styrofoam is good for sighting in because broadheads ruin target butts quickly and are banned on most ranges. Most hunters find that a large fletching better stabilizes the arrows, given the heavy broadhead. They also prefer plastic vanes to feathers because of the range of weather conditions encountered when hunting. Be sure you decide on your fletching before tuning and, if you change your fletching, retune your setup.

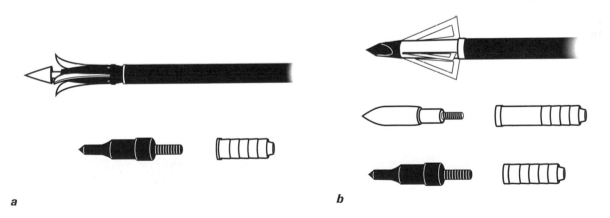

a　　　　　　　　　　　　　　　　　*b*

Figure 11.2　Broadheads and heavy screw-in points for practice: *(a)* expandable broadhead; *(b)* multiblade broadhead.

Selecting Hunting Arrows

1. Determine arrow length.
2. Choose broadhead type.
3. Choose tip weight.
4. Determine arrow size group.
5. Choose type of shaft.
6. Tune broadheads to set up.

The first step in tuning broadheads is to tune your setup with your hunting shafts equipped with field points. The field points should be as close as possible in weight to the broadheads you will use. Once you have tuned with field points, shoot a group of field-tip arrows into your Styrofoam target from 20 to 30 yards. Be sure to ignore poorly executed shots. Using the same aiming spot, now shoot a group of arrows with broadheads installed. Never shoot broadheads with unfletched shafts, since the flight of such arrows is erratic and dangerous.

Compare your two groups of arrows. Make vertical adjustments first. Move the nocking point up if the broadhead group is above the field points and down if the group is below. Once your two arrow groups match vertically, make adjustments for any left-to-right differences. If the broadhead group is left of the field group, you can adjust by increasing the bow poundage, using heavier broadheads, decreasing the tension of a cushion plunger, if used, or moving the arrow rest (or cushion plunger) slightly toward the bow. If the broadhead group is right, adjust in the opposite way. It is best to try only one adjustment at a time.

Bowhunters use a blunt rubber or metal tip when hunting small game such as rabbit or squirrel. These tips kill by impact force, usually instantaneously. A broadhead would destroy too much edible meat.

Misstep

Your field tips and broadheads are of different weights.

Correction

Adjust your field tips to match the weight of your broadheads. With tips and broadheads matched in weight, you will be able to tune your setup and determine your sight settings.

Hunting Equipment Drill 1. *Selecting Hunting Arrows*

Practice reading the arrow selection chart in table 11.1. For each combination of draw weight, tip weight, and arrow length, indicate the shaft size for the type of arrow shaft indicated. (Answer key is on page 190.)

1. Peak bow weight of 38 pounds, tip weight of 150 grains, and 26-inch length

   Aluminum shaft: _____ or _____

   Carbon shaft: _____

2. Peak bow weight of 48 pounds, tip weight of 100 grains, and 28-inch length

   Aluminum shaft (choose one): _____

   Aluminum-carbon shaft: _____

3. Peak bow weight of 42 pounds, tip weight of 125 grains, and 27-inch length

   Aluminum-carbon shaft: _____

   Carbon shaft: _____

Success Check

- Identify draw weight.
- Identify arrow length and tip weight.

Score Your Success

Identify all six arrow sizes correctly = 6 points

Identify five arrow sizes correctly = 5 points

Identify three or four arrow sizes correctly = 3 points

Identify one or two arrow sizes correctly = 1 point

Your score_____

Hunting Equipment Drill 2. *Tuning Broadheads*

If you have a set of hunting arrows, tune them for your bow. Shoot a group of arrows with field tips from 20 yards at a Styrofoam target with an aiming spot marked on it. Then, shoot a group of arrows with broadheads installed from the same distance. Compare the two groups and answer these questions:

- Compared to the field points, was your broadhead group higher or lower? What adjustment would you make?
- Compared to the field points, was your broadhead group left or right? What adjustment would you make?

Success Check

- Adjust vertical before horizontal.

Score Your Success

Identify the correct vertical and horizontal adjustments = 6 points

Identify the correct vertical adjustment only = 3 points

Identify the correct horizontal adjustment only = 3 points

Your score_____

MAXIMIZING HUNTING SUCCESS

Bowhunters trade some precision in shooting for arrow speed and equipment durability. The basic hunting shot, though, has much in common with the basic target shot. Archers who can execute good shots repetitively with good T-form are likely to be successful hunters; those who merely hope everything will fall in place when the time comes are likely to be disappointed.

A difference between target shooting and hunting is the environment. In target shooting it is relatively constant, whereas in bowhunting it is always changing. First, you must adapt your stance to the terrain. Your feet might have to be farther apart or closer than ideal. You might have to straddle a fallen tree. One foot might be higher than another. You might have to crouch or kneel to get a clear shot under a branch. If you hunt from a tree stand, you might even be sitting rather than standing. Start your shot by establishing a stable body position (figure 11.3a). Turn or bend at the waist as necessary to align your shoulders to your target.

You will usually wait for game with your arrow nocked. Any time you must change locations, though, place your arrow with its broad-head in a hood quiver. Injuries from falling on a broadhead can be life threatening! As your game comes into view, begin to estimate its distance from you. You will want to take a shot *only* if the distance is one with which you are comfortable and confident. When the game stops, estimate the distance. Later, we will discuss how to adjust this estimate for the conditions and take into account the game's angle of orientation.

As with target shooting, set your bow hand and your draw hand or mechanical release, and then draw and anchor (figure 11.3b). Leveling your bow is particularly important because slopes, hills, and shadows can cause you to unknowingly cant your bow. Locate your aiming spot and concentrate on it. Difficult as it may be, relax your hands as you aim.

After releasing the bowstring, keep your arm up (figure 11.3c). Following through is as important in hunting as it is in target shooting. When hunting large game, wait 30 minutes to an hour before trailing your game. If a wounded animal senses it is being pursued, it may run, covering a long distance and making it more difficult for you to track.

Figure 11.3   Bowhunting

STANCE

1. Stabilize body position
2. Nock arrow
3. As game moves within range, determine if shot is possible
4. Wait for game to stop
5. Estimate distance
6. Adjust estimate of distance for conditions
7. Decide if angle of game affords a good shot

a

DRAW AND AIM

1. Set bow hand
2. Set draw hand or mechanical release
3. Draw and anchor
4. Align string and shaft and level bow
5. Locate aiming spot and concentrate on target

b

RELEASE AND FOLLOW-THROUGH

1. Maintain back tension
2. Keep hands relaxed
3. Relax draw hand or trigger release
4. Keep bow arm up
5. Wait 30 minutes to one hour to trail game

c

Misstep

Arrow sails over back of target.

Correction

Adjust your estimate of distance to a shorter shot if shooting more than 15 degrees uphill or downhill or down from a tree stand.

Misstep

Arrow tails off downhill on a side-of-hill shot.

Correction

Maintain follow-through on a side-of-hill shot. You can also aim slightly uphill in the kill area.

Judging Distances to Prey

The unique challenge of bowhunting compared to target shooting is judging your distance from your target. To be a successful hunter, you cannot rely on a lucky guess of distance. Rather, you should establish a system for judging distance and practice using it, just as you practice shooting. At least some of your practice should be in the same terrain as where you hunt.

One system you can use is to spot a reference point 20 yards away. Do this by spotting 5-yard increments from your location to the reference point. You can then estimate a distance to a farther or nearer target from this point. Many archers find 20 yards to be a natural reference point because it is common to practice indoors at this distance. You can double-check your estimate

183

by picking a point halfway between your location and the target and estimating your distance to this target. If twice this distance is too different from your first estimate, repeat your judgments.

You should also get to know how many of your normal walking steps correspond to a known distance. When practicing judging distances, take a shot at a target based on your estimate. Then walk off the distance to see how accurate your estimate was. If your shot is off the mark, you will know whether your error was in estimating your distance from the target or in executing your shot.

Some archers realize that they tend to over- or underestimate yardage consistently. They then build this tendency into their decisions. To see a pattern, you should keep a log but probably at 3-D or other unmarked distance shoots and in practice. Record the distance you estimated the target to be and whether your shot was higher or lower than what you aimed. Obviously it takes some time to accumulate enough shots to see a pattern. The pattern might not be the same for all distances. For example, you might overestimate short yardages and underestimate long yardages.

Some hunters use a range finder, a device that measures the distance to a location for you. Others enjoy the challenge of estimating distances and consider this challenge a fundamental part of the hunting experience. To check on your judgments, you can use a range finder when you practice. Range finders are usually prohibited in competitive tournaments for archers practicing their hunting skills.

Finally, some archers use a framing system, although perhaps more often for 3-D shoots than for hunting. Framing is aligning some part of your bow or sight, or even your fingers or hands, to a known distance on your target. An example might be the distance between the top of the back and the belly of a particular deer target. If you find a reference on your hand or equipment that exactly matches this known distance, then you know the target is a particular distance away that you previously determined by measuring. To work properly, the two points creating the gap on your hand or equipment must be held a constant distance from your eye. An archer using a framing system might come to full draw, find the two points on his or her bowsight (such as

two of the pins or a pin and the guard around the bowsight) that frame the known distance on the target, and then let down. The archer draws again, using the sight setting for the distance she had previously determined corresponded to that particular gap.

Some archers have been known to have as many as 14 gaps to use for reference on a five-pin bowhunting sight with a pin guard. Of course, it takes considerable time and a good memory to develop so many references. Most shooters who would use such a system first estimate their distance and use the framing system to check or adjust their estimate, and usually more for longer distances than for shorter ones. Before using a framing system in competition, check the rules of the competition to see if it is allowed.

Shadows in wooded areas sometimes make it difficult for you to judge distance accurately. Some hunters report that they overestimate a distance in the shadows (especially if they are standing in a well-lit area and the target is in the shadows) and underestimate distance shooting from the dark to a well-lit target. Practice in shadows to find out what your tendencies are. Shadows also make it difficult to maintain your aim on game because the natural coloring of game animals provides a camouflage effect. Hunters commonly report that their aim tends to drift low or drift toward a patch of sunlight on the animal's back. Practice with paper animals or 3-D targets in shadowy conditions to learn your tendencies and overcome or compensate for them.

Hunters tend to overestimate distance if they cannot see the ground between them and the target, such as shooting across a valley or small hill. Shooting over water or an open field tends to make hunters underestimate distance. Again, try to practice in such conditions and keep a log of your tendencies so that you can compensate.

Shooting on Hillsides

Shooting on hills affects your shot alignment and your shooting distance. When you shoot up and down hills, especially steep ones, your bow must be pointed acutely up or down. Learn to bend from the waist to shoot so that you can maintain the best alignment of your upper body, keeping your shoulders level and your arms in line (figure 11.4).

The sight setting you use for an up- or downhill shot of approximately 15 degrees or more is slightly off the linear distance from you to your target. You will need to use a sight setting for a shorter distance, about a yard shorter. Exactly how much you adjust depends in part on your arrow velocity, the weight of your arrow, and the angle to the target. Because gravity acts to slow an uphill shot or speed a downhill shot, the arrow does not travel the near-perfect parabolic trajectory as it does with a horizontal shot (figure 11.5).

How much should you adjust for hills? If you shoot light poundage or are taking a long shot, you will need a larger adjustment. Long downhill shots, in particular, call for an adjustment in your sight setting. To learn how much to compensate for this effect on uphill and downhill shots, you must practice these shots regularly. Remember that if you later make an equipment adjustment that affects your arrow speed, you should test the effect of this change on your sight-setting adjustment.

In addition to the actual effect on arrow trajectory, shooting uphill and downhill can affect your distance judgment when the distance is unknown. Hunters tend to overestimate distance when the target is downhill and underestimate it when the target is uphill.

Sometimes you will have shots across the side of a hill. Side hills do not change your distance judgment to the target, but they create illusions that cause many shooters to let the bow drift down the hill during aiming and follow-through. To avoid this drift, aim on the uphill side of your ideal hit zone or use a bowsight with a level. (The rules of competitive tournaments for those with

Figure 11.4 Bend from the waist when shooting on hills.

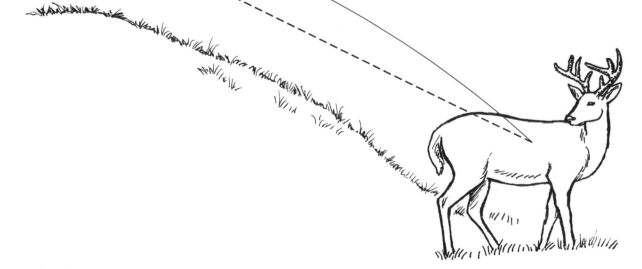

Figure 11.5 An arrow does not travel at a near-perfect parabolic trajectory on hills.

bowhunting equipment often preclude use of a level in competition.) If you are standing on the side of a hill, gravity tends to pull you downhill. When you come to full draw and then attempt to force your bow upright, you can unintentionally torque the bow. It is better to compensate before drawing by leaning slightly into the hill.

Aiming

The goal in hunting is to always kill rather than wound game animals so that the game can be retrieved and the animal dies as quickly as possible. Know the anatomy of the game you are hunting, especially the location of the heart and lungs. The most effective kill shots are those through the heart and lungs, although shots through major arteries, the liver, stomach, or kidneys can cause severe bleeding and result in a successful kill. You should also know the location of major bones in order to avoid shots that would strike bone rather than the chest cavity or vital organs.

One way for you to learn the locations of the vital organs of the game you want to hunt is to practice with paper animal targets, silhouettes, or 3-D targets that have these organs marked. Practicing with 3-D targets also helps you to learn which positions of the animal afford a good shot. If you cannot aim a successful shot to the vital organs without hitting a major bone, you are better off passing up the shot until the animal changes positions or waiting for another opportunity altogether. Working with 3-D targets will also make you realize that when the game is angled rather than broadside to you, the kill zone shrinks in size (figure 11.6).

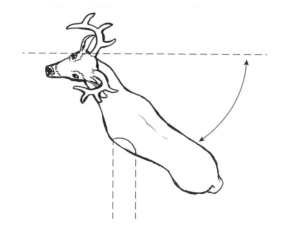

Figure 11.6 The kill zone shrinks in size when the game is angled.

Practicing

Although hunting involves few shots, you must be well practiced to assure yourself success. You can practice for hunting in a variety of ways. First, indoor practice at a short distance is an excellent way to practice shot execution. You can more easily judge whether your shot execution is good when you are indoors rather than outdoors where there are more variables to influence your performance. You know that your scores reflect your shooting and not the elements or a poor estimate of distance. Conditions are better controlled, too, for trying new equipment and tuning equipment.

For a change of pace indoors, hunters can use paper animal targets for practice. Some indoor ranges sponsor bowhunting leagues in which shooters take shots that simulate hunting. For example, some shots may be from a sitting or kneeling position and shooting distances may vary from shot to shot or end to end.

Outdoor target practice can also contribute to your bowhunting skills. You can practice at longer distances and obtain good sight settings. You can practice using your bowsight at odd distances, such as 23 yards or 37 yards. Most bowhunters practice at a maximum distance of 50 yards. At longer distances, even a small error in judging distance can result in your arrow being far off its mark. The risk of wounding rather than killing your game is not worth taking a shot over 50 yards.

Field archery is an effective and fun way to practice for bowhunting. Field ranges are typically 14 targets set out in golf-course fashion, usually in a wooded area. Each target is a different distance and set on different terrain. Distances are marked. You can practice uphill and downhill shots, shots in the shadows and the sun, and shots with level and unlevel footing. You can shoot field archery with the exact equipment setup you would use for hunting, except with field tips in your arrows rather than broadheads.

Three-dimensional rounds are the type of competitive shooting closest to actual hunting. The 3-D refers to the targets, usually foam animals of various sizes placed in natural settings in the woods. You are given a location from which to shoot, but the distance is unmarked. Most

3-D competitions are shot with field tips, too, but occasionally broadhead rounds are held. Three-dimensional targets are helpful when you're learning where to aim at various game animals standing at various angles. They also help you practice maintaining your aim at a location on the dark coat of a game animal, something quite different than aiming at a gold bull's-eye!

If you will be hunting from a tree stand, practice shooting at targets you place around the tree stand. This practice particularly helps with distance judgments. If you must practice away from the woods, consider using an elevated platform.

Although repetitive practice is beneficial for hunting, you should also practice taking single shots at different distances. This type of practice disciplines you to put together one critical shot perfectly the first time. You otherwise may find yourself getting lazy with multiple practice shots from the same location.

Because your footing may be unlevel or awkwardly positioned in hunting or you may be seated in a tree stand, simulate these conditions in practice. You must learn to draw with good upper-body alignment even if you cannot position your lower body as you prefer.

Hunting Success Drill 1. *Indoor Practice*

Indoor practice allows you to perfect your shot without dealing with some of the elements outdoors. You can also simulate hunting conditions to some extent. Obtain five animal targets like the one in figure 11.7 of various types and sizes. Take four shots at each target from different body positions: standing, kneeling, standing on a stable platform or chair, and standing with an open stance. If you can, also vary your distance from the target. Score 5 points for each arrow in the kill zone on the target, 3 points for each arrow in the wound zone, 1 point for hitting somewhere else on the animal, and 0 points for a miss. Total your score.

To Increase Difficulty

- Use smaller targets.
- Change the distance for each shot.
- Change the angle of each shot.

To Decrease Difficulty

- Use larger targets.
- Take all shots from a standing position.

Success Check

- Square shoulders to target.
- Maintain alignment.

Score Your Success

Score 90 points or more = 10 points

Score 80 to 89 points = 8 points

Score 70 to 79 points = 6 points

Score 60 to 69 points = 4 points

Score 50 to 59 points = 2 points

Your score_____

Figure 11.7 Animal target for indoor practice.

Hunting Success Drill 2. *Field Archery*

Locate a field archery range (figure 11.8) and shoot a field archery round. Field ranges typically have 14 targets varying in shooting distance from 20 feet to 80 yards. One end of four arrows is shot at each target. The shooting stakes are marked distances from the targets. If you do not have the equipment or sight settings to allow you to shoot the long distances, you can shoot these targets from a shorter distance. A sign at each target tells you what to do because field ranges do not have to be arranged with targets in any particular order. Field target faces are black and white. Score them with 5 points for the bull's-eye, 4 points for the two white rings, and 3 points for the two black rings. Total your score for the 14 targets.

To Increase Difficulty

- Use 5, 4, 3, 2, 1 scoring for each of the five rings.

To Decrease Difficulty

- Use youth shooting distances.
- Use animal targets.

Success Check

- Maintain upper-body alignment despite footing.
- Adjust for hills.
- Double-check your sight setting for the marked distance.

Score Your Success

Score 200 points or more = 10 points

Score 150 to 199 points = 8 points

Score 100 to 149 points = 6 points

Score 50 to 99 points = 4 points

Your score_____

Figure 11.8   Field archery target.

Hunting Success Drill 3. *Animal Round*

On the field range you located for drill 2, shoot an animal round. Bring a pair of binoculars with you. The shooting stakes for an animal round are at uneven distances, such as 23 or 32 yards, but the distances are marked. Paper targets of game animals are used. Each target is marked with a kill zone and wound zone, usually the outline of the animal (figure 11.9). Shoot an initial arrow. If it lands in the kill zone, record 20 points. If it lands in the wound area, record 18 points. If your first arrow misses, shoot a second arrow. The target might be labeled to move up to a closer stake for the subsequent shot. For your second arrow, record 16 points for a kill or 14 points for a wound. If your second arrow misses, shoot a third and final arrow. For the third arrow, record 12 points for a kill and 10 for a wound. If your third arrow misses, your score is 0 for the target. Shoot a second or third arrow only if you do not score with the previous arrow. Total your score for the 14 targets.

Figure 11.9 Animal targets for an animal round on a field range.

To Increase Difficulty

- Use the bonus X-ring on each target, worth 21 points (first arrow), 17 points (second arrow), or 13 points (third arrow).

Success Check

- Locate the ideal area for aiming.
- Adjust for hills.
- Follow through.

Score Your Success

Score 250 points or more = 10 points

Score 220 to 249 points = 8 points

Score 190 to 219 points = 6 points

Score 160 to 189 points = 4 points

Score 130 to 159 points = 2 points

Your score_____

Hunting Success Drill 4. 3-D Animal Round

Find out from a local bowhunting club when a 3-D round will be held and whether field tips or broadheads will be used. Go through the round on the indicated day and record your score. The center vital scoring area of the animal model is worth 10 points, the outer vital area is worth 8 points, and the remainder of the animal's body is worth 5 points.

Success Check

- Estimate your shooting distance in 5-yard increments.
- Double-check your estimate of distance.
- Adjust for conditions.
- Maintain your aim until steady on the target.

Score Your Success

Score 90 points or more on 14 targets = 10 points

Score 80 to 89 points on 14 targets = 8 points

Score 70 to 79 points on 14 targets = 6 points

Score 60 to 69 points on 14 targets = 4 points

Score 50 to 59 points on 14 targets = 2 points

Your score_____

Hunting Success Drill 5.   *Tree Stand Practice*

If you will be bowhunting from a tree stand, practice from an elevated position so that you learn to judge your distance, taking into account the downhill angle. You can shoot from a platform or from a ladder. Swimming pool ladders with a platform at the top are well suited for this drill. Place the ladder about 20 yards from a target butt. Use an animal target. Shoot four arrows, and then score your shots: 5 points for the inner zone, 3 points for the outer zone, and 1 point for an arrow hitting any part of the animal. Reposition the ladder closer to the target and shoot four more arrows. Repeat this drill until you have shot 20 arrows; total your score.

To Increase Difficulty

- Mix up your shooting distances.
- Include distances up to 30 yards.

Success Check

- Adjust shooting distance for downhill shots.

Score Your Success

Score 80 points or more = 10 points

Score 70 to 79 points = 8 points

Score 60 to 69 points = 6 points

Score 50 to 59 points = 4 points

Score 40 to 49 points = 2 points

Your score_____

Answer Key

Hunting Equipment Drill 1. *Selecting Hunting Arrows*

1. Aluminum shaft: 1916 or 2013; carbon shaft: 600

2. Aluminum shaft (choose one): 2212, 2114, 2115, or 2018; aluminum-carbon shaft: 3-28

3. Aluminum-carbon shaft: 3L-18; carbon shaft: 600

SUCCESS SUMMARY OF BOWHUNTING

Most archers can hardly resist the many ways to enjoy archery. Some target archers never hunt live game but enjoy field and 3-D rounds. Some who only intend to hunt eventually take up target archery. Adapting your equipment and your shot for conditions is part of the challenge of shooting archery.

In this step, you learned how to adapt your shot and your equipment for hunting, and you learned various ways of practicing for bowhunting. If you are planning to bowhunt, you will probably want to read more about hunting techniques, including camouflaging, calling game, trailing game after a successful shot, and field-dressing your kill.

Check to see how far you progressed in taking up bowhunting or the various forms of shooting that simulate hunting. For each drill in this step, record the points you earned. If you earned more than 32 points, you did well for your initial preparations for bowhunting. If you earned fewer than 32 points or you plan to hunt for the first time soon, repeat the hunting success drills. You can continue to use these drills for practice, even after you reach a level of proficiency.

Hunting Equipment Drills

   1. Selecting Hunting Arrows   ___ out of 6

   2. Tuning Broadheads   ___ out of 6

Hunting Success Drills

   1. Indoor Practice   ___ out of 10

   2. Field Archery   ___ out of 10

   3. Animal Round   ___ out of 10

   4. 3-D Animal Round   ___ out of 10

   5. Tree Stand Practice   ___ out of 10

Total   **___ out of 62**

Congratulations on reaching the top of the steps to success staircase in archery! You have come a long way. You know how to select equipment that is matched to your size and strength and is appropriate for your interests. You have established solid T-form adapted to your body shape and strength. You know how to analyze your performance in order to correct flaws in your shooting. With solid form and tuned equipment, you should be able to score well and to improve with additional practice.

Now that you're armed with the information presented in these last two steps, all that remains is to get involved in archery activities. Remember that you can use many of the drills in this text for practice, even as you become a proficient shooter. Varying your practice activities keeps your practice sessions interesting! After all, archery is a sport for a lifetime, and you will be able to enjoy it for years to come.

◧ Glossary

actual draw length—The arrow length needed by an archer; measured from the bottom of the slit in the arrow nock to the back of the bow.

actual draw weight—The energy (expressed in pounds) required to draw the bow to the actual draw length.

address—To assume a stand while straddling the shooting line.

aim—To visually place a bowsight aperture over the target center; if a bowsight is not used, to place the arrow tip over a particular point.

alignment—With regard to the bowstring, the relationship between the string and sight aperture; with regard to shooting form, the relationship of the trunk and the arms.

anchor—To draw the bowstring to the anchor point.

anchor point—A fixed position against the body to which the draw hand is brought.

archer's paradox—The manner in which the arrow clears the bow upon release by bending around the bow handle.

Archery Manufacturers Organization (AMO)—The organization that sets the standards for the measurement of archery equipment.

arm guard—A piece of leather or plastic placed on the inside forearm of the bow arm to protect it from a slap of the bowstring upon release.

arrow rest—A projection from the bow window, above the arrow shelf, on which the arrow lies when drawn.

arrow shelf—A horizontal projection at the bottom of the bow window on which the arrow can lie in the absence of an arrow rest.

barebow—A type of shooting that does not allow use of bowsights, stabilizers, release aids, or other shooting aids.

bare shaft—An arrow shaft without fletching of any kind.

blunt—An arrow with a flat tip used to hunt small game.

bounce-out—An arrow that strikes the scoring area of the target face but rebounds away; also called a rebound.

bow arm—The arm of the hand that holds the bow.

bow efficiency—Ratio of the kinetic energy received by the arrow to that stored by the bow.

bow hand—The hand that holds the bow.

bow scale—A mechanical device that measures the draw weight of a bow at any stage of the draw.

bowsight—Any device mounted on the bow that allows an archer to aim directly at the target or a mark.

bow sling—A strap attached to the bow through which the archer slips the bow hand, thereby preventing the bow from being dropped upon release.

bow square—A device that attaches to the bowstring and lies on the arrow rest to measure brace height and nocking point location.

bowstring—The string on the bow, usually made of Dacron or Kevlar.

bowstringer—A device used for bracing or stringing a bow.

bow window—The recessed area above the grip; the sight window.

brace height—The distance between the bow (measured at the pivot point) and string when the bow is strung; string height.

breakover—The point in the draw of a compound bow when the draw weight reaches its peak and then begins to decrease.

broadhead—A multi-edged sharp arrow point used in hunting game.

bull's-eye—The area on the target face with the highest scoring value; usually in the center.

butt—A backstop for arrows; typically made of grass, excelsior, straw, cardboard, polyethylene foam, or fiber.

cam bow—A type of compound bow with oval-shaped eccentric pulleys.

cant—To tilt the bow to the right or left, as indicated by the top limb tip, at full draw.

cast—The ability of a bow to project an arrow; the distance and speed a bow can shoot an arrow.

center serving—The wrapping thread over the center of the bowstring where the arrow is nocked.

center-shot bow—Bow design wherein the sight window is cut out so that the arrow, sitting on the arrow rest, is at or very near the centerline of the bow.

chest protector—A piece of nylon netting or vinyl worn over the clothing to prevent the bowstring from catching.

clicker—A device attached to the bow or sometimes to the cables of a compound bow that indicates by sound that the arrow has been drawn a certain desired distance; most archers use the sound of the click as an indication to release.

closed stance—A shooting stance in which an imaginary straight line to the target intersects the toes of the rear foot and middle of the front foot.

clout shooting—A type of shooting wherein archers shoot to a large ringed target laid out on the ground, usually from a long distance.

compound bow—A bow that uses a cable system attached to eccentric pulleys mounted at the limb tips, producing peak resistance at middraw and then dropping off to a holding weight less than the draw weight.

creeping—Allowing the draw hand to move forward immediately before or during release.

crest—A decoration painted on arrows, often a colored band, to help archers identify their set of matched arrows.

crossbow—A type of bow that has a barrel and trigger release, similar to a gun; the limbs are short and oriented horizontally rather than vertically.

crosshair sight—A sight with a circular aperture in which two fine lines cross at right angles; the intersection of the lines is aimed at the target.

cushion plunger—A spring-loaded button mounted horizontally through the bow above the handle pivot point to absorb force as the arrow pushes against it upon release.

dead release—A bowstring release in which the hand stays locked in its anchor position and the fingers extend to release the string; back tension is not used to release.

dominant eye—The eye preferred by an archer for sighting or visually fixating on an object.

draw—To pull the bowstring.

draw check—A device attached to the bow to indicate that full draw has been reached.

draw length—The distance between the nocking point and the grip of the bow at full draw; at one time, draw length was measured to the back of the bow.

draw weight—The number of pounds required to draw any bow a given distance.

dry-fire—To draw and release a bowstring without having nocked an arrow; also drawing and releasing a bowstring after an arrow has come off the bowstring.

eccentric pulley or wheel—A round wheel with an off-center axle mounted at the limb tip of a compound bow used to decrease the amount of weight held on the bowstring at full draw.

end—A specified number of arrows shot before archers go to the target to score and retrieve their arrows.

face—The paper or cardboard with a target printed on it.

facewalking—A technique used in barebow or instinctive shooting involving raising or lowering the anchor point to adjust the distance of a shot.

field archery—A type of competitive archery shot outdoors in a wooded area with targets of varying distances and sizes; archers walk from target to target.

field point—An arrow point that is heavier than a target point and similar in weight to a broadhead; it can be unscrewed from a mounting insert in aluminum arrows so a broadhead can be installed.

field round—A competitive round, usually of 14 ends, each shot to a different target from a different distance; similar to golf in that archers walk the round and it is in a wooded or field setting.

finger sling—A piece of leather, plastic, or rope looped at each end through which the archer slips the thumb and a finger after taking hold of the bow; it enables the archer to maintain a loose grip.

finger tab—A piece of leather or plastic worn over the draw fingers to protect them and to ensure a smooth release of the bowstring.

fish point—An arrow point used for bowfishing, usually with movable barbs that open after entry to prevent the arrow from pulling out of the fish.

fishtailing—A back-and-forth motion of the nock end of an arrow on its flight to the target.

fixed pins—The sight pins on a bowhunting sight; in competitive rounds for archers with bowhunting equipment, the pins must be set before competition and remain fixed in position until the end of the round.

fletching—The turkey feathers or plastic vanes mounted on an arrow to stabilize it in flight.

flight shooting—A form of archery in which the object is to shoot an arrow for the greatest distance possible; flight bows are designed with maximum cast so as to shoot maximum distance without great accuracy; flight arrows are small in diameter with small fletching in order to fly as far as possible.

flinching—A form error in which the bow arm moves suddenly upon release, usually flexing horizontally at the bow shoulder.

flu-flu—A type of fletching that is high and wide, often mounted in a spiral, designed to slow an arrow and limit its flight because it is used in aerial shooting or hunting small game.

follow-through—The archer's position after release of the arrow; ideally the body, head, and bow arm position are held steady and the string hand recoils over the string shoulder as a result of continuous back tension.

foot markers—Anything used to mark the exact position of the feet in addressing the target so that the archer can duplicate the position and distance from the target on subsequent shots.

force-draw curve—The graph created by plotting draw weight (vertical axis) against draw length (horizontal axis) for a bow as it is drawn to full draw.

freestyle—A classification for competition that typically allows archers to use bowsights, release aids, and other mechanical devices and shooting aids.

full draw—The position wherein the bowstring is moved back and the draw hand anchors with respect to the head and neck.

gap shooting—An aiming technique used when no bowsight is used; the archer focuses on and adjusts the gap or distance between the target and the tip of the arrow to hit the target.

glove—A leather covering that slips over the fingertips of the string hand and attaches to the wrist to protect the string fingers and allow a smooth release; an alternative to a finger tab.

gold—The center area of the multicolored target often used in target archery.

grip—The part of the bow handle where the bow is held. Also, the removable plastic piece that allows a change in the shape of the bow where it is held.

ground quiver—An arrow holder that sits on or sticks into the ground; some also hold a bow.

grouping—The pattern of an archer's arrows in the target.

handle riser—The middle section of the bow exclusive of the limbs.

heeling—A shooting flaw in which the archer pushes forward suddenly with the heel of the bow hand at release.

high anchor—An anchor position in which the draw hand contacts the side of the face.

high wrist—The bow hold position in which the top of the wrist is held level with the top of the bow arm.

holding—Maintaining steady bow position at full draw during aiming.

holding weight—The pounds of resistance held by the archer at full draw; with recurve bows, the holding weight increases with the length of the draw, whereas with compound bows, the holding weight is less than the peak weight, and therefore holding weight is often reported as part of a compound bow's specifications.

hunting arrow—An arrow used for hunting that is typically longer and sturdier than a target arrow to accommodate a broadhead.

hunting round—A competitive round that mimics hunting conditions; archers typically walk from target to target; the targets are pictures of animals or three-dimensional foam animals, positioned at various, sometimes unmarked, distances.

index feather—The feather mounted on an arrow shaft at a right angle to the nock slit, often of a distinct color; the cock feather.

193

instinctive shooting—A shooting style wherein no bowsight is used and archers aim by instinct and experience in order to shoot targets of various distances.

kisser button—A small disk attached to the bowstring; meant to contact the lips in the anchor position to ensure proper anchor and head positions.

launcher—A shoot-through arrow rest.

let-down—A return to the ready position without releasing the bowstring.

let-off—The weight reduction from peak weight to holding weight on a compound bow. (Sometimes reported as a percentage.)

level—A device attached to the sight or the bow to help the archer maintain a vertical bow position.

limbs—The energy-storing parts of a bow above and below the handle riser section.

longbow—A bow style popular in England in the Middle Ages; long limbs without a recurved shape are characteristic of longbows; although not as efficient in design as a bow with recurved limbs, the longbow does not require the bonding of materials, especially difficult in the past in the damp weather of England.

loose—An older term for releasing the bowstring.

low wrist—A bow hand position wherein the hand is flat against the bow handle and the pressure during draw is through the forearm bone.

minnowing—Side-to-side movement of an arrow in flight, smaller and more rapid than fishtailing, and typically caused by the arrow's fletching contacting the arrow rest after release.

nock—The removable piece, usually plastic, on the end of an arrow with a slit for the bowstring.

nocking—Placing the arrow on the bowstring in preparation for shooting.

nock locator—A stop on the bowstring against which the arrow is placed.

nocking point—The location on the bowstring where the nock locator is positioned.

open stance—A position on the shooting line wherein a straight line to the target passes through the middle of the rear foot and the toes of the front foot.

overdraw—To draw an arrow so that the point passes the face of the bow; also, a device that permits use of arrows shorter than the archer's draw length.

overstrung—A condition in which a bow is strung with a bowstring too short, making the brace height too high.

pass-through—An arrow that penetrates completely through the target face and target butt.

peak weight—The highest weight achieved during the draw of a compound bow.

peeking—A shooting flaw wherein the archer moves the head at release in order to watch the arrow in flight.

peep sight—A plastic or metal piece that has a small hole and is tied into the bowstring so that an archer can look through the hole to line up the bowsight and target.

perfect end—An end in which all arrows land in the highest scoring area.

pin sight—A sight using one or more sight apertures similar to a pinhead.

pinching—Squeezing the arrow nock with the draw fingers during the draw.

pivot point—The place on the bow's grip that is farthest from the string.

plucking—A shooting flaw in which the string hand is pulled away from the face and body upon release.

point—The arrow tip.

point of aim—A method of aiming in which the arrow point is aligned with some point in front of and below the target. Natural point of aim refers to the use of a naturally occurring object, while artificial point of aim employs a stake, cloth, or other device placed by the archer.

porpoising—Up-and-down movement of an arrow in flight, typically caused by a mispositioned nocking point.

post sight—A bowsight with an aperture that has a metal piece projecting vertically up or down, the tip of which is aligned with the bull's-eye.

pressure point—The place on the arrow plate against which the arrow pushes upon release of the bowstring.

pull—To remove shot arrows from the target; also to draw the bow.

push–pull draw—A method of reaching full draw by pushing the bent bow arm away from the body while the string is drawn by the string hand.

quiver—A holder for arrows that may be worn, placed on the ground, or mounted on the bow, particularly when hunting.

range—The place where archery shooting takes place; also the distance to be shot.

rebound—An arrow that hits the target face but bounces back toward the archer rather than penetrating the target; a bounce-out.

recurve bow—A bow with limb tips that are curved forward.

reflexed bow—A bow that appears bent backward when unstrung; it does not necessarily have recurved limb tips, though.

release—Letting go of the bowstring, ideally by opening the string finger hook; also used to describe a particular style of holding the string; for example, the Apache release uses three fingers under the arrow and the primary release uses the thumb and forefinger to pull the arrow itself.

release aid—A handheld device attached to the bowstring; it is used to draw and release the string, minimizing the string deflection otherwise seen with a finger release.

ring sight—A bowsight with an aperture that is an open circle; the bull's-eye is centered in the ring to aim the arrow.

riser—The center handle portion of the bow exclusive of the limbs.

Robin Hood—To shoot an arrow into the end of an arrow in the target; named after the legendary character; also called telescoping.

round—The number of ends shot at designated distances and target sizes to obtain a standard score.

roving—A form of practice wherein the archer walks woods or fields and randomly chooses targets such as a tree stump; the origin of formal field and hunting rounds shot today.

scoring area—The part of the target face made up of scoring circles.

selfbow—A bow made of a single piece of wood.

serving—A heavy thread wrapped around the bowstring at its center and on the loops to protect the string and to add strength.

set arm draw—The method of reaching full draw by first extending the bow arm and then drawing the string.

shaft—The body of an arrow.

shelf—A horizontal projection at the bottom of the bow window upon which the arrow can lie in the absence of an arrow rest.

shooting glove—A leather covering that slips over the fingertips of the string hand and attaches around the wrist, protecting the string fingers and allowing a smooth release; an alternative to a finger tab.

shooting line—A marked line parallel to the targets from which all archers shoot.

sight—Any device mounted on the bow that allows an archer to aim directly at the target or a mark.

sight bar—The part of the bowsight to which the aperture assembly is attached.

sight extension—A bar that allows the bowsight to be extended from the bow toward the target.

sight pin—A bowsight aperture that is a straight piece of metal with a dot or ball at the end.

sight window—The recessed area above the grip; the bow window.

silencer—A clump of yarn or rubber bands attached to the bowstring to reduce vibration and therefore noise; usually used for hunting.

sling—A strap attached to the bow or to the hand holding the bow that prevents the bow from dropping to the ground upon release.

snap shooting—A shooting flaw wherein the arrow is shot immediately as the bowsight crosses the bull's-eye.

spine—The measured deflection of an arrow shaft, established by hanging a 2-pound weight at the center of the arrow.

springy—A small spring with an arrow rest extension substituted for a cushion plunger.

stabilizer—A rod-and-weight assembly mounted on either the face or back of the handle riser to help eliminate torque of the bow around its long axis upon release.

stacking—A rapid, disproportionate increase in draw weight in the last few inches of draw in some recurve bows.

stance—The foot position taken to address the target.

standard draw weight—the draw weight of a bow at the standard distance of 26 1/4 inches from the pivot point or 28 inches from the far side of the bow handle.

stick bow—Another name for a recurve bow, as opposed to a compound bow; sometimes a selfbow made of one piece of wood.

straight-limb bow—A bow with relatively straight limbs.

string—The bowstring; also to attach the bowstring to the limb tip by bending the bow limbs and placing them under tension.

string alignment—The relationship between the bowstring and the sight aperture.

string fingers—The fingers that hold the bowstring in shooting the bow.

string hand—The hand that holds the bowstring; the draw hand.

string height—The distance between the bow (measured at the pivot point) and the string when the bow is strung; brace height.

string pattern—The relationship between the bowstring and the sight aperture.

string walking—A style of shooting wherein the archer moves the position of the string fingers on the string to adjust the vertical displacement of the arrow; no bowsight is used.

tab—A piece of leather or plastic worn over the draw fingers to protect them and to ensure a smooth release of the bowstring; finger tab.

tackle—An archer's equipment.

take-down bow—A bow with detachable limbs.

target butt—The backstop for arrows, typically made of grass, excelsior, straw, cardboard, polyethylene foam, or fiber.

target captain—The person at each target during a tournament designated to call the scoring value of all arrows on that target.

target face—The paper or cardboard scoring area mounted on the target butt.

target panic—Anticipating the release, causing a disruption of a smooth and accurate shot; involves one or more symptoms including, but not limited to, flinching, punching, freezing, and snap shooting.

3-D round—An archery shoot in which the targets are three-dimensional, lifelike foam and are placed at unknown distances to simulate hunting.

3-D target—A lifelike foam shape of an animal, decorated to look like that animal, often with the ideal kill zone marked.

tiller—A measure of even balance in the two limbs; on a compound bow, a tiller is adjustable through the limb bolts, thus varying the distance between the base of the limb and the string.

tip—The end of a bow limb; also an arrow point.

torque—A rotation of the bow about its long axis upon release of the bowstring.

toxology—The study of archery.

toxophily—The art and craft of archery.

tree stand—A platform in a tree that allows a shooter to hunt from an elevation.

tuning—Adjustment of the arrow spine, arrow rest, pressure point, cushion plunger, string height, tiller, and nocking point; used for achieving the truest arrow flight possible.

understrung—A bow with a string too long, resulting in a low brace height and reduced efficiency.

valley—The point of lowest holding weight reached near full draw on a compound bow.

vane—A plastic fletching that is more windproof and weatherproof than feathers but often is heavier.

weight—The number of pounds required for drawing the bowstring a given distance.

windage—Horizontal correction of the bowsight setting to compensate for drift caused by wind.

wrist sling—A strap that wraps around the archer's wrist and the bow, thereby preventing the bow from falling to the ground at release.

X-ring—A small circle at the center of the bull's-eye; the number of arrows landing in the X-ring is often used as a tiebreaker among archers achieving identical scores in competition.

◨ About the Authors

Kathleen M. Haywood (right) is a teacher preparation educator. She has taught archery at three universities and completed a National Archery Association instructor certification course. An eight-time Missouri state archery champion, she is now retired from competition. During her years of competing, she was a member of the Professional Archers Association (PAA) and the National Field Archery Association (NFAA).

A member of the American Alliance for Health, Physical Education, Recreation and Dance (AAHPERD), Dr. Haywood was presented the Mabel Lee Award by AAHPERD and the Scholar Award by the Central District of AAHPERD. She is also a past president of the North American Society for Psychology of Sport and Physical Activity and a fellow of the American Academy of Kinesiology and Physical Education.

Dr. Haywood is the associate dean for graduate education in the College of Education at the University of Missouri at St. Louis. She earned her PhD in motor behavior from the University of Illinois at Urbana-Champaign in 1976. A resident of St. Charles, Missouri, she enjoys playing tennis and desktop publishing for the Missouri AHPERD.

Catherine F. Lewis (left) is an elementary physical educator at Moline Elementary School in the Riverview Gardens School District, St. Louis County, Missouri. A former member of the PAA and NFAA, Ms. Lewis has more than 15 years' experience in archery instruction and had a successful career in archery competition. She has taught archery in the professional preparation program at the University of Missouri at St. Louis and to youths in school, scouting, and camp programs.

Ms. Lewis is also a member of AAHPERD and of the Missouri AHPERD. She earned her master's degree from the University of Missouri at St. Louis in 1986 and is currently writing her doctoral dissertation. Ms. Lewis lives in Des Peres, Missouri, where she spends her leisure time camping, fishing, and reading.